AMERICAN NATURE WRITING 1994

AMERICAN NATURE WRITING 1994

Selected by John A. Murray

SIERRA CLUB BOOKS
San Francisco

The Sierra Club, founded in 1892 by John Muir, has devoted itself to the study and protection of the earth's scenic and ecological resources—mountains, wetlands, woodlands, wild shores and rivers, deserts and plains. The publishing program of the Sierra Club offers books to the public as a nonprofit educational service in the hope that they may enlarge the public's understanding of the Club's basic concerns. The point of view expressed in each book, however, does not necessarily represent that of the Club. The Sierra Club has some sixty chapters coast to coast, in Canada, Hawaii, and Alaska. For information about how you may participate in its programs to preserve wilderness and the quality of life, please address inquiries to Sierra Club, 730 Polk Street, San Francisco, CA 94109.

The three quotations on page vi come from a symposium on nature writing edited by John A. Murray that appeared in "Manoa: A Pacific Journal of International Writing," Fall, 1992.

Page 227 serves as an extension of this copyright page.
ISBN: 0-87156-479-3
ISSN: 1072-4273

Production by Robin Rockey
Cover and text design by Amy Evans
Composition by Wilsted & Taylor

Printed in the United States of America on acid-free paper containing a minimum of 50% recovered waste paper, of which at least 10% of the fiber content is post-consumer waste

10 9 8 7 6 5 4 3 2 1

For Robert D. Richardson, Jr.

scholar, mentor, friend

And for Harry Middleton,

in memory

American nature writing is energized by our most urgent social and political questions: how to live in right relationship. In learning to pay respectful attention to one another and plants and animals, we relearn the arts of empathy, and thus humility and compassion—ways of proceeding that grow more and more necessary as the world crowds in. I'm trying to say nature writing is in a period of great vitality because it is driven by a political agenda, as good art always is.

William Kittredge

In my opinion, nature writing, including mine, is enjoying popularity because humans sense their need for reality, for physical challenge, for nature itself . . . nature, and by association the nature writer, is seductive. Our views are altered by our perceptions, prejudices, experiences; we can level forests, asphalt meadows, poison air. But wherever nature is left alone, she reasserts herself rather quickly and definitely. In a world of quicksand, she is constant, and writers who learn from her can provide audiences with considerable hope and confidence, as we draw her lessons into poetry, politics, and, eventually, posterity.

Linda M. Hasselstrom

In broadest terms, "natural history writing" addresses a breach between human culture and landscape, formalized in the agricultural and industrial revolutions. It seeks to define, in truly myriad ways, just relationships, not simply with all that composes the Earth but between conquering and conquered peoples, for example . . . I'd like to think that as a "natural history writer" I am addressing issues of prejudice, of dignity, and of tolerance. That with others I am bent on the creation of a literature of hope.

Barry Lopez

Contents

Preface

One touch of nature makes the whole world kin.
William Shakespeare,
Troilus and Cressida (III, 3)

With this collection, Sierra Club Books begins a new series dedicated to bringing you some of the best nature writing of the previous twelve months. For many years, readers have enjoyed annuals devoted to short stories, poetry, essays, plays, and other literary forms. Now they can sample a portion of the finest nature writing as well. Some of the authors in this anthology are well established (Barry Lopez and Annie Dillard), others are just becoming widely known (David Petersen and Linda Hasselstrom), and at least two are being introduced to a national audience for the first time (Sherry Simpson and Jennifer Brice). All have mastered their voice and craft and have something compelling to say about nature. You will find a variety of genres here: fiction (Annie Dillard), journal (Edward Abbey), poetry (Pat Matsueda), essay (most of the selections), and article (Annick Smith). The book is also geographically diverse and includes areas both inside and outside the United States: Mexico, Montana, Iceland, North Carolina, the Galápagos Islands, Norway, Alaska, Japan, New York City, Honduras, Arizona, Hawaii, Cuba, and Los Angeles, to name a few. The range of topics is as rich as the range of literary styles. You can ride in a helicopter and shoot anesthetic darts at an Alaskan grizzly bear with Sherry Simpson. Explore the botanical and paleontological wonders of the Central American land bridge with David Rains Wallace. Watch a peregrine falcon in action over the skies of Utah with Terry Tempest

Williams. Visit the Grand Canyon with Barry Lopez. Take a walk on a Pacific Northwest beach with Brenda Peterson. Structurally, the book also takes a new turn for anthologies as it alternates male and female voices (twelve women and twelve men) to provide a natural rhythm that will hopefully add to your reading pleasure.

Next year's collection is already being planned. If you have a selection, or know of a selection, that you believe would contribute to that anthology, by all means send it to me in care of Sierra Club Books, 100 Bush Street, 13th Floor, San Francisco, California 94104. I am particularly interested in nature writing (i.e., writings of any genre with a strong natural content) from the following groups: (1) writers known only locally or regionally but with national potential, (2) writers from the Midwest, Northeast, and Deep South, (3) writers with experiences in nature abroad, (4) writers concerned with nature in an urban or suburban context, and (5) writers from ethnic groups offering alternative perspectives on nature (such as African American, Asian American, Hispanic American, and Native American). I promise to respond to each submission. Working together—readers and editor—we can build anthologies in the future that, like this one, hold both literary excellence and thematic and stylistic diversity as the standard.

I have many thanks to give. Frank Stewart at the University of Hawaii introduced me to the exemplary work of Pat Matsueda and Adele Ne Jame, and also provided a forum in an issue of *Manoa* last year for a symposium on nature writing that generated some valuable responses. Annie Dillard brought the writings of Harry Middleton to my attention several years ago. Amy Ling at the University of Wisconsin provided helpful guidance. My students in a graduate seminar in nature writing at the University of Alaska, Fairbanks, in the spring of 1993 worked hard to make the class productive, and I learned much about the genre from our discussions. I thank Barry Lopez for generously spending an evening with the seminar group at my home. As always I must thank the many authors, agents, and editors without whose enthusiastic cooperation a book like this would be impossible. David Spinner and Jon Beckmann at Sierra Club Books immediately saw the value of such a series, and I am grateful to them. As a matter of fact, the anthology was David Spinner's idea, generated in the course of one of our long, rambling telephone conversations. The dedication acknowledges a promise made to Professor Richardson in graduate school, that I would one day dedicate a book to him as he dedicated his biography of Thoreau to his mentor, Walter Jackson Bate. Finally I must give thanks to the Murray family, especially to my four-year-old son, who is part of the generation that will inherit this world in the next century, a century to whose birth all of us nature writers are now attending.

J. A. M.

Harry Middleton

In Memoriam

Fear no more the heat o' the sun,
Nor the furious winter's rages;
Thou thy worldly task hast done,
Home art gone, and ta'en thy wages.
Shakespeare, *Cymbeline (IV, 2)*

I learned about Harry Middleton in 1990 from Annie Dillard, whose praise for his fly-fishing essays on the Smokies was unqualified. For several years Harry and I visited over the phone. Harry called me from Alabama to thank me for including him in this book. Days after we spoke Harry died of a heart attack. I would ask readers to buy as many of his books as possible, because they are the only legacy he left two teenage sons in need of a college education. They are: *The Bright Country* (Simon and Schuster), *Rivers of Memory* (Pruett Publishing Company), *The Starlight Angling Society* (Meadow Run Press), *On the Spine of Time* (Simon and Schuster), and *The Earth Is Enough* (Simon and Schuster). To further assist the family a fund has been set up on their behalf: Harry Middleton Memorial Fund, c/o Pruett Publishing, 2928 Pearl Street, Boulder, Colorado 80301 (800-247-8224).

These are some lines Harry wrote before he died:

> More and more these days my dreams are of rivers, of wild waters, water that carries me away.

I will miss this big generous man, who wrote so beautifully of the mountains and waters he loved.

Introduction

Nowhere Ridge

I.

It is not down on any map; true places never are.
Herman Melville

I lay down in the rock bunker and found it served a useful purpose. Whoever carried the talus to the knoll understood the effects of wind at twelve thousand feet. The structure faced west, along the axis of the prevailing Pacific storm track, and was shaped like the entrance to the womb, with the enclosed end pointing toward the wind and the open end toward the rising sun. Lying inside the shelter with my hands behind my head and my feet sticking out the entrance, I looked up and saw only the cold Colorado sky. Passing clouds. A curious golden eagle. The chirp of a pika. The sweet fragrance of high-altitude clover. The blue curve of infinity.

What was this thing? Certainly not a frost heave or meandering rock channel. Too symmetrical for that. Nor was it a cairn. Too elaborate to mark a trail, and I was miles from the nearest trail. How old was it? The gray hoary chunks of granite, at least those at the base, had rested *in situ* for centuries. The lichens, which grow more slowly than human consciousness, attested to that. Dull iridescent red, they covered the foundation cobble like dried blood. Who built it? Yes, that was the question. Whoever or whatever, I could have remained a while. For one thing, the grassy bed was well suited for a nap. For another, the thin mountain air always acts like a narcotic, especially after ascending two thousand feet in about an hour. But I had another mountain, farther off, to climb that bright August day. I stood up, walked around, scratched my head in befuddlement, dug the camera out of the pack and took a picture. The reconnaissance complete, I methodically surveyed the horizon, as I had been taught in the Marines long ago, to orient myself should it become necessary to make a report.

To the west were the Never Summer Mountains, the same classic range that Ansel Adams memorialized in a well-known photograph during the Great Depression. Mount Stratus (12,520 feet). Mount Nimbus (12,706 feet). Mount Cumulus (12,725 feet). Mount Cirrus (12,797 feet). The supreme work of some 30 million years was subsequently mutilated by the Denver Water Board and the Grand Water Ditch, a monumental act of hubris that diverted the headwaters of the Colorado River to the parched East Slope. Imagine Thomas Moran's 1875 painting *The Mountain of the Holy Cross* with a well-engineered gash running the width of the canvas. Aeschylus comes to mind: "Those that the gods would destroy, they first make mad with power." To the north was the Mummy Range, on the far side of which you will find a lost country—the Comanche Peak Wilderness—as beautiful as anything I have seen in six years of exploring the Alaskan interior. To the south was Middle Park. Cold clear streams falling swiftly out of the high country. Low rocky ridges of quaking aspen and Douglas fir. A sportsmen's paradise, where I fished and hunted in my youth, before the ski resorts, the dam project, the clear-cuts, the summer home sprawl, and the general tourist blight turned the wild democratic valley into Little Europe.

Below Mount Baker (12,397 feet) I could just make out Baker Gulch, where in 1973 a large male black bear killed and partially ate a Wisconsin man sleeping in his tent. Ray Lyons, a World War II bomber pilot and West Slope outfitter I later worked for as a hunting guide in 1977, was summoned from his Grand Mesa cattle camp to track down and kill the bear. He and his Plott hounds (a modern version of the Greek Furies) accomplished that task in one day. More recently, green activists successfully halted the logging of old-growth forest in Baker Gulch. To the east, where the far ponderosa foothills dropped like headlands, was the vanished buffalo prairie of the Pawnee and the Arapahoe, colored a light blue like the sea. Somewhere beyond that oceanic horizon were the distant cornfields and buckeye woodlots of Ohio where I spent a childhood looking west. The rising smog of rush-hour Denver coffee-stained the southeastern portion of the compass. To those familiar with the Colorado Front Range, it has now become apparent that I was somewhere in Rocky Mountain National Park. The place? Let us call it Nowhere Ridge.

I did not tarry long that day, did not tear apart the sod looking for immaculate arrowheads or upend ancient dignified rocks to locate that well-preserved axehead or grinding stone. My ignorance was total, blissful. Without so much as a backward glance, I hurried on my way, singing all the songs from Bob Dylan's *Blood on the Tracks* I could remember, not realizing, like so many discoverers, that I had even made a discovery. I dutifully climbed my appointed mountain, sat cross-legged at the summit, found a bighorn sheep skeleton on the descent, befriended a brown-feathered ptarmigan while eating an orange, spotted a herd of elk in a nameless valley, watched them graze and play and splash in a tarn through binoculars, and then trotted the five miles out to the road and drove back to Boulder. That night I saw a band named the Johnny Three at the Blue Note and shared a table with my high school buddy Jimmy Miller, who played lead guitar in a rival rock group called the Sensations, and his girlfriend Maxine, who still works as a fashion model in Denver. In between sets we talked about such things as whether Wade Boggs or Don Mattingly would win the American League batting championship in 1985, and, if they made it to the Super Bowl, whether the Denver Broncos would lose by 21 or 28 points. The bunker on the Continental Divide seemed so inconsequential I never brought it up.

Sometime in late December, when all my neighbors were skiing to the grocery store, I decided to sort my slides from the previous summer. When the forgotten image flashed on the screen I puzzled over it for a long time. Outside the house snowflakes fell, and the wind howled. Somewhere a tape of John Lennon's last album played. Belatedly, I made a duplicate and sent it to Glen Kaye, Chief Park Naturalist, along with a letter. He probably knew about it, I wrote, but just in case here was a photo and map. I wondered if it might be part of an Indian game drive system. The bunker was located in such a way that game could be pushed past it by drivers working at timberline. A hunter could wait, concealed from view, with a bow and arrow, a spear, or an atlatl. I'd done the same thing while bow-hunting for mule deer in the Mount Evans Wilderness Area with my old college friend Greg Fife.

Within the week, a letter arrived. No record of the bunker existed, Kaye said. A team of archaeologists from Colorado State University and the National Park Service would be dispatched next summer as soon as the snow melted. Please inform no one of the exact location as undisturbed sites are rare and "so much pre-history in the park has already been lost." In a general way, as I am telling you, I told my roommates Dave Student (real name) and Jeff Swedlund, both of whom tied flies for a living, about the site. We were excited and happy; it was refreshing to know that Rocky Mountain National Park still kept secrets with 2.2 million annual visitors (now more than 3 million). As I recall, John Gierarch and Ed Engle came over later in the week for dinner and read Kaye's letter. Both have since gone on to become pretty well known nature writers; John with books such as *Trout Bum* and *The View from Rat Lake* and Ed with his essay collection *Seasonal*. At the time, like so many nature writers who are actively publishing today, we were still dabbling in a sort of transplanted Chinese nature poetry, unaware that there was this other genre growing faster than fireweed through a burned forest.

The results of the field study were sent to me about a year later, on the eve of their publication as a scientific monograph. As it turns out, the U-shaped structure was a vision quest site built upon a prehistoric (10,000-year-old) fasting bed. Both were used by Native Americans for meditative purposes. In some cases, as we know from Sitting Bull and Black Elk, self-mutilation with sharp obsidian blades was also practiced, the pain being seen as a way to further liberate the spirit. An idea of how far the participants would go is evident in George Caitlin's 1837 painting *Self-Torture in Sioux Ceremony,* which depicts a Teton Sioux hanging from a pole by tongs connected to sharp spikes piercing the skin and muscle of his chest. This ritual was part of the Sun Dance, which sought to acquire power from Wakan Tanka (the Great Mystery). Some of the last historic vision questers were interviewed by George Bird Grinnel, the naturalist who accompanied General Custer on his 1874 Black Hill expedition. Grinnel wrote of the Cheyenne in his 1923 book:

> In those old times, young men used to go off on the hills and fast for four nights. This was called wu wun, starving. They did this in order that they might be fortunate, and might not be hit in battle . . . they had no shelter and no covering. . . . If he fasted to the end, after four days, the old man went to him and brought him down to the camp. They did this only in the summer. This is said to have been purely a sacrifice, and not an attempt to dream for power; but often those who lay there did have dreams, and what they dreamed surely came to pass. Not everyone starved and to only a part of those who starved did the vision come.

As I had expected, there was also evidence that the site had been used in connection with a game drive system. The archaeologists discovered sixteen additional cairns on the ridgeline as well as a second, though much less evident, stone structure in the shape of a small circle. All totaled they unearthed 21 arrowheads, 7 butchering tools, 202 chipping flakes, and 2 grinding slabs. The oldest of these was a white chert projectile point dated to about ten thousand years before present, and the most recent was a quartzite point that was about five hundred years old. The artifacts came from quarries as close as Specimen Mountain in the Mummy Range and as far away as lower Middle Park near present-day Kremmling (where Louisiana-Pacific had until 1992 a facility that turned my favorite aspen groves into toxic waferboard and their associated beaver ponds into flooded quagmires). To read this monograph is to be humbled with the knowledge that a vibrant human culture occupied the Colorado Rockies when the ziggurats of Ur were still just a distant dream along the Euphrates.

Every summer since finding the site, almost ten years now, I have climbed a mountain or prominence on the summer solstice, the longest day of the year, and fasted from dawn to dusk. I take only water, a pencil and paper, perhaps a book of poetry, and my foul weather gear. I think about the preceding year and the year to come, who remains and who has passed on, what I have done right and what I have done wrong, what is important and what is not. Each year is different. Some years I come down exhausted. Other years I return uplifted. I look not for the false euphoria of the cult follower or the forced equanimity of the Stoic, both of which are illusions. I try only to better understand myself and my world. To see clearly, in the sense that the French philosopher Albert Camus understood the concept when he wrote in "The Wind at Djemila" that, above all, he wanted to "keep my lucidity to the last." To achieve balance and moderation as Aristotle used the terms. I believe the Plains Indians had a good idea in their pursuit of the vision quest as a mode of personal reflection. I also believe it would not be an entirely bad idea, in such a secular age, if more people did this. I certainly intend to take my son up to the hills and show him what I have learned when he reaches the age of awareness around thirteen or fourteen. The mountains have much to teach us, in their great resonant silences, in the spectacular beauty of their wide horizons, in the way the cloud shadows brighten and darken the ridges and valleys. To sit all day upon a heavy, solid mountain is to feel anchored. Do not get up and leave early. The more fatigued you become, the closer you are to achieving that which you seek. Stay until you take on the color of the earth and grow roots and sprout flowers that you can take back as gifts to share with loved ones, as evidence, to them and others, that there are worlds inside each of us that make the richest men and women seem idle fools and paupers.

II.

They crossed seven mountains before they came
to the gate of the forest;
they approached it with wonder.

The Epic of Gilgamesh, Book II,
("The Forest Journey"), circa 2300 B.C.

I began this prologue with the account of the fasting bed site because it seems to me that many of the essays in this collection are also concerned with the sacred in nature. This thematic consistency is not the result of any intentional effort on my part as editor, but has long been a characteristic of the genre. Indeed, the optimism and hope referred to by both Linda Hasselstrom and Barry Lopez in the epigraphs taken for this book are at the very heart of the human experience of nature.

Several authors among those gathered here come to mind on this theme of the sacred. Rick Bass, for example, in his essay on the Yaak Valley of northwestern Montana, deplores the greed that could decimate his pristine, albeit unprotected, mountains: "Even though there would be only about three weeks' worth of timber for the local sawmill if every last standing tree on Roderick Mountain were cut down . . . the local timber industry wants into Roderick, as they have gotten into every other forest up here." Like a latter-day Jeremiah, Bass urges his readers to take action to protect the sacred mountains from the secular forces of despoilation. "If I sound angry," he writes frankly, "it's because I am. And wild. Wild." When Rick and I were camping in Denali National Park several years ago (I'll never forget the storm that blew our tents down), he spoke often about the beauty and wildness of the Yaak Valley. His devotion to the region reminded me of the passion you find in the writings of John Muir. It was exciting to see such vitality, such purposefulness, in a writer so young and full of promise.

Dan O'Brien, writing from a viewpoint of indignation and outrage kindred to that in Bass, finds in a new electric light on top of a previously dark mountain near his home in the Black Hills a metaphor for what human civilization is doing to the entire planet. The light represents the imposition of human technology, the artificial, on the natural, an old mountain on the Sioux homeland. While interviewing O'Brien in 1988 for *The Bloomsbury Review* I remember him emphasizing the restorative power of the Dakotas, how the country helped him through a personal crisis as it had once helped Theodore Roosevelt; you could feel his passion for the landscape and its unique values. Anyone who has ever gazed up at the starry heavens, and had that view marred by the lights of orbiting space satellites and transcontinental jets, understands the lament of Dan O'Brien. There are certain scenes the viewing of which should be considered a basic human right, along with the right to life, liberty, and the pursuit of happiness.

One hundred years ago, in 1893 (Grover Cleveland was president), the beliefs expressed by these two writers—antipathy toward unlimited growth and suspicion of "progress" as defined by the bottom line—would have been considered radical and perhaps even subversive. At the very least they would have been on the margins of discourse. Today they have become mainstream views, with a wide political consensus behind them. The extent to which they have become institutionalized is seen most dramatically in the fact that the incumbent vice-president, Albert Gore, has himself written a best-selling nature book. This change represents the beginning of an historic intellectual revolution, reversing a perspective of dominion over nature that has prevailed in Western civilization for thousands of years. That these writers are male is all the more interesting, in light of the fact that it has been a patriarchal order that has perpetuated the exploitative view of nature.

Linda Hasselstrom, a neighbor and good friend of Dan O'Brien, strikes a similar chord in her essay: "If the earth were a single country, it might well consider itself under attack—by humanity as a whole." She suggests that much of what we are doing constitutes crimes against nature, against Gaia, the character from Greek mythology sometimes identified with the Earth's biosphere. "Many Indian tribes," Hasselstrom writes, "have held this belief [that the Earth is a god] for centuries. We might do worse than emulate them." When I interviewed Linda Hasselstrom for *The Bloomsbury Review* last year she spoke at length about this theme in her writing, a view that is so prevalent in her book *Land Circle*. In that book, as in this essay, Hasselstrom makes a case for what she calls a "covenant." She quotes Black Elk, an eminent religious figure of the Oglala Lakota for whom a wilderness area in the Black Hills around Harney Peak is named:

> You have noticed that everything an Indian does is in a circle, and that is because the Power of the World always works in circles, and everything tries to be round. . . . The sky is round and I have heard that the earth is round like a ball and so are all the stars. The Wind, in its greatest power, whirls. Birds make their nests in circles, for theirs is the same religion as ours. The sun comes forth and goes down in a circle. The moon does the same, and both are round. Even the seasons form a great circle in their changing, and always come back again to where they were. The life of a man is a circle from childhood to childhood and so it is in everything where power moves. Our tipis were round like the nests of birds and these were always set in a circle, the nation's hoop, a nest of many nests where the Great Spirit meant for us to hatch our children.

Sherry Simpson provides a variation on this theme by reminding us of the sacredness of the northern brown bear, an animal worshipped long ago by both Neanderthal and Cro-Magnon cultures in Europe. A newspaper reporter, she takes an assignment to follow biologists as they sedate and radio-collar a bear: "I don't tell anybody the real reason I asked for this story: so I can touch with my own hands what frightens me most." What she finds is that the bear is beautiful and powerful and "is a furnace, burning with life." Afterward, as the helicopter lifts off from the remote site, the bear "looks clownish with a yellow and a white tag punched into each ear and a white leather radio collar circling her neck." The author feels that "we have stolen something from her." What has been stolen is the bear's innocence, its dignity, its sacredness, and Simpson expresses mixed feelings about the experience:

> A sense of beauty and loss pierces me as I struggle to tell myself something important, something lasting about this night, about how I have glimpsed the way bears live here, high above the world, and yet not nearly far enough away from roads, chainsaws, guns, helicopters. . . . If this mountain top is wilderness, then it is wilderness that rubs so close to civilization that I can feel it fraying beneath my feet.

Linda Hogan, of Chickasaw Indian descent, writes from a similarly reverential point of view in her essay "The Voyagers":

> To dream of the universe is to know that we are small and brief as insects, born in a flash of rain and gone a moment later. We are delicate and our world is fragile.

Hogan turns her eyes toward outer space, the greatest wilderness of all, and writes of the flight of the *Voyager* spacecraft, which has now sped past Pluto, lifted off the plane of the solar system, and entered the lonely gulfs of interstellar space. The *Voyager* carries a golden record with everything on it from Beethoven to Chuck Berry, but, Hogan ironically notes, "even the metals used in the record tell a story about the spoils of inner earth, the laborers in the hot mines. Their sweat is in that record, hurtling away from our own galaxy." Hers is a humble admonition, shed of all hubris:

> We have come so far away from wisdom, a wisdom that is the heritage of all people, an old kind of knowing that respects a community of land, animals, plants, and other people as equal to ourselves. . . . We hardly know who we are. We face the search for ourselves alone. In spite of our search through the universe, we do not know our own personal journeys. We still wonder if the soul weighs half an ounce, if it goes into the sky at the time of our death, if it also reaches out, turning, through the universe.

The book ends, fittingly, on a birth, as Jennifer Brice writes from personal experience about the sacred process that forms the ultimate basis for nature and civilization. Both her grandmother and mother were avid flower gardeners and in her pregnancy Brice regards her mother's fertile garden as "a healing tonic, a hymn to the regenerative power of the earth, a drunken celebration of life under the midnight sun." She also seeks advice and counsel from her mother on the birthing process:

> Deeply afraid of giving birth, I yearn for the only solace my mother cannot—or will not—give. Casually . . . I ask about labor. She tells me a story about water that breaks in the middle of the night, timed contractions, the urge to push, the moment when the baby wakes in her arms. She never uses the word "pain."

Later, Jennifer Brice learns all about pain: "The first contraction tears through me at midnight. I feel a giant hand reach inside and try to claw my baby out. . . . For a baby, the violent, bruising passage through the birth canal must be like expulsion from paradise." Entering life is no less painful than leaving life; both are sacred and both are part of what Black Elk called the circle of nature.

One has the sense, in these and other writings, that nature writing is poised at the beginning of a period of wonderful exuberance. All of the excitement that attends the beginning of a new century, and the start of a new millennium, together with a growing awareness of the interdependence of nature and culture, cannot help but fuel this historic genre. I believe that as the genre attracts more and more gifted young writers, and addresses increasingly the compelling political and social issues of our time, it will gain in stature and maturity, offering what Barry Lopez so eloquently calls "a literature of hope." Nature teaches humility, generosity, and balance, and nature writers, in turn, share these immutable values with a world often lost in hubris, greed, and disorder. The best works of nature writing are yet to come, and they will most certainly be concerned with these and other eternal verities.

III.

Nature is that which we observe in perception through the senses.
Alfred North Whitehead, from *The Concept of Nature*
(Tarner Lectures delivered at Trinity College, November 1919)

There is a prominent rock outcropping along the Sanctuary River in Denali National Park. Since moving to Alaska in 1988, I have sat on that knob for the summer solstice a couple of times. The view is particularly good in late June, when the midnight sun sets due north and shines down the valley to illuminate the north-facing glaciers at the head of the Sanctuary River. This is nature, alright, and about as wild as you'll find among the national parks that are road accessible. The country is lean, hard, and has the long low contours of all ancient grounds. What trees you see are either thin or very thin. A spruce tree fifty feet tall would be something to camp under. Timberline is astonishingly close to the valley floor. From the salience you can see all sorts of animals—bear, caribou, moose—though never in the biblical numbers of twenty or thirty years ago (except the profligate mosquitoes). Occasionally a wolf trots by, looking not like those robust captive wolves you see on the covers of magazines, but rather like a homeless person who has taken the form of a wild animal. I read once that the Sanctuary outcropping was used almost continuously for ten thousand years before the arrival of white people; from the windy vantage the forefathers of the Iroquois and the Inca could spot animals and direct hunts, or, like me, simply take in the view. From what we know of human life before agriculture and domesticated animals, a lot of time was spent simply taking in the view.

This year, about two weeks ago, I spent the solstice up there. Not much exciting happened, compared to past years. In the morning the mosquitoes were pretty bad for the first hour. The second hour is difficult to describe. About nine nature showed her mercy and created a wind. Later, I watched a ragged band of caribou cross the valley from west to east and then turn back west again. It took them all afternoon to accomplish this, and they looked about as directionless as a group of congressmen. Caribou are not known for their intelligence, a fact I became acquainted with while hunting them last September in the Arctic Refuge. This group was shedding their winter coats, and their antlers were only partially formed, and they looked, in a word, beleaguered. By mid-August the bulls are so beautiful that long-lens photographers, myself included, will chase them all afternoon, but in late June they look like something that can't decide if it is alive or dead.

I had with me that day Paul Kennedy's new best-seller *Preparing for the Twenty-first Century* and from time to time dipped into the tome. His augurings are like those of Malthus, only less hopeful: vast urban slums, decimated forests, global warming, loss of the ozone layer, illiteracy, a population of 10 or 20 billion, wars, plagues, insect infestations, pollution, economic calamities, agricultural failures. Finally I realized I had read this all before in the Old Testament and put the book away. Toward evening a merlin hunted mice on the rolling green tundra, gliding just inches above the ground in graceful smooth lines that paralleled those of the Earth. The merlin did not catch one thing in the time I watched, which was long enough for several tour helicopters to pass overhead on their way to Denali. About an hour before the sun went down I thought I saw a bear, but the binoculars showed it to be a moose. A cow moose, still gaunt from giving birth. Her calf was nowhere to be seen. In the evening everything looks like a bear.

It was one-thirty in the morning when I returned to camp. The sky was still luminous with arctic light, the color of the fur on the belly of a wolf, which is always ten shades lighter than whatever is on the back. The river made its music behind the white spruce, as it has since before the human race came out of Africa, as it will when English is spoken only by scholars. Some of today's writers will endure to that distant time. The best among us write for that audience, write for the ages, for the unborn. The best among us also work to provide a vantage for the reader, a point like the Sanctuary outcropping from which to better view the landscape, both figurative and literal. Above all, contemporary nature writers are respectful of nature, as the human race was for many millennia before acquiring the technology to control nature. It is entirely possible that some of the writers included in this book may be remembered in those distant times, when the solstice sun will still be shining on the headwaters of the Sanctuary. I pray that there will still be Dall sheep on those glaciers that will let you sit among them, as they did in the beginning, fifteen thousand summers ago, when men and women and children with Asian faces first walked into this great land of ours.

Barry Lopez

Replacing Memory

from *Georgia Review*

I. *Manhattan, 1976*

The hours of coolness in the morning just before my mother died I remember for their relief. It was July and it had been warm and humid in New York City for several days, temperatures in the high eighties, the air motionless and heavy with the threat of rain.

I awoke early that morning. It was also my wife's thirtieth birthday, but our celebration would be wan. My mother was in her last days, and the lives of all of us in the family were contorted by grief and tension—and by a flaring of anger at her cancer. We were exhausted.

I felt the coolness of the air immediately when I awoke. I walked the length of the fourth-floor apartment, opened one side of a tall casement window in the living room, and looked at the sky. Cumulus clouds, moving to the southeast on a steady wind. Ten degrees cooler than yesterday's dawn, by the small tin thermometer. I leaned forward to rest my arms on the sill and began taking in details of movement in the street's pale light, the city's stirring.

In the six years I had lived in this apartment as a boy, from 1956 until 1962, I had spent cumulative months at this window. At the time, the Murray Hill section of Manhattan was mostly a neighborhood of decorous living and brownstone row houses, many of them not yet converted to apartments. East 35th Street for me, a child newly arrived from California, presented an enchanting pattern of human life. Foot-beat policemen began their regular patrol at eight. The delivery of residential mail occurred around nine and was followed about ten by the emergence of women on shopping errands. Young men came and went the whole day on three-wheel grocery cart bikes, either struggling with a full load up the moderate rise of Murray Hill from Gristede's down on Third Avenue, or hurtling back the other way, driving no-hands against light traffic, cartons of empty bottles clattering explosively as the bike's solid tires nicked potholes.

In the afternoon a dozen young girls in private-school uniforms swirled in glee and posed with exaggerated emotion across the street, waiting to be taken home. By dinnertime the street was almost empty of people; then, around eleven, it was briefly animated again with couples returning from the theater or some other entertainment. Until dawn, the pattern of glinting chrome and color in the two rows of curbed automobiles remained unchanged. And from night to night that pattern hardly varied.

Overlaying the street's regular, diurnal rhythm was a more chaotic pattern of events, an unpredictability I would watch with unquenchable fascination for hours at a time. (A jog in the wall of The Advertising Club of New York next door made it impossible for me to see very far to the west on 35th Street. But if I leaned out as far as I dared, I could see all the way to the East River in the other direction.) I would study the flow of vehicles below: an aggressive insinuation of yellow taxis, the casual slalom of a motorcycle through lines of stalled traffic, the obstreperous lumbering of large trucks. The sidewalks, with an occasional imposing stoop jutting out, were rarely crowded, for there were neither shops nor businesses here, and few tourists. But with Yeshiva University down at the corner of Lexington, the 34th Street Armory a block away, a Swedenborgian chuch midblock, and 34th Precinct police headquarters just up from Third Avenue, I still saw a fair array of dress and captivating expressions of human bearing. The tortoise pace of elderly women in drab hats paralleled the peeved ambling of a middle-aged man anxious to locate a cab. A naïf, loose-jointed in trajectory down the sidewalk, with wide-flung strides. A buttonhooking young woman, intently scanning door lintels and surreptitiously watching a building superintendent leaning sullenly against a service entrance. Two men in vested suits in conversation on the corner where, rotund and oblivious, they were a disruption, like a boulder in a creek. A boy running through red-lighted traffic with a large bouquet in his hand, held forth like a bowsprit.

All these gaits together with their kindred modulations seemed mysteriously revealing to me. Lingering couples embraced, separated with resolve, then embraced once more. People halted and turned toward each other in hilarious laughter. I watched as though I would never see such things again—screaming arguments, the otherworldly navigations of the deranged, and the haughty stride of single men dressed meticulously in evening clothes.

This pattern of traffic and people, an overlay of personality and idiosyncrasy on the day's fixed events, fed me in a wordless way. My eyes would drift up from these patterns to follow the sky over lower Manhattan, a flock of house sparrows, scudding clouds, a distant airplane approaching La Guardia or Idlewild with impossible slowness.

Another sort of animation drew me regularly to this window: weather. The sound of thunder. Or a rising hiss over the sound of automobiles that meant the streets were wet from a silent rain. The barely audible rattle of dozens of panes of glass in the window's leadwork—a freshening wind. A sudden dimming of sunshine in the living room. Whatever I was doing, these signals would pull me away. At night, in the isolating light cone of a streetlamp, I could see the slant, the density, and sometimes the exact size of raindrops. (None of this could I learn with my bare hands outstretched, in the penumbral dark under the building's cornices.) I watched rainwater course east in sheets down the calico-patched street in the wake of a storm; and cascades of snow, floating and wind-driven, as varied in their character as falls of rain, pile up in the streets. I watched the darkness between buildings burst with lightning, and I studied intently the rattle-drum of hail on car roofs.

The weather I watched from this window, no matter how wild, was always comforting. My back was to rooms secured by family life. East and west, the room shared its walls with people I imagined little different from myself. And from this window I could see a marvel as imbued with meaning for me then as a minaret—the Empire State Building. The high windows of its east wall gleamed imperially in the first rays of dawn, before the light flared down 35th Street, glinting in bits of mica in the façades of brownstones. Beneath the hammer of winter storms, the building seemed courageous and adamantine.

The morning that my mother would die I rested my forearms on the sill of the window, glad for the change of weather. I could see more of the wind, moving gray clouds, than I could feel; but I knew the walk to the subway later that morning, and the short walk up 77th Street to Lennox Hill Hospital, would be cooler.

I had been daydreaming at the window for perhaps an hour when my father came downstairs. The faint odors in the street's air—the dampness of basements, the acrid fragrance of ailanthus trees, the aromatics in roof tar—had drawn me off into a dozen memories. My father paused, speechless, at the foot of the stairs by the dining table. As determined as he was to lead a normal life around Mother's last days, he was at the beck and call of her disease almost as much as she was. With a high salute of his right hand, meant to demonstrate confidence, and an ironic grimace, he went out the door. Downstairs he would meet my brother, who worked with him, and together they would take a cab up to the hospital. My brother, three years younger, was worn out by these marathon days but uncomplaining, almost always calm. He and my father would eat breakfast together at the hospital and sit with Mother until Sandra and I arrived, then leave for work.

I wanted an undisturbed morning, the luxury of that kind of time, in which to give Sandra her birthday presents, to have a conversation not shrouded by death. I made breakfast and took it into the bedroom. While we sipped coffee I offered her what I had gotten. Among other things, a fossil trilobite, symbol of longevity. But we could not break the rind of oppression this terminal disease had created.

While Sandra showered, I dressed and returned to the window. I stood there with my hands in my pockets staring at the weathered surface of the window's wood frame, with its peeling black paint. I took in details in the pitted surface of the sandstone ledge and at its boundary, where the ledge met the color of buildings across the street. I saw the stillness of the ledge against the sluggish flow of early morning traffic and a stream of pedestrians in summer clothing below. The air above the street was a little warmer now. The wind continued to blow steadily, briskly moving cloud banks out over Brooklyn.

I felt a great affection for the city, for its tight Joseph's coat of buildings, the vitality of its people, the enduring grace of its plane trees, and the layers of its history, all of it washed by a great tide of weather under maritime skies. Standing at the window I felt the insistence and the assurance of the city, and how I was woven in here through memory and affection.

Sandra touched my shoulder. It was time we were gone, uptown. But something stayed me. I leaned out, bracing my left palm against the window's mullion. The color I saw in people's clothes was now muted. Traffic and pedestrians, the start-up of myriad businesses, had stirred the night's dust. The air was more rank with exhaust. A flock of pigeons came down the corridor of the street toward me, piebald, dove gray, white, brindled ginger, ash black—thirty or more of them. They were turning the bottom of a long parabolic arc, from which they shot up suddenly, out over Park Avenue. They reached a high, stalling apex, rolled over it, and fell off to the south, where they were cut from view by a building. A few moments later they emerged much smaller, wings pounding over brownstones below 34th Street, on a course parallel to the wind's.

I left, leaving the window open.

When Sandra and I emerged a half-hour later from the hospital elevator, my brother was waiting to meet us. I could see by the high, wistful cast of his face that she was gone.

II. *Arizona, 1954*

Our train arrived at Grand Canyon Village on the South Rim late on a summer afternoon. With my brother Denny and a friend of my mother, a young woman named Ann, I had come up on the Santa Fe spur line from Williams, a town about thirty miles west of Flagstaff. We had left Los Angeles the evening before, making a rail crossing of the Sonoran Desert so magical I had fallen silent before it.

The train itself was spellbinding. I do not remember falling asleep as we crossed the desert, but I know that I must have. I only remember sitting alone in a large seat in the darkened observation car, looking at the stars and feeling nearly out of breath with fortune—being able to wander up and down the aisles of the streaking train, sitting in this observation car hour by hour staring at the desert's sheer plain, the silhouettes of isolated mountain ranges, and, above, the huge swath of the Milky Way.

Near midnight we stopped for a few minutes in Needles, a railroad town on the lower Colorado across the river from the Fort Mojave Indian Reservation. The scene on the platform was dreamlike, increasing my sense of blessing. The temperature was over one hundred degrees, but it was a dry heat, pleasant. I had never been up this late at night. Twenty or thirty Indians—I didn't know then, but they would have been Chemuwevis as well as Mojaves, and also Navajos, who worked on many of the Santa Fe repair crews—craned their necks, looking for disembarking passengers or cars to board. Mexican families stood tightly together, stolid, shy and alert. The way darkness crowded the platform's pale lamplight, the way the smoky light gleamed on silver bracelets and corn-blossom necklaces, leaving its sheen on the heavy raven hair of so many women—all this so late in the heated night made Needles seem very foreign. I wanted to stay. I could have spent all the time I had been offered at Grand Canyon right here.

But we left. I returned to my seat in the now completely empty observation car. I am sure I fell asleep shortly after we crossed the river, on the way to Kingman.

John, Ann's husband of only a few months and a seasonal ranger at the park, met the train at the canyon. My brother and I were to have two weeks with them before Mother came up to join us. (The three of them taught together in the secondary school system in Southern California's San Fernando Valley.)

On the way up from Williams, the train had climbed through piñon and juniper savannah. As I descended the train car's steps, I saw fully for the first time the largest trees I had ever looked at—ponderosa pines. In the same moment, their fragrance came to me on the warm air, a sweet odor, less sharp than that of other pines.

John embraced Ann fiercely and said, "I will never be separated from you, ever again, for this long." Their passion and his words seemed wondrous to me, profound and almost unfathomable. I stared at the huge ponderosas, which I wanted to touch.

During those two weeks, Denny and I traveled the South and East rims of the canyon with Ann while John lectured daily to visitors. The four of us lived in a small log cabin with a high-pitched roof. Sometimes I rose early, before the sun, and went outside. I would just stand in the trees or wander nearby in the first light. I could not believe the stillness.

A short distance from the cabin was a one-room museum with an office. I spent hours there, looking at pinned insects, stuffed birds, and small animals. Some of these creatures seemed incredibly exotic to me, like the Kaibab squirrel with its tufted ears—perhaps a made-up animal.

I read pamphlets about the geology of the canyon and its Indian history, and I went with my brother to some of John's lectures. The most entrancing was one in which he described the succession of limestones, sandstones, and shales that make up the visible canyon walls. The precision and orderliness of his perception, the names he gave so easily to these thousands of feet of wild, unclimbable, and completely outsized walls, seemed inspired, a way to *grasp* it all. I think this was the first such litany I committed to memory:

Kaibab, Toroweap,
Coconiño, Hermit;
Supai, Redwall,
Temple, Muav.
Bright Angel.
Tapeats.

On John's days off we drove out to picnic at Shoshone Point, a place on the East Rim set aside by the Park Service for its employees. Here, far from the pressing streams of visitor traffic, the silence within the canyon reverberated like silence in the nave of a large cathedral. The small clearing with its few picnic tables was a kind of mecca, a place where the otherwise terrifying fall-off of the canyon seemed to comfort or redeem. I saw a mountain lion there one afternoon. It leaped the narrow road in one long bound, its head strangely small, its long tail strangely thick, a creature the color of Coconiño sandstone.

I did not go back to the canyon after that summer for twenty-six years. In the spring of 1980, I joined several other writers and editors at a workshop there in the Park Service's Albright Training Center. I arrived at night by plane, so did not see much until the next morning. I got up early, just after sunrise, thinking I would walk over to the El Tovar Lodge on the rim of the canyon for breakfast. The walk, I thought, would be a way to reenter the landscape, alone and quietly, before the activities of the workshop caught me up in a flow of ideas and in protracted discussions.

I didn't remember the area well enough that morning to know where I was, relative to the cabin we'd stayed in, but I set off through the woods toward what felt like the canyon's rim. The gentle roll of the land, the sponginess of ponderosa needles beneath my feet, familiar but nameless odors in the air, the soft twitter of chickadees up ahead—all this rounded into a pattern my body remembered.

At a certain point I emerged from the trees onto a macadam road, which seemed the one to take to the lodge. I'd not gone more than a few yards, however, before I was transfixed by the sight of a small building. It was boarded up, but it had once been the museum. An image of its interior formed vividly in my mind—the smooth, glass-topped display stands with bird eggs and prehistoric tools, the cabinets and drawers full of vials of seeds and insect trays.

I walked on, elated and curiously composed. I would come back.

At the foot of the road was a wide opening in the trees. Once it might have been a parking lot. I was only part-way across when I realized that the young pines growing here were actually coming up between train rails. Again I stood transfixed. It was here, all those years ago, that I had gotten off the train. I held tightly to that moment and began stepping eastward along the tracks, looking up every few steps to pure stands of ponderosa growing a hundred feet away to the south. Then I recognized a pattern in the trees, the way a dozen of the untapered, cinnamon-colored trunks stood together on a shallow slope. It had been here exactly that I had stepped off. I stared at them for many minutes, wondering more than anything at the way memory, given so little, could surge so unerringly.

I walked up to the trees and put my fingers on the bark, the large flat plates of small, concave scales. Far above, the narrow crowns were still against the bluing sky.

On the other side of the tracks I walked past the entrance to the lodge and stood at the edge of the canyon before a low, broad wall of stone. The moment my knees touched the wall, my unbounded view was shot with another memory—the feel of this stone angle against my belly when I was nine, and had had to hoist myself up onto the wall in order to see deep into the canyon. Now, I stood there long after the desire to gaze at the canyon had passed. I recalled suddenly how young ponderosas, bruised, smell like oranges. I waited, anxious, for memories that came like bursts of light: the mountain lion in its leap; the odor and jingle of harness mules and saddle horses in the hot sun at the top of Bright Angel Trail; my brother, light footed as a doe, at the wall of an Anasazi ruin. These images brought with them, even in their randomness, a reassurance about time, about the unbroken duration and continuous meaning of a single human life. With that came a sense of joy, which I took with me to breakfast.

III. *Bear River, Idaho, 1991*

Cort bought a potted sulfur buckwheat in the Alberton's in Jackson and he and John and I left for Idaho by way of Afton, Wyoming, passing through Montpelier and then Paris, Idaho. We turned off the main road there, drove west through Mink Creek and then Preston and swung north on US 91, crossing the bridge over Bear Creek, where we pulled off.

Cort had been here before. Neither John nor I had, but I had wanted to see the place for a long time. In this river bottom, rising away from me to the Bannock Range in the northwest and, more precipitously, to the Bear River Range behind me in the southeast, several hundred people had been violently killed on a bitter cold morning in January 1863. This obscure incident on the Bear River, once commonly called a "battle" by Western historians, has more often been referred to in recent years as a massacre, an unnecessary killing. Twenty-two men of the Second Cavalry and the Third Infantry, California Volunteers, under the command of a Col. Patrick Connor, were shot dead by Northern Shoshone. No one knows how many Shoshone were killed, but most estimate it was well over three hundred—more Indians than were killed in any other massacre in the West, including those at Sand Creek, Colorado (1864), Washita, Oklahoma (1868), or Wounded Knee, South Dakota (1890).

Connor's stated reason for bringing three hundred troops north from Salt Lake City that winter on a forced march was to protect the Overland Mail Route. The incident that triggered his decision was the death of a white miner in a skirmish involving several miners and Indians near Preston, a few days after Christmas, 1862. In his official report, Connor said he meant to "chastise" the Shoshone. He permitted a federal marshal to accompany him, carrying arrest warrants for three Shoshone men reputedly involved in the fatal incident with the miners, but Connor told the marshal it was not his intent to take any prisoners.

The Shoshone, 400 to 450 of them, were camped in willow thickets at the mouth of a ravine formed by Beaver Creek, several hundred yards short of its confluence with the Bear River. The spot was a traditional winter campsite, well protected from a prevailing north wind, with hot springs and with winter grazing for about two hundred horses. The night before the massacre, a man named Bear Hunter was in the nearby village of Franklin with his family, purchasing and loading sacks of wheat. He saw Connor's troops arriving, surmised their real purpose, and brought word back to the encampment.

Early the following morning, realizing he had lost the advantage of surprise, Connor massed his cavalry openly on the south side of the river, across from the Indian camp. The temperature was probably in the low teens. Connor then waited impatiently for his infantry, which had bogged in heavy snow on the road out of Franklin.

The Shoshone were by now all awake and digging in, for Connor's intentions had become plain. (Connor, of course, had no evidence that these particular Shoshone people had done anything wrong, only the suspicion that the men the US marshal wanted were among them.) One of the Shoshone men shouted out in perfect English, "Come on you California sons-of-bitches. We're ready for you." Provoked by the remark, Connor surged across the icy river and ordered the cavalry to charge. Fourteen of his soldiers were cut down almost instantly. Connor retreated to regroup and to help his foot soldiers, now arriving, get across the river.

Once they were over, Connor divided his forces, sending one column up the west slope of the ravine and another up the east slope, achieving a double flanking of the Indian camp. From these elevated positions the soldiers raked the camp with a furious, enfilading fire. The Shoshone, lightly armed, fought back with sporadic shots and in hand-to-hand combat for three or four hours, until late in the morning, by which time most of them were dead. Connor ordered his troops to kill every wounded Indian and to set fire to all seventy tepees, scattering, burning, or fouling all the food they could find as they did so. (Historians believe as many as sixty Shoshone might have escaped, most of them by swimming the partly frozen river.) In the final stages of the fight, Shoshone women were raped. Bear Hunter was tortured to death with a white-hot bayonet.

Connor reported 224 Indians killed. Residents of Franklin, six miles away, riding through the smoldering camp and into the willow thickets the next morning, counted many more dead, including nearly one hundred women and children. They took a few survivors back, housing them and treating their injuries. Connor, who returned immediately to Salt Lake City, denounced the Mormon people of Franklin in his official report as unhelpful and ungrateful. For their part, the Mormans may only have been heedful of Brigham Young's official policy: it was better to feed Indians than to fight with them.

John and Cort and I read in silence the historical plaques on a stone obelisk at the roadside. I felt more grief than outrage, looking across at the mouth of what is no longer called Beaver Creek but Battle Creek. An interpretive sign, erected in October 1990 by the Idaho Historical Society, seeks to correct the assumption that the fight here was a battle. It calls the encounter "a military disaster unmatched in Western history." A 1990 National Park Service plaque, designating the undistinguished ravine across the river bottom as a National Historical Landmark, says with no apparent irony that the spot "possesses national significance in communicating the history of the United States of America."

We left the highway, drove up a dirt road, and parked at the site of the encampment, which is not signed or marked. Where the Shoshone tepees once stood, in fact, the creek is now clogged with debris and refuse—a school locker, a refrigerator, a mattress, scorched magazines and tin cans, lawn furniture riddled with bullet holes. Violet-green swallows swooped the muddy water, only eight or ten feet across. On what is today called Cedar Bluff—the west side of the ravine—an iron-wheel combine and a walking-beam plow stood inert in sage and buckbrush. Overhead we heard the mewing of Franklin's gulls. From bottom flats near the river came the lowing of beef cattle.

Cort took the sulfur buckwheat from the truck, and the three of us started up the east side of the creek. The ravine, crisscrossed with horse and cattle tracks, was badly eroded. A variety of exotic grasses barely held in place a fine, pale tan, friable soil. Suddenly we saw a red fox. Then a muskrat in the water. Then the first of nine beaver dams, each built with marginal materials—teasel stalks and shreds of buckbrush, along with willow sticks and a few locust limbs. As we moved farther up the creek we heard yellow-headed blackbirds and mourning doves. In the slack water behind each succeeding dam, the water appeared heavier—silt was settling out before the water flowed on to the next dam, a hundred feet or so downstream. The beaver were clarifying the watercourse.

We finally found a small, open point of land near the creek. Cort put the buckwheat down and began to dig. He meant the planting as a simple gesture of respect. When he finished, I filled a boot with water and came back up the steep embankment. I poured it through my fingers, slowly, watching the small yellow flowers teeter in the warm air. Cort had gone on up the creek, but I met John's eye. He raised his eyebrow in acknowledgment, but he was preoccupied with his own thoughts and stepped away.

I climbed to the top of the ravine on the east side and walked north until I came to a high bluff above the creek where hundreds of bank swallows were nesting. I sat watching them while I waited for my friends to emerge from the willow thickets below. A few months before, Cort had lent me his copy of Newall Hart's scarce history, *The Bear River Massacre,* which contains reproductions of military reports and other primary materials. He recommended I read Brigham Madsen's

The Shoshoni Frontier and the Bear River Massacre. Cort himself had written about the incident in his *Idaho for the Curious.* When he and John joined me, Cort said he wanted to cross the creek and look over a section of Cedar Bluff he'd not walked on an earlier visit. I wanted to watch the swallows a while longer. John essayed another plan, and we each went our way again.

I worked back south along the creek bottom, pausing for long moments to watch for beaver, which I did not see. Frogs croaked. I came on mule-deer tracks. The warm air, laced with creek-bottom odors, was making me drowsy. I climbed back to the top of the ravine at the place where we had planted the buckwheat. A road there paralleled the creek, and its two tracks were littered with spent 12-gauge shotgun shells, empty boxes of .308 Winchester ammunition, and broken lengths of PVC pipe. I followed a barb-wire fence past a bathtub stock tank to the place where we'd parked.

I opened Hart's book on the hood of the truck. Tipped against the back endsheet is a large, folded plat map of the "Connor Battle Field," made in 1926 by W. K. Aiken, the surveyor of Franklin County, Idaho. I oriented it in front of me and began matching its detail to the landscape—Aiken's elevations, the sketchy suggestion of an early road to Montana, and a spot to the south where Aiken thought Connor had caught his first glimpse of the Shoshone encampment that morning. In the upper-right corner of his map Mr. Aiken had written, not so cryptically, "Not a Sparrow Falls."

The river's meander had since carried it nearly three-quarters of a mile to the south side of its flood plain. Otherwise the land—ranched and planted mostly to hay crops, dotted with farm houses and outbuildings, and divided by wire fences—did not, I thought, look so very different. You could see the cattle, and you could smell pigs faintly in the air.

John came back. He took a bird guide out of the truck and began slowly to page through it. Cort returned with the lower jaw of a young mule deer, which we took as a souvenir. We drove back out to the road and headed north for Pocatello.

IV. *Southern California, 1988*

Sandra and I were in Whittier, California, for a ceremony at the town's college. It was the sort of day one rarely sees in the Los Angeles basin anymore: the air gin-clear, with fresh, balmy winds swirling through the eucalyptus trees, trailing their aromatic odor. The transparency of the air, with a trace of the Pacific in it, was intoxicating.

As we left the campus, Sandra said she could understand now what I meant about the sunlight, the clear air of my childhood.

"Yes," I answered. "It was like this often in the spring, after the rains in February. Back then—well, it was a long time ago. Thirty years, thirty-five years ago."

It was obvious anyway, she said, how this kind of light had affected the way I saw things.

I told her something Wallace Stegner wrote: whatever landscape a child is exposed to early on, that will be the sort of gauze through which he or she will see all the world afterward. I said I thought it was emotional sight, not strictly a physical thing.

The spanking freshness of the afternoon encouraged a long drive. I asked Sandra if she wanted to go out to Reseda, where our family had lived in several houses, starting in 1948.

In November 1985 I had come down to Los Angeles from my home in Oregon. I was meeting a photographer who lived there, and with whom I was working on a story about the California desert for *National Geographic*. Flying into Los Angeles usually made me melancholy—and indignant. What I remembered from my childhood here, especially a rural countryside of farms and orchards out toward Canoga Park and Granada Hills, was not merely "gone." It had been obliterated, as if by a kind of warfare, and the remnant earth dimmed beneath a hideous pall of brown air.

A conversation with people in Los Angeles about these changes never soothes anyone. It only leaves a kind of sourness and creates impedence between people, like radio static. On the way to eat dinner with my friend, ruminating nevertheless in a silent funk about the place, I suddenly and vividly saw a photograph in my mind. It was of a young boy, riding the cantilevered support of a mailbox like a horse. On the side of the mailbox was "5837." I wrote the numerals down on the edge of a newspaper in my lap. I was not sure what they meant, but I recognized the boy as myself.

During dinner, I just as suddenly remembered the words "Wilbur Avenue," a street in Reseda. We had lived in three different houses in that town, the last one on Calvert Street. I had visited it several times in the intervening years, but hadn't been able to remember where the other two houses were.

The next day I rented a car and drove out to the Calvert Street home. Some thirty citrus and fruit trees my brother and I had planted in the mid-fifties had been dug out, and the lot had been divided to accommodate a second house, but parts of the lawn we had so diligently watered and weeded were still growing. I had raised tumbler pigeons here, and had had my first dog, a Kerry Blue terrier.

I inquired at a gas station on Victory Boulevard and found I was only a few blocks from crossing Wilbur Avenue. I made the turn there but saw the house numbers were in the six thousands and climbing; coming back the other way, I pulled up tentatively in front of 5837. I got out slowly, stared at the ranch-style house, and was suffused with a feeling, more emotion than knowledge, that this had been my home. Oleander bushes that had once shielded the house from the road were gone, along with a white rail fence and about fifteen feet of the front yard. In the late forties, before flood-control projects altered the drainage of this part of the San Fernando Valley, Wilbur Avenue had been a two-lane road with high, paved berms meant to channel flood water north to the Los Angeles River. In those days it also served as a corridor for sheep being moved to pasture. Now it was four lanes wide, with modest curbs.

One walnut tree remained in the yard, and a grapefruit tree closer to the house. I glimpsed part of the backyard through a breezeway but kept moving toward the front door, to knock and introduce myself.

There was no answer. I waited awhile and knocked again. When no one answered I walked around to the breezeway, where there was a kitchen door. I nearly collided with a small, elderly woman whose hands flew up involuntarily in defense. I quickly gave my name, explaining I had grown up here, that I only wished to look around a little, if I could. Fright still gripped her face.

"Do you know," I said to her, "how, from the family room, you have to take that odd step up to the hallway, where the bedrooms are?"

Her face relaxed. She waved off her anxiousness, seemingly chagrined. She explained that the owner of the house, a woman named Mrs. Little, was inside, dying of cancer. I remembered the name. She had lived out near Palmdale when we rented the house. I said that I was sorry, that there was no need for me to go inside.

"Well, please, have a look around," she said. She was relaxed now, serene, acting as though we were distant relatives. She walked into the backyard with me. At nearly each step, having difficulty stemming the pressure of memories, I blurted something—about a tree, about a cinderblock wall (still unfinished) around a patio. I pointed to some aging apricot and grapefruit trees, and to a massive walnut tree. We were standing on a concrete path, where I squatted down to peer at a column of ants going in and out of a crack. I had watched ants in this same crack forty years before. These were their progeny, still gathering food here. The mystery of their life, which had once transfixed me, seemed in no way to have diminished. I felt tears brim under my eyes and spill onto my cheeks. The woman touched my forearm deliberately but lightly, and walked away.

The horse stalls, a barn, and a row of chicken coops were gone, but I found scraps of green rolled roofing and splinters of framing lumber from them in the tall grass. I remembered mischief I had created here as a five-year-old. And then, like a series of sudden inflorescences, came memories first of the texture of tomatoes I had raised in a garden beside the chicken coops, and then of the sound of bees—how my friends and I had dared each other to walk past a hive of feral honeybees behind the barn where it ran close to the back fence.

Tempted to pick apricots and a grapefruit, I decided I had no right to do so. I said goodbye to the woman and asked her to convey my good wishes to Mrs. Little, whom I could not think would remember me.

Driving straight from the house to Anza-Borrego State Park in the western Sonoran Desert, a hundred and fifty miles away, I felt a transcendent calm. I promised myself I would return and try to find the first house, the location of which was lost to me.

Sandra and I came over from Whittier on the freeways, turning north off the Ventura onto Reseda Boulevard, then cutting over to Wilbur, which ran parallel. The house could not hold for her what it held for me, and I felt selfish using our time like this. But I wanted to share the good feeling I had had. The neighborhood still has about it something of the atmosphere of a much older San Fernando Valley—a bit rundown, but with no large housing developments, no landscaped and overwatered lawns. I drove past the house and had to turn and come back. The mailbox with its numbers was gone. The lot was empty: the house and all the trees had been razed; the bare, packed, red-brown earth had been swept clean. Only the tread marks of a single tractor were apparent, where it had turned on soft ground.

I got out of the car and walked back and forth across the lot, silently. On the ground near a neighbor's cinder-block fence I saw an apricot pit. I put it in my pocket.

"I've been thinking," I said to Sandra, once I was standing beside the car again. "The first house may have been way out on Wilbur, toward the Santa Susannas." She looked off that way.

"Would you mind driving? That way I could look. I might get the pattern of something, the way it looked."

"Yes," she said. "Certainly."

We turned around and headed north on Wilbur, windows open to the fresh breeze. We drove past the house where my friend Leon had lived, where I had first bitten into the flesh of a pomegranate, and then slowly past other places that I knew but which I could not recognize. The air all around was brilliant.

Terry Tempest Williams

Peregrine Falcon

from "Refuge: An Unnatural History of Family and Place"

Lake Level: 4205.40′

Not far from Great Salt Lake is the municipal dump. Acres of trash heaped high. Depending on your frame of mind, it is either an olfactory fright show or a sociological gold mine. Either way, it is best to visit in winter.

For the past few years, when the Christmas Bird Count comes around, I seem to be relegated to the landfill. The local Audubon hierarchy tell me I am sent there because I know gulls. The truth lies deeper. It's an under-the-table favor. I am sent to the dump because secretly they know I like it.

As far as birding goes, there's often no place better. Our urban wastelands are becoming wildlife's last stand. The great frontier. We've moved them out of town like all other "low-income tenants."

The dump where I count birds for Christmas used to have cattails—but I can't remember them. A few have popped up below the hill again, in spite of the bulldozers, providing critical cover for coots, mallards, and a variety of other waterfowl. I've seen herons standing by and once a snowy egret, but for the most part, the habitat now is garbage, perfect for starlings and gulls.

I like to sit on the piles of unbroken Hefties, black bubbles of sanitation. It provides comfort with a view. Thousands of starlings cover refuse with their feet. Everywhere I look—feathered trash.

The starlings gorge themselves, bumping into each other like drunks. They are not discretionary. They'll eat anything, just like us. Three starlings picked a turkey carcass clean. Afterward, they crawled inside and wore it as a helmet. A carcass with six legs walking around—you have to be sharp counting birds at the dump.

I admire starlings' remarkable adaptability. Home is everywhere. I've seen them nesting under awnings on New York's Fifth Avenue, as well as inside aspen trunks in the Teton wilderness. Over 50 percent of their diet is insects. They are the most effective predators against the clover weevil in America.

Starlings are also quite beautiful if looked at with beginner's eyes. In autumn and winter, their plumage appears speckled, unkempt. But by spring, the lighter tips of their feathers have been worn away, leaving them with a black, glossy plumage, glistening with irridescences.

Inevitably, students at the museum will describe an elegant, black bird with flashes of green, pink, and purple.

"About this big," they say (holding their hands about seven inches apart vertically). "With a bright yellow bill. What is it?"

"A starling," I answer.

What follows is a dejected look flushed with embarrassment.

"Is that all?"

The name precedes the bird.

I understand it. When I'm out at the dump with starlings, I don't want to like them. They are common. They are aggressive, and they behave poorly, crowding out other birds. When a harrier happens to cross-over from the marsh, they swarm him. He disappears. They want their trash to themselves.

Perhaps we project on to starlings that which we deplore in ourselves: our numbers, our aggression, our greed, and our cruelty. Like starlings, we are taking over the world.

The parallels continue. Starlings forage by day in open country competing with native species such as bluebirds for food. They drive them out. In late afternoon, they return in small groups to nest elsewhere, competing with cavity nesters such as flickers, martins, tree swallows, and chickadees. Once again, they move in on other birds' territories.

Starlings are sophisticated mimics singing songs of bobwhites, killdeer, flickers, and phoebes. Their flocks drape bare branches in spring with choruses of chatters, creeks, and coos. Like any good impostor, they confuse the boundaries. They lie.

What is the impact of such a species on the land? Quite simply, a loss of diversity.

What makes our relationship to starlings even more curious is that we loathe them, calling in exterminators because we fear disease, yet we do everything within our power to encourage them as we systematically erase the specialized habitats of specialized birds. I have yet to see a snowy egret spearing a bagel.

The man who wanted Shakespeare's birds flying in Central Park and altruistically brought starlings to America from England, is not to blame. We are—for creating more and more habitat for a bird we despise. Perhaps the only value in the multitudes of starlings we have garnished is that in some small way they allow us to comprehend what vast flocks of birds must have felt like.

The symmetry of starling flocks takes my breath away, I lose track of time and space. At the dump, all it takes is the sweep of my hand. They rise. Hundreds of starlings. They wheel and turn, twist and glide, with no apparent leader. They are the collective. A flight of frenzy. They are black stars against a blue sky. I watch them above the dump, expanding and contracting along the meridian of a winged universe.

Suddenly, the flock pulls together like a winced eye, then opens in an explosion of feathers. A peregrine falcon is expelled, but not without its prey. With folded wings he strikes a starling and plucks its body from mid-air. The flock blinks again and the starlings disperse, one by one, returning to the landfill.

The starlings at the Salt Lake City municipal dump give us numbers that look good on our Christmas Bird Count, thousands, but they become faceless when compared to one peregrine falcon. A century ago, he would have seized a teal.

I will continue to count birds at the dump, hoping for under-the-table favors, but don't mistake my motives. I am not contemplating starlings. It is the falcon I wait for—the duckhawk with a memory for birds that once blotted out the sun.

Edward Abbey

Sheep Count

from "Confessions of a Barbarian"

From 1946, when he was nineteen, until days before his death at age sixty-two on March 14, 1989, Edward Abbey kept meticulous personal journals—thirty-eight years' worth in all, twenty volumes. From these journals, many of his essays and articles came essentially whole cloth. The following "Sheep Count" is excerpted from volume 20 of the Confessions of A Barbarian: Pages from the Journals of Edward Abbey *and has never before seen print.*

By way of stage-setting: Cabeza Prieta—"Dark Head" in Spanish, for a prominent local mountain—is a desert bighorn sheep preserve and, ironically, an Air Force gunnery range in extreme southern Arizona. Most summers, the preserve conducts a bighorn sheep count, with volunteer observers spending several days alone, hunkered in sweltering saguaro-rib blinds near various isolated wildlife watering holes. This is the story—the unpolished field notes—of Abbey's tragicomic participation in the 1988 count, less than nine months before his death.

David Petersen

Thursday, June 23, 1988—Eagle Tank, Cabeza Prieta

Camped out near Ajo Sunday night; all seemed well.

Attended an orientation meeting Monday morning, after having breakfast with Bill Broyles and Byrd Baylor. Met them later on the road to Papago Well: Byrd bound for Basiric Tank, Bill for Las Tinajas Altos—the high tanks. Me, I took off north up Mohawk Valley and by 1600 hours was stuck deep in the sand of a roadside wash about sixteen miles north of Papago Well, ten miles short of Eagle Tank.

And there, for the next three nights and days, I struggled with the horror and despair of trying to jack, crank, wedge my goddamn exasperating two-wheel-drive, free-wheel (no positraction) truck out of the sand and dust. The horror of it. The hopelessness. I even called for help on the CB radio the second night—Tuesday. Nobody heard me. Or nobody responded.

I tried brush under the tires. Tried the bench covers, plywood and dacron plush, from the camper shell in the bed of the truck. (Ruined them. Should have deflated the tires to five p.s.i., driven out, reinflated with the hand pump.) I tried fins from [military] tow-targets. I jacked and shoveled, jacked and shoveled, gunned the motor. Dug in again. Brief flurries of progress followed by static spells of failure.

And all of this in the godawful heat—110 in the shade of a tree, up to 116 in the cab of my truck.

I finally gave up and decided to walk the sixteen miles to Papago Well, at night, in hopes of catching Bill Broyles there on his return to Ajo. The walk itself was an appalling prospect, with the temperature at 2200 hours still up around ninety. And me exhausted. No sleep in three nights. All my ice and cold drinks gone the first day.

Nightmare!

How I was beginning to *hate* the sight of that Hi-Lift jack, those rear wheels sunk to the hubs in sand, the shovel, the ragged bench covers, the tattered and scattered and half-buried fragments of target fins, the piles of hand-chopped mesquite brush. Hate. Despair. *Fear*.

How long would my water last in this horrible inferno? (I had about eighteen gallons with me, actually, and some ten gallons of it still untouched.) Always thirsty. I reached for my faithful Desert (brand) water bag last night, in the dark, where I'd hung it on a scrawny mesquite—no decent trees anywhere around, no real shade either—and found the bag alive with tiny ants as I raised it to my lips. Instantly, hundreds of them were swarming over my hand, arm, face, whiskers.

Well, OK, about 2230 I went to bed with my shoes on. Slept badly.

Awoke about 0130—after the moon was down—and went for a little walk to see if I could follow the dirt road in the dark.

Maybe. But suppose I broke an ankle, got snake-bit, and the rising sun found me still miles from Papago? I'd be a goner for sure; a horrible death in the heat. Thoughts of easing the process: I'd carry a knife, of course. And a flashlight. And two gallons of water, at least. Some food.

I returned to bed about two in the morning, slept fitfully if at all, and rose at 0400 with the first glimmer of dawn.

So? Resolve! Desperation!

In one final spasm of effort, I took my leather gloves and my little hatchet and walked off into the pre-dawn twilight to find another aluminum and fiber target. Found one a mile from camp, still standing, nose buried in the ground. I chopped off two big bright fins and dragged them back through the wash to my truck.

Came then that awful moment when the red desert sun appears, over the Mohawk Mountains, around 0530 fucking hours. The instant heat.

With more jack-work, more shoveling, I finally got the truck almost in line with the road and on the bank, set the fins under the rear wheels, started the motor, popped the clutch and . . . ?

Hooray! Progress: got halfway across the wash before bogging down again.

Well then, let's repeat the whole process: try again. And this time I *succeed*, reaching hard ground at 0700.

And thus I escaped—deeper into Hell, where I am now, sitting in this saguaro-rib [wildlife] observation blind before Eagle Tank. I'm now twenty-six sandy miles from Papago Well, fifty or sixty from Ajo. But at least there's water here. I'll live—if I stay.

I've seen no live sheep yet. Nothing but doves, Gambel's quail, a few other birds, and lots of wild honeybees.

The "tank" is actually a cave blasted into granite, about ten feet deep and six feet high, with maybe two or three feet of green warm water in the basin. Cleverly shielded from the sun to retard evaporation.

The tank is *roaring* with bees. Masses of drowned bees float on the water, others creep upon its edge, and swarms swirl and buzz in the cool shade of the cave. They seem not at all disturbed by my presence.

Still no sheep, but much fresh sheep dung in the area, as well as coyote scat, and maybe others—bobcat? Raccoon? Lion! (One hopes.)

On the job—three days later. A disaster. I only hope nobody heard my radio plea for help.

Jet-jockeys screaming overhead all day. Several sonic booms. What does a sonic boom do to a bighorn sheep? They could never *get used* to it—nobody could.

So here I sit all broken-hearted.

Nineteen-hundred hours: Twilight creeping in, into Eagle Canyon, and not a single fucking sheep in sight yet. Why not?

In four days in this awful heat I've eaten almost nothing. Why? Ain't hungry. Too busy drinking water. *Survival*, that's the thing.

Boring here. No action: no bighorns, no lions, not even an eagle or rattlesnake.

Maybe I'll go home tomorrow. This expedition is a failure. Next time I'll bring three or four iceboxes packed with ice and at least one gallon of juice per day—I dream of cold cider, icy orange juice, chilled milk, cold cranberry juice, all of it mixed with club soda, garnished with lemon or lime—and, of course, a fucking four-wheel-drive fucking truck!

0600, Friday, June 24, 1988—Eagle Tank, Cabeza Prieta

Overslept, enjoying strange happy rollicking dreams. Arose at sunup, thick and groggy, and padded quietly up here to my sheep-count blind: sat, ate an orange and read the conclusion to Santayana's *Three Philosopher Poets* [Lucretius, Dante, Goethe]. Such sweet fine precious writing! So finicky and fastidious a fellow! But all right . . . I liked his remarks on Homer—the sycophant—in the essay on Dante.

Passed a coyote on my way up to the blind, [he was] headed down-canyon on the other side—where bound? [I continue] into the morning sun, into the grisly heat, the sweet stink of *bursera* [elephant tree] and the arid waterless waste of rocks.

Half an hour in the blind, and I've seen nothing but the usual doves and bees—then suddenly, a quick gray fox appears at the lip of the cave. Nervous, restless, annoyed by the bees, it dashes to and fro—pointy nose, pointy ears, long bushy tail—dropping down, now and then, into the cave for a quick drink. Anxious, agitated, constantly checking for danger, the fox seems quite different from the relatively calm, self-assured and at times even brassy and insolent coyote.

But where be da phukkin ships [sheep]?

The fox is gone. A second coyote has come and gone. No action at the tank now [except for] the usual flocks of white-wing doves ("Who cooks for you? Who cooks for you?") coming and going. They descend, enter the cave, come hurtling out excited and crying, then race down-canyon past me in my saguaro-rib blind like fat, gray-feathered bullets.

I am homesick, sick for home, I think of little Benno [the author's young son]. . . .

Linda M. Hasselstrom

The Covenant of the Holy Monkey Wrench

from *Hembra*

Every year eruptions of earth's forces in the form of volcanoes, hurricanes, tornadoes, monsoons, earthquakes and floods kill and maim millions of people. We call these events "natural disasters" to differentiate them from the deliberate and premeditated murder we practice on other humans. "Natural" disasters are caused by forces we do not control, even though we'd like to.

No one I know has been crazy enough to suggest that "natural" disasters may be our fault.

Primitive peoples sought to control calamity by prayer, sacrifice and study. Now that we're sophisticated, we believe most natural disasters can't be stopped; we concentrate instead on warning systems so that we may evacuate before a flood, and on our ability to mobilize personnel and machinery to clean up the mess after the earthquake is over. But no matter how scientifically we approach it, "natural disaster" has a way of eluding us. It's almost as though some intelligence was outwitting our best scientists.

Lately, more people have become aware of the concept embodied in the term "Gaia," a world goddess who *is* the world. According to this theory, everything on or in the earth is alive: not only animals, humans and plants, but rocks, minerals, sky, clouds. Others agree with Frederick Turner that "we are promoting nature because *we are nature.*"[1] And all must be treated with respect; all these lives must be protected if the whole is to survive, because all are a part of a collective consciousness, an integrated body. James Lovelock, who has written much about Gaia, believes that the health of the planet is what matters, "not that of some individual species of organisms," and that "nuclear radiation, fearful though it is to individual humans is to Gaia a minor affair."[2]

The concept of a planet of dissimilar species joined into a single entity should not seem outlandish to us; when people collaborate for mutual aid, we call them a city, a country, a club, a political party, or a minority. Although independent individuals exist within the unified whole, a prime goal is to make the whole strong through unity. Businesses pay taxes for an army to defend the country's borders; individuals may be drafted to serve in the army. Products of one country are bartered to others for goods and services not otherwise available. Certain individual rights may exist only until they threaten to harm the country, the whole.

And when another entity declares war, the entire populace mobilizes, reorganizing its priorities for the defense of all. An individual who fails to show proper enthusiasm for the call to arms is in trouble; the society doesn't see that as exercising a legitimate individual right, but as committing treason, becoming a threat to the entirety. Choosing not to fight becomes a threat, antisocial and illegal.

If we view the earth and its various life forms as a single unified country, might we not say that it is under siege? Japanese fishermen kill dolphins, one of the gentlest and most intelligent species; miners and

1. Frederick Turner, in "Only Man's Presence Can Save Nature," forum including several environmental commentators in *Harper's,* April, 1990, p. 48. Turner is Founders Professor of Arts and Humanities at the University of Texas at Dallas.

2. James Lovelock, *The Ages of Gaia: A Biography of Our Living Earth* (New York: W. W. Norton & Co., 1988), p. xvii.

developers destroy grizzly bear habitat; oil spills daily into the oceans from ruptured tankers; vehicle exhaust, smokestacks, radiation "accidentally" vented from nuclear power plants, all pollute the air we all must breathe.

If the earth were a single country, it might well consider itself under attack—by humanity as a whole, the Nation of Humans. If you were the earth, would you fight back? Are "natural disasters" killing humans *because* of the crimes we've committed against nature, against Gaia?

Many Indian tribes have held this belief sacred for centuries. We might do worse than emulate them. And if our goddess is really our world, someone will immediately want to organize it, appoint a priesthood, and preach against nonbelievers.

Perhaps Gaia's church might be called the Covenant of the Holy Monkey Wrench. Some unofficial worshippers have already undertaken pilgrimages to defile the gods of the desecrators by putting grinding compound in gas tanks, and removing the survey stakes proclaiming where they'll strike next. No doubt some of these individuals felt very alone, out there in the dark. Naturally, I cannot encourage illegal activities. But I wonder if Gaia watches such folks with a smile, while she's monkey wrenching on a grand scale.

The first ecological warfare I noticed was practiced by "The Fox" in the 1960s; columnist Mike Royko inadvertently became his publicist and protector.[3] Concerned about pollution, the man first tried to talk to heads of corporations that were dumping waste into streams and Lake Michigan. Often he would fail to get past a receptionist, or would be put off with some form letter. So he decided to "become an ecological warrior and take direct action to dramatize the problem." He chose his name from his home territory, Michigan's Fox River Valley, and because foxes are sly, elusive creatures; and he approached his self-appointed task with a logic, clarity, and a refreshing sense of humor missing from some recent monkey wrenching.

3. All quotations in reference to "The Fox" are from "Fox was sly but not dangerous," Mike Royko, *The Chicago Tribune,* published in *The Rapid City Journal,* April 30, 1990, p. A4.

"The Fox" specialized in dramatic acts to call attention to pollution; "He stopped up drainage outlets of big polluters; he draped derogatory signs on highway overpasses near their plants, and he plugged a few factory chimneys. Once, he crawled under the fence of an asphalt plant, turned a few knobs, and shut down the plant. Whatever his action, he left a note of warning to the polluter, with his signature—a drawing of a fox." And, says Royko, "He never did anything that endangered anyone." His final publicized act was to "go to the outlet of a company that was dumping slop into Lake Michigan. He managed to get a jar of the discharged waste. Then, as a flourish, he added some scallops, oysters, shrimps and minnows to the jar of glop to symbolize what the steel company was doing to wildlife. He then went to the Loop corporate headquarters of the steel company and asked to see the vice president for public relations. The secretary became suspicious, and The Fox got nervous, so instead of dumping the stuff on the desk of the vice president, he took it out of his briefcase and dumped it on the plush office carpet, then escaped before the cops got there, while the secretary screamed in horror." After that, The Fox decided to "work within the system and try to educate people about environmental concerns." And presumably, he has been doing that for the last twenty years.

But I miss him. His activities, so precisely aimed at polluting companies, focused attention on polluters. If his nonviolent tactics were widely copied, dozens of corporate executives would have to answer to dozens of reporters, and, ultimately, to citizens.

Generations of people worshipped their gods with offerings of still-pulsating hearts torn from the breasts of living humans. Even more generations worshipped—and still worship—a god who allowed the brutal crucifixion of his only son. Millions of adherents bow down to gods who demand women be uneducated, veiled, cast out of their homes for barrenness, prevented from preaching the word of their particular god, or forced to bear an unlimited number of children to be raised in poverty. Each of these churches supports, sometimes lavishly, a prestigious priesthood who interpret the god's wishes on earth. Each is based on a code of laws or customs sanctified by god and time. Each qualifies for enormous tax deductions.

If one were to establish the Church of Gaia, it would not be the strangest religious institution ever proposed. In time, its adherents might write, or receive as revelation, a body of laws governing members' behavior, might establish a priesthood, vestments, traditions, holidays. By all these methods, its members would work their way toward a definition of Gaia, their Goddess, toward a system for pleasing Her, worshipping Her, converting others with Her message.

The god of the Christians, as conveyed through the Old Testament, demanded loyalty in return for everlasting life in heaven. He also loved to make bargains with his followers, and was famous for clever and painful retribution. If we accept his example of godly behavior as applicable to Gaia, the consequences might be shocking. If, for example, an eye is exacted for an eye, a tooth for a tooth, what has the loss of the dodo and the passenger pigeon cost us? Both died because of human greed and insensitivity to life.

Is an earthquake that kills 150 people part of the payment for the bubbling chemical poisons dumped in landfills by companies that know better? Is the current pollution nightmare being quietly recorded on the debit side of the ledger, for payment in full as the poisons reach our children's drinking water, their air?

How did—or will—we compensate for the loss of Glen Canyon, its unique sequence of lives destroyed forever by the waters of Lake Powell? Have we already paid the price, or is the bill coming due any day now?

And what terrible price might be required of white people for destroying entire red, black, and brown tribes of human beings by our haste, by our inability to fit their simple existences into the complex weave of our developing societies?

We've already lost territory; Times Beach surrendered, its citizens became refugees. California is shaky, west of the San Andreas Fault.

Are natural disasters direct retribution for our crimes against nature? Is Gaia punishing us for our casual torture and ruination of her flesh?

The flaw, of course, is that those who do the damage don't always pay the bill. Union Carbide's carelessness and greed were responsible for the deaths of thousands of Indians, but so far I've seen no news reports of terrible deaths among Union Carbide officials. Is Gaia simply too big, too complex, to keep track of these details? Still, a master computer is intricate, but it manages to credit payments to the right accounts most of the time.

How convenient if payment were swift and direct: a man driving down a highway tosses a beer can out of the car. An instant later (sorry, Ed Abbey), the beer can slaps him in the ear, and a neon sign in the sky glows: "Don't do that again or I'll shove it down your throat!" Alas, adults learn that few truths can be expressed in simple terms, and justice is not often swift and simple.

Perhaps the answer lies in Gaia's own systems. If we believe Gaia to be a single interrelated system, injury to one part of her injures the whole. The death of a single species of spider may mean disaster to an entire ecosystem in a generation or two, as the effects of that loss radiate. Each injury spreads destruction, like the circles on a pond after a stone is thrown into it. Every part of Gaia's system jangles alarms with each destruction, each oil spill, each slaughter of a species.

Perhaps Gaia believes humans are similarly in sympathy with one another, a single intelligence in millions of separate bodies. Perhaps she doesn't realize our pathetic ignorance, and our pitiful isolation from one another and from our universe. The Iowa housewife sipping coffee in her cozy kitchen may shiver for a moment when another acre of jungle is bulldozed in South America, but she can't define the feeling, because she's lost touch with jungle, with nature. When an oil spill kills some of the birds that are part of Gaia's body, perhaps she twitches a mountain in Mexico and brings buildings down on hundreds of individuals, assuming we'll see the connection.

Unfortunately, we're not a collective intelligence. We simply don't understand; most of us don't even know we're soldiers fighting in a war, let alone that we're losing. If we did, perhaps we'd mobilize with the spirit we show in times of war.

If Gaia is anything like the other gods worshipped during our short history on the planet, she's bound to get annoyed one of these days. When gods and goddesses are angry, affairs can get distinctly and thoroughly unpleasant. The Egyptians turned down Moses' request for an exit visa, and endured plagues of blood, snakes and death. If Gaia, our only home, decides to make her message more plain, we may be in more trouble than we can imagine. Some scientists already are contemplating the possibilities of a drought on the Great Plains that would create the Great American Desert of early explorers; Lovelock and others predict that the consequences of annihilation of tropical rain forests and the greenhouse effect will be upon us within ten years in the form of "storms of vastly greater severity than anything we've ever experienced before, disruptions in the ozone layer, events for which no amount of expensive computer simulation could properly prepare us."[4]

The alternative? Perhaps we should all behave as though we're members in good standing of the Church of Gaia: treat everything in our world with the love and care we lavish on our children. We won't need to issue membership cards for our church; you're a member if you behave like one. And if you don't, Gaia may get you. It's an old threat, but it works with children, and it also works with executives thinking of embezzlement, senators thinking of bribes, or a rapist who grabs an armed woman. Some people can be persuaded; others understand only greater force.

Look at the advantages of membership in Gaia's army, even if the church doesn't immediately qualify for tax exemptions. We won't have to build churches; surely a goddess of the world can be worshipped anywhere. We won't have to tithe; we can plant trees instead. We can throw away our little gold crosses, symbolic of torture, and wear tiny gold monkey wrenches, or leaves, or birds. On second

4. James Lovelock, *Harper's,* p. 47.

thought, no gold. Make that tiny clay monkey wrenches, or bird feathers, or leaves carved of wood from a tree that has already fallen in the woods.

Our elected priesthood would need no elaborate robes, no shepherd's crook. If any symbol were needed, the warrior priests could carry a greasy monkey wrench, or an empty syrup bottle. The true saints among our fellowship might prefer a more positive symbol such as a bag of seeds.

No, I can't prove the theory, and I can't prove my solution will work. But no single priest of any of humanity's myriad religions has ever been able to show followers heaven, either. It's a matter of faith.

Rick Bass

The Fringe

First publication

I dreamed of Grizzly Peak last night. I dreamed of the ferns and the creek and the burned area where the giant Ponderosa pines are. I dreamed of the hawks and eagles. I dreamed of moose. Sometimes when I hike into the Grizzly Peak country, I see bears; other times, coyotes. I've seen mountain lions in Grizzly Peak's woods.

There's this one log I like to sit on, in a high hanging grassy valley near Grizzly Peak's center. I like to eat lunch there, near Flattail Creek, and watch the trout pass beneath my feet. I like to hike in through the Grizzly Peak country, up the steep ravines, through the forest, and then sit in that lonely valley and eat my lunch: a handful of raisins, a sandwich. I sit facing west, and know that as big as the trees are out here, they get even bigger farther west.

In the late summer, there's this one larch tree on the ridge that turns gold a week before any other tree in the forest, and in the late afternoon you can see it glowing up there on that ridge with the sun behind it, lighting it like a candle in the dark forest of green. And though you will never reach it before dark, you can aim for it, navigate by it, until the sun goes down. . . .

I'm at the edge of something up here, the electrified, galvanized seam where two landscapes crash into each other: a Pacific Northwest low-elevation rain forest, and the cliffs and mountains of the northern Rockies. This low-elevation rain forest is the last of its kind in Montana, and it's at the very outer fringe of the Pacific Northwest. Every atom in this valley is special, is sacred, has a ringing to it: is different from any other place on this green earth. Once, though it's a hell of a long way from the ocean, salmon ran near here. The Yaak River drains this country, empties into the Kootenai River, which empties into the once-magnificent Columbia. The salmon used to be able to get all the way out here, passing beneath the big cool cedars and larch. In the Kootenai there is still a handful of sturgeon—twenty of them are thought to be left up here. And twenty bull trout, too, about ten miles from Grizzly Peak's center.

Every species in and around the Grizzly Peak country seems to be down to single- or at best double-digit populations. Nine or ten grizzlies—you can bet they range through this country—and five or six wolves.

In this magic zone, this fringe, two worlds combine, and it is here that the wildest of the wild things meet: those species that have been driven from the Northwest and those that are still hiding out in the Rockies.

Wolf, wolverine, grizzly, raven, badger, weasel, marten, mink. Moose, deer, elk, and even woodland caribou. Great gray owls standing four feet tall. Golden eagles, with six-foot wingspans. Bald eagles, their snowy heads brilliant, like those of angels, as they wheel in the blue sky of winter.

I'm making it sound like a big place. It's not. The valley itself is only 371,000 acres. Grizzly Peak and the uncut woods around it comprise only 6,000 acres, making it the smallest proposed wilderness in Montana. But if you've got a heavy pack, crossing the peak can take three days, dawn till dusk in the summertime. It's *jungle.* And steep.

This isn't good country for people. It's too cold in the winter, too rainy in the summer, and there aren't any jobs up here. No *infrastruc-*

ture, other than the jungle itself. But the relatively low elevations in the valley and the heavy rains produce big trees—or used to, before the virgin forests were cut down. Because of this, year after year after year, more timber comes out of the Yaak Valley than any other valley in Montana.

For reasons of inaccessibility, no roads have yet been built through the three-day wilderness of Grizzly Peak Mountain. The top half of the peak is a treeless, grassy flat-topped mesa, and the timber below is wind-stunted piss-ant trunk-split lodgepole. But grizzlies live in there. And other things. It's *thick*.

If every standing tree in Grizzly Peak core were cut, there would probably be enough saleable timber to last the local mill about two weeks. The mill's hurting, having been jerked around by management; it could use some wood. But to trade a whole mountain, for two weeks?

Still, it seems that's what may happen.

There are no designated wilderness areas in Yaak; of the 371,000 acres, the most species-diverse wilderness in the Lower Forty-Eight, not a single acre is protected as wilderness. In a bill now pending, 20,000 acres of the bare-topped Roderick Mountain, near Grizzly Peak country, is being proposed for wilderness, but not tiny Grizzly Peak itself. Six thousand acres! What kind of a country can't afford to add 6,000 acres to its wilderness system, when grizzlies live there?

For a long time, the local timber industry up in the northwestern part of the state has been feasting on the federal wildlands in this valley, sawing more than a thousand miles of road into this forest, and cutting the big trees, clearcutting entire mountainsides. Now the hills are washing away and the Yaak River is silting up and the trout are disappearing. . . . Out of 100 mountains in this valley, only two small roadless cores—Grizzly Peak/Roderick and the Mt. Henry/Pink Mountain country—are uncut on all four sides, top to bottom.

You don't need to visit the jungle to write a letter on its behalf—to Pat Williams in the House, and Max Baucus in the Senate, and to your own people. All you need to do is respond to the poetry, the diversity of the *words,* describing what is still left there on that one three-day mountain, the last untouched one in the valley.

Peregrine falcon Boreal owl Townsend's big-eared bat Harlequin duck Woodland caribou Lynx Flammulated owl Common loon Bald eagle Golden eagle Merganser Black-backed woodpecker Pileated woodpecker Pallid sturgeon. . . .

Wavy moonwort Mingan Island moonwort Small lady's slipper Round-leaved orchid Sparrow's egg Lady's slipper Kidney-leaved violet Maidenhair Spleenwort Bog birch Crested shield-fern Green-keeled cottongrass Spalding's catchfly Linear-leaved sundew Northern golden-carpet. . . .

You can look at the words without ever having to see the place and know that, even if you are not a letter writer, this is a time when you must be, before we slide over into the twenty-first century, and Grizzly Peak is lost. Maybe this year, after only a hundred years of white folks living in this valley, with outside help we can get Grizzly Peak and the other last mountains of the world protected.

Grizzly Peak keeps coming into my dreams, but if you are going to get there on foot, in real life, and are a wild thing—a grizzly, a wolf, a caribou—you have to come in (via Canada) from either the northwest or the northeast, via Mt. Henry.

I favor the northeast approach, out of the Mt. Henry country.

The wildest thing I've come across in the Mt. Henry country—wilder than the black bear with cubs that chased me up a tree, wilder than the mountain lion that stalked me by ducking down in the grass and flipping its tail back and forth, up and down, like a question mark—is a beautiful and elegant spirited actress named Jeannette McIntire. Fifty-plus years ago, she and her husband, John McIntire, took time off from their radio work to buy some land in this foolish wild valley, which at that time, people say, was exactly like Alaska.

The two had a son, Tim, and a daughter, Holly, and for a long time, lived happily ever after. Tim's gone now, in the beautiful night stars above the valley and the woodcock's haunting spring calls over the marshes, and tough old John McIntire (he played the wagonmaster on the television series "Wagon Train") is gone too. Holly, a photographer, married the poet Charles Wright, and they have a son, Luke, and live in Virginia. But Mrs. McIntire—Jeannette—is still living way up north in the valley, on the northernmost piece of private property, fifteen miles from her nearest neighbors, which are us.

In the forever light of long summer evenings, we go up to Jeannette's place and drink gin-and-tonics with her. Her cabin smells of rawhide and sweet leather, of woodsmoke and deerskin. There is another woman in the valley, Nancy, who tans hides, and Jeannette likes to wear Nancy's makings. Jeannette will fix an elk or venison roast for an early supper, and together we'll watch the green meadows of head-high virgin grasses while she tells us about her radio days in New York City. With John she worked on the radio show "The March of Time," with Orson Welles. She and John had fans all across the country, all over the world.

But every chance they got, they came back up here, not just to hide, the way I do, but to live a life together. They came to embrace their meadow, to see a million stars on ten thousand nights, to see mountain lions, wolves, and bears, and swans flying over the valley. She came fifty-plus times to watch the ducks and geese migrating south—and saw them come back, too, fifty-plus times.

When Jeannette and John first homesteaded the meadow below Mt. Henry, they came across an old trapper's cabin at the back of the property: more of a root cellar than a real cabin. The trapper had evidently spent a winter or two there, because inside were an old stove and a pile of rusting-out canned goods.

And in the middle, a pit—a great hole—where things had been shoved and then buried. One day Jeannette and John began to unearth all the stuff that was down in that earthen basement.

An old desk. A handmade chair. And stacks of papers—reams and reams.

"He was writing *plays,*" Jeannette told us. "And they were beautiful. We sat there and thought about him being up here at the turn of the century, during those hard winters, all alone, writing these gorgeous plays—and then *burying* them, and, well, with us being actors, we just broke down and wept. . . ."

Mt. Henry's the tallest mountain in this valley. Sometimes there's snow on its top even in the summer, and that's a beautiful thing to see. The peak is sheer rock, bare like a volcano, but just below are forests, and right at treeline are two little lakes, deep and cold.

Up on top of Mt. Henry is an old fire lookout tower. It's been abandoned in favor of satellite surveillance of digitally and color-displayed thermal variations—*fires*—but back in the not-so-old days, an old guy would sit high up in that tower at the top of the world and watch for smoke. He'd pack in with his mule string and stay up there a month or more at a time. Grizzlies would come claw and bite at the stout legs of the lookout tower, trying to topple it. At first it was only ten feet off the ground, but because of the grizzlies, the lookout guy extended the tower, making his perch twenty feet off the ground.

He'd come riding through the McIntires' meadow on his way up to the lookout each summer—the snows lingering even on into July. He'd eat dinner with them, listen to hand-cranked Victrola music, and stay the night before going on up into the real wilderness—the one that's still there, though smaller, like a memory. And it became a tradition, year after year, for the McIntires, all through the summer, to go out onto their porch at the edge of that meadow and look toward the top of that lonely, windy mountain. They'd see the lantern burning there—one tiny light at the top of the mountain—and would imagine the old man reading, or writing letters. Holly and Tim would light their own lantern: hold it up for him to see and then extinguish it.

And they'd watch, as up on the mountain the light in the lookout tower dimmed, then flickered, then disappeared, only to come back on again: once, twice, goodnight.

In the spring, the river would run fast again as the woods woke once more and the singing birds returned. The meadow would burst out as green as limes, shimmering with life—blackbirds cackling in the reeds, beavers building backwater trout pools, and always the big creatures—the deer, the elk, the moose—coming out of the wilderness to bear their June-young in the meadow at the edge of the woods.

Smoke rising straight and clean from the single chimney. Jeannette cooking on the wood stove or going out for a walk. John working in the barn on some piece of equipment or out riding in the woods—etching it all into his mind, as if to take it with him when he left for the stars, so many years later. And the two of them sharing it—sharing all of it.

In the spring, to make the meadow more lush and pleasant for the elk, and to grow a cutting or two of hay, the McIntires would plunge in with their two draft horses and an iron sled, called a stoneboat, and would lift each round stone, each glacial boulder, onto the stoneboat until it was full. In that manner, load by load, the McIntires pulled all the moraine from the meadow and dumped it at the meadow's edge.

The meadow grew purer and greener, and became more and more of a line, an edge, at the border of the wilderness: a comfortable transition between what was wild and what was not. You would certainly have to call the McIntires' love for each other wild, in the best sense of the word: *alive.* So perhaps the green meadow below Mt. Henry marked not a line between the wild and the not-wild but a zone between wildness and wilderness. And perhaps that was why the McIntires themselves were able to live there together so comfortably and for so long: because they also belonged to what was just across the line. . . .

Northern bog lemming Wolverine Moose Turkey Pine marten Fisher Elk Black bear White-tailed deer Mink Mule deer Muskrat Bobcat Weasel Beaver Ruffed grouse Blue grouse Franklin's grouse Gray wolf Coeur D'Alene salamander Torrent sculpin Inland (redband) rainbow trout Shorthead sculpin Westslope cutthroat trout Bull trout White sturgeon. . . .

In the 1970s, wars raged throughout northwest Montana over which federal lands would be protected as wilderness and which released to private industry and the hounds of corporate (and often subsidized) overlogging. The McIntires fought valiantly for the protection of the Mt. Henry wilderness. They stood up in the face of the local timber mill and asked that just that one mountain—just one core, out of a hundred—be spared. Jeannette and John went back and forth to Washington, testifying to Congress about the wild nature of the valley and asking that Mt. Henry be designated a wilderness. But in the end the local politicians won, and animosity over Mt. Henry—what's left of it—still lingers.

Lingers, hell; it's emblazoned in the earth. As if to answer "Don't hack the Yaak," a rallying cry for those protective of the wilderness, the Forest Service permitted timber sales whose boundaries, when clearcut into the mountain across from the McIntires' meadow, appear to spell the word *HACK*.

And they hacked. They scalped every mountain within view of the McIntires' meadow, except for the crown of Mt. Henry—they haven't arrived there yet, but they're coming. The letters stand more than a thousand feet high: the *H* and then the *A* and then the *C*. (They ran out of mountain, clearcut the letters too huge to add the *K*.)

Twenty-five years ago, Caribou Mountain (no caribou now!) was carved away almost entirely, and still very little is growing up there, just the bare, scarred faces of entire mountainsides. The soil washed away after all the trees were cut off, and in only one year the beautiful centuries-old forest soil was stripped away by the Pacific storms and spring runoff, leaving behind a lunar-gray, runny kind of pus-looking bareness, a forever-bareness. The timber companies left only enough spindly lodgepoles to surround and frame those empty letters, those last-laugh letters: *H-A-C*. . . .

The McIntires had a beautiful love and for the most part a beautiful life. They tried to protect one mountain—one out of a hundred—a thing of beauty and wildness, for those who would come afterward, but they came away with zero, in this, the wildest place.

The McIntires' work was not in vain—they lived their life together in beauty. But their basement is full of boxes and boxes of letters, articles, and documents, a paper struggle to protect a real place, a place at the fringe of everything; a place easy to forget, easy to give up on.

I know it's not noble or artistic of me to ask readers of this essay to write letters. It's not thought of nicely in literary circles to call for action. But I don't have time for any of that crap. Maybe in the next century. Maybe, if the last of this valley's three-day wildernesses are protected—Grizzly Peak, and part of the Mt. Henry country—then I can cedar-thrash my way into the woods and sit on that log up above the creek, the one I keep dreaming about, and write a pretty poem or two. But not now. Right now there isn't time for any of that fairy-dust shit. I'll tell you flat-out that the way to stop the destruction is to write Congress, write the Representatives (U.S. House, D.C., zip code 20515) and Senators (U.S. Senate, D.C., zip code 20510) and tell them to protect these 6,000 acres of federal wildland. Write Montana's Max Baucus, in the Senate, and Montana's Pat Williams in the House, and Minnesota's Bruce Vento in the House, who chairs the subcommittee.

The words on this page, or any page, whether literature or not, are just stick-figures, abstract etchings in dust. But letters to Congress—reams of them—are the pure musculature, a pure and reckoning force of which even the grizzly would be proud. Letters now are what is needed—letters, not poems.

Linda Hogan

The Voyagers

from *Prairie Schooner*

I remember one night, lying on the moist spring earth beside my mother. The fire of stars stretched away from us, and the mysterious darkness traveled without limit beyond where we lay on the turning earth. I could smell the damp new grass that night, but I could not touch or hold such black immensity that lived above our world, could not contain within myself even a small corner of the universe.

There seemed to be two kinds of people; earth people and those others, the sky people, who stumbled over pebbles while they walked around with their heads in clouds. Sky people loved different worlds than I loved; they looked at nests in treetops and followed the long white snake of vapor trails. But I was an earth person and while I loved to gaze up at night and stars, I investigated the treasures at my feet, the veined wing of a dragonfly opening a delicate blue window to secrets of earth, a lusterless beetle that drank water thirstily from the tip of my finger and was transformed into sudden green and metallic brilliance. It was enough mystery for me to ponder the bones inside our human flesh, bones that through some incredible blueprint of life grow from a moment's sexual passion between a woman and a man, walk upright a short while, then walk themselves back to dust.

Years later, lost in the woods one New Year's eve, a friend found the way home by following the north star and I began to think that learning the sky might be a practical thing. But it was the image of earth from out in space that gave me upward-gazing eyes. It was that same image that gave the sky people an anchor in the world, for it returned us to our planet in a new and loving way.

To dream of the universe is to know that we are small and brief as insects, born in a flash of rain and gone a moment later. We are delicate and our world is fragile. It was the transgression of Galileo to tell us that we were not the center of the universe, and now, even in our own time, the news of our small being here is treacherous enough that early in the space program, the photographs of earth were classified as secret documents by the government. It was thought, and rightfully so, that the image of our small blue earth would forever change how we see ourselves in context with the world we inhabit.

When we saw the deep blue and swirling white turbulence of our earth reflected back to us, says photographer Steven Meyers, we also saw "the visual evidence of creative and destructive forces moving around its surface, we saw for the first time the deep blackness of that which surrounds it, we sensed directly, and probably for the first time, our incredibly profound isolation, and the special fact of our being here." It was a world whose intricately linked-together ecosystem could not survive the continuing blows of exploitation.

In 1977, when the Voyagers were launched, one of these spacecraft carried the Interstellar Record, a hoped-for link between earth and space that is filled with the sounds and images of the world around us. It carries parts of our lives all the way out to the great Forever. It is destined to travel out of our vast solar system, out to the far, unexplored regions of space in hopes that somewhere, millions of years from now, someone will find it like a note sealed in a bottle carrying our history across the black ocean of space. This message is intended for the year 8,000,000.

One greeting on board from Western India reads: "Greetings from a human being of the Earth. Please contact." Another, from Eastern China, but resembling one that could have been sent by my own

Chickasaw people, reads: "Friends of space, how are you all? Have you eaten yet? Come visit us if you have time."

There is so much hope in those greetings, such sweetness. If found, this message will play our world to a world that's far away. It will sing out the strangely beautiful sounds of earth, sounds that in all likelihood exist on no other planet in the universe. By the time the record is found, if ever, it is probable that the trumpeting bellows of elephants, the peaceful chirping of frogs and crickets, the wild dogs baying out from the golden needle and record, will be nothing more than a gone history of what once lived on this tiny planet in the curving tail of a spiral galaxy. The undecipered language of whales will speak to a world not our own, to people who are not us. They will speak of what we value the most on our planet, things that in reality we are almost missing.

A small and perfect world is traveling there, with psalms journeying past Saturn's icy rings, all our treasured life flying through darkness, going its way alone back through the universe. There is the recorded snapping of fire, the song of a river traveling the continent, the living bent of wind passing through dry grasses, all the world that burns and pulses around us, even the comforting sound of a heartbeat taking us back to the first red house of our mothers' bodies, all that, floating through the universe.

The Voyager carries music as well. A Peruvian Wedding Song is waiting to be heard in the far, distant regions of space. The Navajo Night Chant travels through darkness like medicine for healing another broken world. Blind Willie Johnson's slide guitar and deep down blues are on that record, in night's long territory.

The visual records aboard the Voyager depict a nearly perfect world, showing us our place within the whole; in the photograph of a snow-covered forest, trees are so large that human figures standing at their base are almost invisible. In the corner of this picture is a close-up of a snow crystal's elegant architecture of ice and air. Long-necked geese fly across another picture, a soaring eagle. Three dolphins, sun bright on their silver sides, leap from a great ocean wave. Beneath them are underwater blue reefs with a shimmering school of fish. It is an abundant, peaceful world, one where a man eats from a vine heavy with grapes, an old man walks through a field of white daisies, and children lovingly touch a globe in a classroom. To think that the precious images of what lives on earth beside us, the lives we share with earth, some endangered, are now tumbling through time and space, more permanent than we are, and speaking the sacred language of life that we ourselves have only just begun to remember.

We have sent a message that states what we most value here on earth: respect for all life and ways. It is a sealed world, a seed of what we may become. What an amazing document is flying above the clouds, holding Utopia. It is more magical and heavy with meaning than the cave paintings of Lascaux, more wise than the language of any holy book. These are images that could sustain us through any cold season of ice or hatred or pain.

In *Murmurs of Earth,* written by members of the committee who selected the photographs and recordings, the records themselves are described in a way that attests to their luminous quality of being: "They glisten, golden, in the sunlight, . . . encased in aluminum cocoons." It sounds as though, through some magical metamorphosis, this chrysalis of life will emerge in another part of infinity, will grow to a wholeness of its own, and return to us alive, full-winged, red, and brilliant.

There is so much hope there that it takes us away from the dark times of horror we live in, a time when the most cruel aspects of our natures have been revealed to us in regions of earth named Auschwitz, Hiroshima, and My Lai, a time when televised death is the primary amusement of our children, when our children are killing each other on the streets.

At second glance, this vision for a new civilization, by its very presence, shows us what is wrong with our world. Defining Utopia, we see what we could be now, on earth, at this time, and next to the images of a better world, that which is absent begins to cry out. The underside of our lives grows in proportion to what is denied. The darkness is made darker by the record of light. A screaming silence falls between the stars of space. Held inside that silence are the sounds of gunfire, the wailings of grief and hunger, the last, extinct song of a bird. The dammed river goes dry, along with its valleys. Illnesses that plague our bodies live in this crack of absence. The broken link between us and the rest of our world grows too large, and the material of nightmares grows deeper while the promises for peace and equality are empty, are merely dreams without reality.

But how we want it, how we want that half-faced, one-sided God.

In earlier American days, when Catholic missions were being erected in Indian country, a European woman, who was one of the first white contacts for a Northern tribe of people, showed sacred paintings to an Indian woman. The darker woman smiled when she saw a picture of Jesus and Mary encircled in their haloes of light. A picture of the three kings with their crowns and gifts held her interest. But when she saw a picture of the crucifixion, the Indian woman hurried away to warn others that these were dangerous people, people to fear, who did horrible things to each other. This picture is not carried by the Voyager, for fear we earth people would "look" cruel. There is no image of this man nailed to a cross, no saving violence. There are no political messages, no photographs of Hiroshima. This is to say that we know our own wrongdoings.

But there is not even a true biology of our species on board because NASA officials vetoed the picture of a naked man and pregnant woman standing side by side, calling it "smut." They allowed only silhouettes to be sent, as if our own origins, the divine flux of creation that passes between a man and a woman, are unacceptable, something to hide. Even picture diagrams of the human organs, musculature, and skeletal system depict no sexual organs, and a photograph showing the birth of an infant portrays only the masked, gloved physician lifting the new life from a mass of sheets, the mother's body hidden. While we might ask if they could not have sent the carved stone gods and goddesses in acts of beautiful sexual intimacy on temple walls in India, this embarrassment about our own carriage of life and act of creative generation nevertheless reveals our feelings of physical vulnerability and discomfort with our own life force.

From an American Indian perspective, there are other problems here. Even the language used in the selection process bespeaks many of the failings of an entire system of thought and education. From this record we learn about our relationships, not only with people, but with everything on earth. For example, a small gold-eyed frog seen in a human hand might have been a photograph that bridges species, a statement of our kinship with other lives on earth, but the hand is described, almost apologetically, as having "a dirty fingernail." Even the clay of creation has ceased to be the rich element from which life grows. I recall that the Chilean poet Pablo Neruda wrote "What can I say without touching the earth with my hands?" We must wonder what of value can ever be spoken from lives that are lived outside of life, without a love or respect for the land and other lives.

In "The Foundations of the Voyager Record," one of the co-authors writes about hearing dolphins from his room, "breathing, playing with one another. Somehow," he says, "one had the feeling that they weren't just some sea creatures but some very witty and intelligent beings living in the next room." This choice of words places us above and beyond the rest of the world, as though we have stepped out of our natural cycles in our very existence here on earth. And isn't our world full of those rooms? We inhabit only a small space in the house of life. In another is a field of corn. In one more is the jungle world of the macaw. Down the hall, a zebra is moving. Beneath the foundation is the world of snakes and the five hearts of the earthworm.

In so many ways, the underside of our lives is here. Even the metals used in the record tell a story about the spoils of inner earth, the laborers in the hot mines. Their sweat is in that record, hurtling away from our own galaxy.

What are the possibilities, we wonder, that our time capsule will be found? What is the possibility that there are lives other than our own in the universe? Our small galaxy, the way of the milk, the way of sustenance, is only one of billions of galaxies but there is also the possibility that we are the only planet where life opens, blooms, is gone, and then turns over again. We hope this is not the case. We are so young we hardly know what it means to be a human being, to have natures that allow for war. We barely even know our human histories, so much having unraveled before our time, and while we know that our history creates us, we hope there is another place, another world we can fly to when ours is running out. We have come so far away from wisdom, a wisdom that is the heritage of all people, an old kind of knowing that respects a community of land, animals, plants, and other people as equal to ourselves. Where we know the meaning of relationship.

As individuals, we are not faring much better. We are young. We hardly know who we are. We face the search for ourselves alone. In spite of our search through the universe, we do not know our own personal journeys. We still wonder if the soul weighs half an ounce, if it goes into the sky at the time of our death, if it also reaches out, turning, through the universe.

But still, this innocent reaching out is a form of ceremony, as if the Voyager were a sacred space, a ritual enclosure that contains our dreaming the way a cathedral holds the bones of saints.

The Interstellar Record is a testament to the unacknowledged holiness with which we see our earth, and to our own roles as caretakers. The people of earth are reaching out. We are having a collective vision. Like young women and men on a vision quest, we seek a way to live out the peace of the vision we have sent to the world of stars. We want to live as if there is no other place, as if we will always be here. We want to live with devotion to the world of waters and the universe of life that dwells above our thin roofs.

I remember that night with my mother, looking up at the black sky with its turning stars. It was a mystery, beautiful and distant. Her body I came from, but our common ancestor is the earth, and the ancestor of earth is space. That night we were small, my mother and I, and we were innocent. We were children of the universe. In the gas and dust of life, we are voyagers. Wait. Stop here a moment. Have you eaten? Come in. Eat.

William Kittredge

Lost Cowboys (But Not Forgotten)

from *Antaeus*

We are, most of us, ethnologists in our own house, working to locate ourselves amid the clutter. Some of us are quite self-consciously working to remake ourselves in the image of some imaginary long-ago land where people were healed to their lives.

But you have to think we have always been aware of our awareness and incessantly trying to avoid acknowledging how much everything, including ourselves, is on-the-spot invention and make-believe.

When I came to Montana I was always tracking, but I didn't know what animal I was after. I would drift through taverns like an anthropologist; I believed my life and the lives of people I knew were not of much significance because we lived in the insulated city of our middle-class affiliations. Lives of consequence, I thought, were being lived down the road among the drunks and Indians and working stiffs (as in, "Their lives are more *real*"; it was as condescending as could be).

Like a lot of people, I imagined life in its most significant cadences was taking place somewhere on our political peripheries. I was after that occasional tavern which becomes a hideout for radical funniness and the juxtaposition of dissimilar elements. A life in taverns can be like art, I thought; it can help us see freshly, as is our sacred duty.

Humiliation and sentimental nostalgia were dominant in the cowhand music I listened to as the days drifted away. But I wasn't responsible; I was invisible and artistic, and close to paralyzed by my disengagements.

First you find a metaphor, such as the lost-wax process in bronze casting (the idea of a residual metallic shell around a core which has melted and drained away—that is, cowboys in image instead of actuality), and then you name your manifestation of that metaphor (something like "Lost Cowboys"). You construct your entire piece of writing to fit the name. It's one way of trying to make sure your piece is reasonably coherent, and has a title you can live with.

There are at least four great memoirs about life on the Plains: *Goodbye to a River* by John Graves; *Old Jules* by Mari Sandoz; *Wolf Willow* by Wallace Stegner; and *We Pointed Them North* by Teddy Blue Abbott and Helena Huntington Smith.

The last time Teddy Blue ever saw Calamity Jane was in Gilt Edge, Montana, just up from the Judith Basin. "I joked her about her trip and asked her: 'How'd you like it when they sent you east to get reformed and civilized?'

"Her eyes filled with tears. She said: 'Blue, why don't the sons of bitches leave me alone and let me go to hell my own route?' "

When Teddy Blue talked, it was always cowboying. The later stuff was only life. "I started young and I am seventy-eight. Only a few of us are left now, and they are scattered from Texas to Canada.

"Such is life," Teddy said, "in the Far West."

Sliced apples, and pears, various cheeses, decent wine: As evening came down over the tree-lined boulevards on the north side of Great Falls, there was a well-lighted reception in the Charlie Russell Museum.

A raggedy man came in off the street, boots wrapped with duct tape. Somebody told him the feast was free. He smiled and poured for himself.

Somebody else wanted to show him out, but nobody did. What I remember is his judicious expression as he sipped his wine and studied a Russell painting, and the uneasiness in that hall full of the enfranchised (we the people with okay automobiles and new shirts).

The tension softened after somebody said the old man was probably the only person in the place Charlie Russell might have tolerated. Everybody smiled and knew it was true.

On summer evenings the year I turned six, my father would catch a bay gelding called Moon, lift me to the saddle, and lead me out along the irrigation ditch at the head of the garden, where he would instruct me in the arts of horseback. If I came unseated, he would knock the dust off my shirt and lift me up again; crying was unthinkable; this was my start in the real life, and I knew it.

I remember daybreak on the high deserts of eastern Oregon and my father and some other men who are dead now. They would ease into a round willow-walled corral, where sixty or so spooky geldings were circling counterclockwise around the rock-solid juniper center post. The cowboss threw his seagrass riata in an effortless overhanded way and dropped a loop on a stocking-footed bay, and I watched as my father eased down the taut rope toward the trembling animal.

You see men like him in the Salt Lake City airport, surrounded by businessmen wearing polished snakehide boots and skiers bound for the mountaintops with peacock feathers tucked into their hatbands. Not long ago I saw Wilford Brimley in the Delta concourse at that airport, backed against a wall, studying the crowd. (There, I thought, the first time I saw him on a movie screen, so actual amid the silliness of *The Electric Cowboy,* they got one of the real ones.)

Another lank old broke-up buckaroo made his way past, limping and walking a little sideways like a crab, paying us none of his attention. It's my illusion that those old farts learned their rules in a rigorous school not many of us try anymore ("Get back on your horse"). They know their time is over, and hate the notion, as anybody would, as my father did; they see us as imitation, and pitiful in our dislocations. Wilford Brimley has become a movie star. I think of him as the first Old Post-modern Cowhand Fart, trapped in our zoo, keeper and kept. I wish I knew what he thought.

My father believed his second wife was as good and capable as a human could be, and yet he was willing to say no woman should ever be elected to political office. "They're not fit for it," he would say.

He despised the unemployed on principle, because they were weak, but he was legendary for his generosity, and men who worked for him stayed for years. He loaned them money, bought them whiskey, hired them back, but he never imagined they were his equals. The list of things my father came to despise started and ended somewhere in the neighborhood of people who overwork the goodwill of others. The motto of the country where I come from in southeastern Oregon ought to be "Take care of your own goddamned self."

Snow was skittering across the highway at Lost Trail Pass in early November. I was backtracking Lewis and Clark south across the Bitterroot Range between Montana and Idaho. What I was seeking, in my lonely-boy state of mind, with Elvis plugged into the tape deck, was a cure for my fragmentations, and another growing season.

It's a dis-ease that can overcome you with first evidence of winter in the northern Rockies, when the world seems entirely distant from hummingbirds in the blooming lilacs. I'm nearing sixty and people I know are dying of major afflictions; we're learning to accommodate the notion that closure, as in the way stories end, has something to do with the people we are.

It is coming evening as I drove upstream along the Salmon River, out of isolated meadowlands along the great watersheds and into the deep forested canyons that rise toward the Stanley Basin. It's a drive everybody in Montana seems to try once in a while, seeking relief from cherished isolations and heading south toward what is understood as heedlessness in Sun Valley, or gambling in Jackpot and Reno, and then on to the alien blooming richness of the Sonoran deserts in early spring.

My friend John Rember tells me that, for the first time in fifteen years, he found dead spawned-out salmon on gravel bars along the Salmon River. Not enough of them yet to raise the old-time rotting stench, but the big fish are coming back, thanks to the Sawtooth Fish Hatchery. The native sea-run salmon are mostly gone, but hatchery programs have worked in Alaska, and they beat the hell out of the alternative, which is no salmon at all.

But I want more, and I grieve for the sad old terrible grizzly bears. The grizzlies in this part of the world are easy to kill. There was no need to go search them out in the bushwhack mountains. A hunter could just sight in his high-velocity rifle and wait for the salmon to run. The grizzlies would come down to fish, and you could sit three hundred yards away with a scope and kill them like pests. I pray that deep in these mountains there are grizzlies living invulnerable lives in a paradise of their own discovering, where we will never go.

In Stanley the white-water-rafting tycoons had gone back to wherever they originate, and the village was settled in to enjoy a long season of rural privacy. John Rember is a native who left the family ranch south of Stanley in the late 1960s, graduated from Harvard, and learned to live in the land of the rich while he taught in a private school in Ketchum. He climbed in the Sawtooths, and skied, season by season. And then he cashed out. When I visited he was living with his folks while he built a house of his own.

The locals are returning to roots. I did the other thing, left the valley where I grew up and never went back except to drive through on my way to somewhere else.

John and I walked the rough flooring in his new house. Out a hole in a wall, to be his bedroom window, in wintertime moonlight, the icy Sawtooths were glowing under a creamy, swirling sky, and I contemplated the classical, serious, fool-making mysteries. How to proceed? Can it be true we suffer a nostalgia for which there is no remedy on earth?

My nerves were wrecked. I imagined the morning light was breaking through the great windows in the Sun Valley Lodge like shattered glass. It should have been the sweetest of times, mayflies hovering in golden light under shimmering birch, the waters mysterious with eveningtime trout, and nights of ease and merriment among the winsome and perfectly enfranchised folk who inhabit the Wood River Valley.

I bribed the chambermaid for a peek into the third-floor bedroom where Hemingway is reputed to have written *For Whom the Bell Tolls.* It overlooked a year-round ice rink famous from 1930s Sonja Henie movies. What I found was intimacy with the kind of fracturing that drove Hemingway to his shotgun. *Many must have it.* I stood on the balcony, listening to birds. Their calling sang of dislocations.

So I eased myself downstairs. This was the summer of 1976. A western film conference was under way: actors, old-time directors, scholars, stars, Harry Dean Stanton, Strother Martin, Buster Crabbe. I was there to learn something about the dominant mythology of my homeland.

That afternoon there were only a half-dozen meditative souls in the bar. I found myself in conversation with a couple of legendary men, the Native American actor Iron Eyes Cody and Colonel Tim McCoy of the Wyoming National Guard and MGM. As young men they had both gone to Hollywood from the Thermopolis country in Wyoming. They were bemoaning modernist inauthenticity, as old men will.

Don't mistake me, I respected them. Tim McCoy was one of the seven great stars at MGM before the invention of sound, he and John

Gilbert, Lon Chaney, Ramon Novarro, Buster Keaton, Marion Davies, and Lillian Gish. It was perfect, there we were, remnants, me and those once-upon-a-time moving-picture stars.

Then a green-eyed handsome man moved in. He was wearing an orange jogging outfit, deck shoes, no socks, and a Rolex watch. He eyed us like a hired pathologist. "What you need," he said to me, "is a line."

As in, we all thought, and we were right, cocaine.

As in, I think now, politics, line of work and intention.

Colonel Tim McCoy just froze. Iron Eyes Cody looked away in sorrow. But it was true, I needed to be tethered. Many must have it. I smiled, and there I was, in complicity with the green-eyed guy, cut off from those old men and what I see to have been a chance at right relationship and true reverence. But the cocaine was also a try at connection.

In Ketchum, over breakfast, a friend told me about traveling to Santa Barbara four days a month to train as a lay analyst. Our talk led to notions of *familia*, the Latin word that unites home and family in that cluster of narratives which is our most inclusive name for who we are.

We are all "making story." It is the most important thing we do. We constantly tell ourselves the story that is our life; when we forget the plot, we lose track of ourselves. In psychological circles this is called "narrative dysfunction." It is no fun.

We invent fine, brave, but sometimes wrongheaded stories to live by and people to be. These can be teaching stories, good and useful, about learning always to seek humility and compassion. But the people inventing these stories, any of us, are often wounded and frightened by the loneliness inherent in our lives, and our stories are often deeply selfish.

Many of us are heading out to the hills. To hell with public responsibilities. Maybe, we whisper, we can find a hideout paradise, water from a hot spring showering down from a cliff above a wilderness river. We are talking about nature as a true resort, a place in which we might find refuge. We are talking about privilege.

> The road took us to the most distant fountain of waters of the mighty Missouri in surch of which we had spent so many toilsome days and wristless nights.
> Meriwether Lewis

In motel rooms I replayed the video of Elvis singing "Hound Dog" to a real dog on *The Steve Allen Show* in 1956. Meditating on Elvis's last, sad rewards got me to Meriwether Lewis, and the high hopes that surrounded beginnings in the American West.

On Monday, August 12, 1805, Lewis was laboring uphill, heading west toward the Continental Divide. Earlier in the afternoon a man named McNeal "exhultingly stood with a foot on each side of this little rivulet and thanked his god that he had lived to bestride the mighty & heretofore deemed endless Missouri."

Lewis "proceeded to the top of the dividing ridge from which I discovered immence ranges of high mountains still to the West of us with their tops partially covered with snow."

It was an instant of vast importance. The Corps of Discovery had been moving upriver from St. Louis for two days short of fifteen months, since May 14, 1804. One of the objectives assigned by President Jefferson was the discovery of an overland route for transcontinental trade and traffic. At last men from the United States were at the great watershed.

Lewis was expecting to gaze down on the River Columbia, a free-flowing highway that would carry them to the Pacific in triumph and ease. What he saw was timbered ridge after timbered ridge, some snow-covered, feathering off to a sky that must have seemed more infinite with possibility than anyone had hoped.

Lewis and William Clark returned to the East and told Jefferson that the way to the West lay over a three-hundred-mile maze of mountains, sixty miles of which were covered with perpetual snows. Their message was taken to heart. The federal government did not venture into the northern Rockies again until the Stevens railroad survey of 1855. An endlessness of mountains was left as an enclave to be inhabited by Indians, trappers, and prospectors, bypassed by civilization and civic order. Part of that enclave remains as wilderness in the intermountain West. It is vitally important to our sense of ourselves as a people, central in the story we tell about our national willingness to preserve that which is most natural in our lives, if only by accident.

The entire West may be thought of as states on the cusp. If political boundaries had been laid out by a sensible formula, entities like Montana and Wyoming and Idaho wouldn't exist at all.

Almost a hundred years ago, in his *Report on the Lands of the Arid Region of the United States,* John Wesley Powell pointed out that natural political empathies in the American West lay within the major watersheds. By cutting up the West along boundaries determined by the artificial four-square grid survey, which didn't reflect anything real, Powell said, we were forcing our populations into artificial alliances. It was a brilliant, accurate insight, and nobody paid him much attention. As a result, we have conglomerations of unlikely allies.

Montana, Wyoming: What's in a name? As Ezra Pound pointed out, nouns are not real, nothing is static; verbs and processes are real. In the act of naming we are constantly involved in transmogrification, making unreal.

A friend, something of a poetic fop, once stopped in a tavern in Hailey, Idaho, where Ezra was born, and asked if anything had any idea who Pound might be. The barkeep, who looked like some kind of logging-camp Wobbly nihilist, grinned and recited:

> Learn of the green world what can be thy place
> In scaled invention or true artistry
> Pull down thy vanity.

At least that's the story. Point is, I believe it. My friend says he fled up the road about fifteen miles, to his own kind, and happy hour at the Sun Valley Lodge.

In Boise there's a woman named Nancy Stringfellow, who spent much of her life creating one of the two or three finest bookstores between

Chicago and the West Coast. She writes, "We came here in 1914, when I was four years old. Oh, it's changed since I was a girl, but there are still little towns a girl wants to get away from and a woman wants to get back to."

In May 1982 Annick Smith and I were driving home along the upper reaches of the Lochsa River, and we elected to bide a while and ease the miseries of travel at an undeveloped wilderness spa called Jerry Johnson Hot Springs. We counted our blessings; the steaming creekside pools were deserted.

Then we noticed a speckling of ominous gray-white residue accumulating on the rocks. It seemed to be falling from the clear sky. Have you ever been back in the western wilds, and imagined the technocratic world has ended?

Maybe it was true, nukes at last, and we were the saving remnant, alive there where the hot water bubbled at the edge of a snow-melt creek coming down from the western slopes of the Bitterroots. Maybe we were the last uncontaminated people on earth.

But it was Mount St. Helens, and we were not actually alone. In those mountains, mellowing out in other hide-away hot springs, there were many like us, seeking after something actual and vital in the touch of the world. Gary Snyder has said, "And that's the real work: to make the world real as it is and find ourselves real as we are within it."

By which he seems to mean that it is hard to believe in ourselves as real. It is commonplace to despair over children from inner city enclaves who come to believe in nothing but moral chaos, in which notions of justice seem one contrivance after another, and the consequences of their actions appear almost perfectly arbitrary. In such situations, our lightness of being is indeed unbearable. And it's not just a dis-ease of the ghettos; it's uptown and everywhere, and those of us who can, we flee, we seek out the hot springs. We try to be at ease, and accept the grace we find.

But it seems unearned, and we are tempted to despise ourselves, even while we cultivate our decencies. It's just that it's all too easy, and so many of us are so willing to collapse into direct, welcoming connection with things we claim to love, like creek-bed stones.

Mount St. Helens turned out to be disappointingly dusty, but it counted as a small apocalypse in our part of the world. That first evening, as we drove in from Jerry Johnson Hot Springs, the arc lights cast an orangey shimmering aura through the volcanic ash which was settling in small drifts along the streets of Missoula. We seized the opportunity to join a long rolling knot of party which lasted the three or four days until the rains came.

Some of us followed the action, resort to resort, Sun Valley, Boulder, Telluride, Sedona, Santa Fe, Moab, wondering where it would go next. And some of us ended up two-hearted as we could be, understanding that life breaks more easily than we imagined and trying to reconnect ourselves to the rhythms of place and family, at the same time trying to ignore the whispering of what might be actual guilt. God knows some problems were left blowing in the wind, like, What about everybody else, the people we've all seen who couldn't afford the trip?

There is a story about Paris and Gertrude Stein and Picasso and Matisse, and a migration of their followers to the American West, in search of a union between the aesthetic and the practical, and a healing connection to the natural world.

The Modernist Rich fall for the Cowboys' native work-oriented sense of style (Oscar Wilde said the miners in Leadville were more interesting than anyone else he encountered in America, because of their floppy hats and great ground-sweeping coats) and fail to understand that Cowboys and Loggers and Miners are Rednecks at heart.

Rednecks, as they are mostly understood in the American West, tend to be working-class white folks whose people have been in the country for at least a couple of generations. They cannot be defined by class or where they grew up or profession. If one characteristic defines Rednecks, it is, I think, a deep sense of disenfranchisement—they feel, quite justifiably, cut off from the sources of power in their culture.

At first the Modernist Rich are driven to overdress as Dudes or pseudo-Cowboys; but they realize actual Cowboys despise them, and besides, Cowboys are deeply involved in unsound grazing practices which speed the destruction of the very nature that has proven to be so healing. It is a sad realization which leads to betrayal. The Rich revert to Ruling-Class instincts and buy the land, become Dude Ranchers and Rancher/Conservationists, and everything is saved except for the Cowboys.

We operate in systems of story and metaphor which we use to define the world (both natural and social) for ourselves, and we must always seek to remodel the mythology (model) that we have inherited from society because each synthesis always fails.

Artists in the American West (as everywhere), from Timothy O'Sullivan to Charlie Russell to the duck-stamp painters to the people who planted half-buried nose-down Cadillacs in the Texas deserts, have always worked toward helping us in that process by inciting us to witness a version of the moment with blinders off. It's what artists are for: they help us *see;* they drive society through the process of coming to fresh recognitions; it is a political responsibility.

At midmorning in the valley where the Madison River flows through southwestern Montana, the light was absolute and pure, as it would be in paradise if I could imagine such a place.

Shadows cast by the mountains of the Madison Range were receding across the sagebrush foothills; a country man was baling with his New Holland hay-baler.

A Montana highway patrolman smiled a good-old-boy smile when I asked about the road to the Earth First! encampment.

"Newspaper?" he said. Fifty-seven-year-old white citizen, summer haircut and a rented Toyota: Maybe I was FBI. "No," I said.

I was looking for Dave Foreman, the main Earth First! spokesperson. FBI agents had gone to his house in Tucson, showed .357 magnum pistols, and dragged him, in nothing but his shorts and handcuffs, to jail.

Now he was out on bail, awaiting trial, formally charged with *conspiracy to sabotage a nuclear facility and destruction of an energy facility.*

As I understood the story, it was a kind of morality play, a good man brought down by his own heedlessness. But my story wasn't working out. I had visited a charismatic leader and found him retired from charisma; I found he had never believed in charisma; he thought charismatic leaders were a step toward fascism, always had. In theory, he despised them.

There is a story about Wovoka, the Paiute whose visions inspired the Ghost Dance rebellion, a spiritual movement that swept across the West like a great wind, and culminated in the massacre at Wounded Knee in December 1890. A year or so later a group of Plains Indians traveled horseback over great distances to consult with Wovoka at Walker Lake in Nevada. His wife came to the door of his ranchhand house. "The Messiah is tired," she said, "and wishes you would all go home."

My dealings with Dave Foreman had gone like that, sort of. There was an old Volkswagen van parked alongside the gravel road, Texas plates and a bumper sticker that read *Succeed: Get the US out of Texas.*

The hippie-looking driver and his friends were stopped and talking to four flat-faced official types (we called them "hair-cuts" when I was a kid in the West; we were talking about deputy sheriffs).

Three rope-haired, dusty-legged young men and a woman were guarding the gate into the campground. They were a decade younger than my own children; I wondered whether they were taking names, or what.

I didn't get out of my Toyota; I didn't speak to anybody except a Forest Service ranger. "Just driving around," I said. I wondered whether he wrote down my license plate numbers so some computer jockey could check it back to Budget Car Rental at the Jackson, Wyoming airport and get my name. The odor of new-cut alfalfa reminded me of childhood mornings when it was easy to know what I thought.

Who did he imagine I was? Adult citizen on a public road? Was that good enough? Was it clear I was disgusted with my government and myself and about to cause an old-fart scene? I wondered whether the young people in the VW bus were being harassed, if this was harassment. I wondered whether those young people were anarchist badasses, their names all over FBI lists; I wondered why I wasn't anything but pissed off at myself.

I don't want my name on lists. To hell with you, I thought, cursing my culture, you shouldn't get to have my name, this land belongs to me and my people, I don't need to be on your lists, I don't need your permissions, your stinking badges.

Remember those old stories about native people who were afraid to be photographed? They thought their souls were being stolen. I felt like that. There I was in the valley of the Madison River, and somebody was trying to steal my soul.

Remember grade school, when they started telling you about Manifest Destiny? Did you sense a rat? Did it ever sound like the same story you heard around the house, from adults, in which power equals wisdom?

Thomas Jefferson would have loved this agrarian wonderland at the far edge of his Louisiana Purchase and likely thought well of these radical children. He wrote, "I hold it that a little rebellion, now and then, is a good thing, and as necessary in the political world as storms in the physical." And, "The tree of liberty must be refreshed from time to time with the blood of patriots and tyrants."

There we were, me and all the other *haircuts,* telling ourselves we were trying to love this gorgeous morning across the world in our way, but actually gone tyrant. I hated my own incapacities; I hit the road; I was out of there.

Let's try one more turn at making story. Under an early-winter moon it is possible to imagine witnessing the world in ancient clear-minded ways, without the dreaded self-conscious irony of the literate classes. There is not a single electric light in this dream. We study the stars and remember their old patterns as remnants of a language we forgot a long time ago, when the animals all knew how to lie down with one another.

In the American West our society has never been in any sense fair (our ways have been notoriously imperialistic, sexist, and racist); now our society is spinning apart (again).

Old men like my father are furious; they conspired all their lives to fashion a society that suited them. My mother was the boss's moneyed wife; she is confined to her bed; she watches politicians on the TV news and laughs. Those boys, she says.

The well is running dry. Where do we start this time in the continual process of remodeling our selves and culture? How do we understand the society forming around us? What is being made?

1.) The West was an enormous empty (innocent?) stage waiting for a performance. Sometimes it was already a paradise, but more often it was a place that needed remaking (irrigating).

2.) The West has been performed (written) upon; we see the history of our performance everywhere; we see our societal and personal mythologies inscribed on the landscape (fences, roads, canals, power lines, city plans, bomb ranges).

3.) Many of us think much of the West has been ruined. What does this mean—ruined in what sense, ecologically or what? Ruined in terms of what models? By which injustices? Much that we see resembles a kind of chaos (the physical and emotional environs around Las Vegas).

In *America,* Baudrillard says America is a dream. Of course it is, life always is, we inhabit dreams. Then he says a thing that is more interesting: He says life in the American West is a dream of life after the crisis.

What was the crisis? "All that fascinates us is the *spectacle* of the brain and its workings." Out West we see a society in the midst of reinventing itself. Everyone is aware of this. We are all watching. An ironic society is making itself up in a sometimes quite self-reflexive way.

Our crisis is psychological, a crisis of awareness and guilt (through greed, we have ruined our paradise; we knew we were doing it) which has driven us to a deep sense of powerlessness.

Anomie is the easy result (all that counts in the long run is selfishness; I watch myself watch myself; all actions are equal; too many drugs). In response to this crisis of will, a society we don't understand is evolving with terrific speed (inscribing itself on us and our landforms).

Out of control (again), as in our semigenocidal history of conquest and settlement. What to do? Maybe we want to live inside a new story, but how do we define it, how do we choose it, how can we make it come to be?

On our first visit together at Glacier National Park, Annick Smith and I and her eleven-year-old twin boys, Alex and Andrew, hiked more than six miles up to the Sperry Chalet—a 3,700-foot rise in elevation from the paved parking lot at the McDonald Lake Lodge. The boys ranged ahead like wolves when word came down the hill that we were in danger of missing supper.

The second day we traipsed over to the Sperry Glacier, only about four miles and a 1,500 foot rise in elevation; it was like walking in the pastures of heaven. The twins ran their eleven-year-old routes. Annick and I rested on the cool glacial ice.

For a while we didn't notice the condom. It had been used and tossed away, collapsed, slippery and luminous in the morning; someone had been testing our ice; couples wandered the glacier; Annick wondered who it could have been—them, or them? I wondered exactly how much self-absorbed theatricality had been involved. It was my way of condescending to the moment.

Sometimes I live to see the single thing light up. But when I am hounded and strange, looking to hide and perfect my revenge (my living well), then I cleave to obsessive purity, another place to be, in which nothing is forgiven.

Above the treeline in the stony highlands it is possible to imagine that the absolute clarity of crystalline light over the glacial cirques is a moral imperative: Be correct—it is a way of killing possibility. We should go out under the blue-white skies, throw down a blanket, and make love on the glaciers (and carry out the parts that are not biodegradable).

We are a far way into devastation of the interwoven system of life on our planet—the single environment in which our race will ever be able to live. Many of us are seeking ways to stop that devastation; we think it is an enterprise of uttermost urgency. We at least think we are trying to save the world, which is a particularly powerful way of saving ourselves.

We are reinventing our notion of what is most valuable to us, as individuals and as a species, redefining what we take to be sacred; it is our most urgent business, our major communal enterprise. We are deeply afraid of trying to exist on some starship, alone in the universe; we refuse to go on with business as usual.

If we have some luck, we want to believe (and why not?), and stay smart as we can, we may someday find ourselves living inside the solace of a coherent self. Miners and cowhands and unmarried mothers and married mothers and insurance salesmen and old-woman tattoo artists and nature freaks and timber fallers and everyday downtown drunks and so on unto glory, we must learn empathy (we tell ourselves), and cherish and forgive each other.

A young man went to an abandoned house where he had lived with his family, and found a bird trapped inside the empty white-painted rooms, batting at the windows. The sunny spaces where he had run to his mother as a child were thick with this terror. Even when he opened the windows, and the bird escaped, there was no cure.

Imagine a life in which the meadowlarks and magpies come down from their trees and look in our windows at night and study us in our sleep, and then fly away, thinking, tomorrow we must talk and sing to them because nothing else ever helps.

Jan DeBlieu

Into the Dragon's Mouth

from *North Carolina Monthly*

It begins with a subtle stirring, and the falling of sunlight on the vapors that swaddle the earth. It is fueled by extremes—the stifling warmth of the tropics, the bitter chill of the poles. Temperature changes set the system in motion: Hot air drifts upward and, cooling, slowly descends. Knots of pressure gather strength or diminish, forming invisible peaks and valleys in the gaseous soup.

Gradually the vapors begin to swirl as if trapped in a simmering cauldron. Air particles are caught by suction and sent flying. They creep across mountainous ridges and begin the steep, downward descent toward the barometric lows. As the world spins it brushes them to one side but does not slow them.

Tumbling together the particles of air become a huge, unstoppable current. Finally some of them rake against the earth, tousling grasses and trees, slamming mountains, pounding anything that stands in their way. By now they are a force unto themselves, one that shapes the terrestrial and aquatic world. They bring us breath and hardship. They have become the wind.

I stand on a beach near sunset, squinting into the dragon's mouth of a gale. The wind pushes tears from the corners of my eyes and across my temples. Ocean waves crest and break as quickly as I have ever seen them, rolling onto the beach like tanks, churned to an ugly, frothy blue-brown. The storm is a typical March northeaster, most common in spring but just as apt to occur in January or June.

Where I live, on the North Carolina Outer Banks, the days cannot be defined without wind. The roar of the surf would fall silent as the ocean grew as languid as a lake. Trees would sprout wherever their seed happened to fall, cresting the frontal dune, pushing a hundred feet up with spreading crowns. We would go about our lives in a vacuum, as content somewhere else as here. That is how it feels on the few moments when the wind dies: ominous, apocalyptic. As if the world has stopped turning.

I lounge on the beach with friends, enjoying a mild afternoon. A light west breeze lulls and then freshens from the east. Its salty tongue is cooling and delightful at first, but as the gusts build to fifteen miles an hour we begin to think of seeking cover. We linger a while—how long can we hold out, really?—until grains of sand sting our cheeks and catapult into our mouths. As we climb the dune that separates us from the parking lot I am struck anew by the squatness of the landscape. Nothing within a half mile of the ocean grows much higher than the dune line. Nothing can stand the constant burning inflicted by salty wind.

On a thread of soil twenty miles from the mainland, every tree and shrub must be designed to tolerate wind that is both laden with salt and ferociously strong. Gusts of sixty miles an hour or more will shatter limbs that are any less pliant than rubber. Weather is not normal here; we are too far out to sea. There is nothing between the coast and the Appalachian Mountains, two hundred fifty miles inland, to brake the speed of building westerly breezes. There is nothing between the Outer Banks and Africa to deaden the blows of easterly gales.

Any weather book will tell you that winds are caused by the uneven heating of the earth. Pockets of warm and cold air circle each other, create an air flow, and *voilà!* the wind begins to blow. Air moves from high pressure to low pressure, deflected a little by the Coriolis effect. It is a simple matter of physics. I try to keep that in mind as I stand on the beach bent beneath the sheer force of the air being thrown at me, my hair beating against my eyes. Somehow, out in the elements, conventional wisdom falls a bit short. It is easier to believe that wind comes from the roaring breath of a serpent who lives just over the horizon.

The wind, the wind. It has nearly as many names as moods. There are siroccos, Santa Anas, foehns, brickfelders, boras, willywaws, hurricanes, northeasters, chinooks, monsoons. There are bands of wind and calm that girdle the earth. At between thirty-five and thirty-six degrees parallel, the Outer Banks lie just north of the Horse Latitudes, in which, legend holds, light winds slowed the sailing ships of European explorers and hot weather killed many of their horses. But in winter the weather of this coast is shaped by the prevailing westerlies that scream across the continent, pushing calmer, milder air far south.

Offshore, the wide, warm Gulf Stream ropes its way north past Cape Hatteras and turns back out to sea after a close swipe at land. It mingles briefly with the cold tongues of the Virginia Coastal Drift, a spin-off of the southbound Labrador Current. In terms of weather, the junction of these two flows is enough to stop the show. In winter when a dome of high pressure from the arctic drifts southeast, it may come to the edge of the Gulf Stream and stall.

Will it linger or be pushed over the Gulf Stream and out to sea? Suppose there is a core of warm air off the coast, just to the east of the stream. At the same time, suppose the jet stream has grown unusually strong and is flowing to the northeast. The two air masses bump against each other like huge bubbles, the cold air fighting to move east, the warm air prodded north by the jet stream. A pocket of turbulence develops in the crook between them. Wind flows east, then is bent quickly to the north. Unable to resist the centrifugal force, it begins to move full circle, creating a system of low pressure that deepens violently.

The barometer plummets; rain descends in torrents. Up north snow falls thick and fast. The edge of the Gulf Stream is where great winter storms are made. They drift north, bequeathing to the Outer Banks rain, usually, but sometimes snow. And wind.

In the spring of 1962 an explosive low-pressure system developed unexpectedly over the Outer Banks. In the wake of fierce northeast winds the ocean pounded the shore for three days, spilling over the dunes and through the little towns tucked behind them. During that particular meteorological episode, known as the Ash Wednesday storm, people woke to find the ocean sloshing into their beds. This cycle of weather has been repeated many times since, though never with equal force.

Such sudden, lashing northeasters have always intrigued the forecasters at the Cape Hatteras Weather Station, who as recently as a decade ago were at a loss to explain them. Now, with the help of sophisticated probes and satellite photos, meteorologists can often tell when a winter low-pressure system threatens to form over the coast. They can warn island residents, with some confidence, to buckle down for a squall.

More typically the wind blows fickle, and its swings of mood are devilishly tricky to foretell. At the center of a pressure system wind speed slows, but at the edges it quickens. A strong core of high pressure, sliding over the coast, may bring light wind that lasts for days. The system may stall long enough to dissolve, or it may venture out to sea, stirring up gales as it passes.

How much wind tomorrow? The technicians at the weather station make their educated guesses, knowing all along that the wind may fool them. Knowing that, whatever else it does, the wind will call the day's tune.

Before the advent of sophisticated forecasting equipment, islanders watched for subtle changes to predict the behavior of weather and wind. They studied the sky and the animals the way a mother might look for the telltale signs that her young child is growing tired and cross. If, in a light, variable wind the gulls stand facing north, watch for steady north wind by nightfall. If clouds form a halo around the moon, count the stars within the halo. If there are three, expect bad weather for the next three days.

A mackerel sky—one with thick clouds that look like fish scales—means rain is on the way. A sun dog at sunset foretells a bad storm. A mild spell in December or January is a "weather breeder"; it brings penetrating cold before winter's end. "A warm Christmas," an elderly island man once told me, "makes a fat cemetery."

Only fools lived on the ocean, back before hurricanes could be spotted on radar. The houses of Outer Banks natives nestled together in wooded sections just off the Albermarle and Pamlico sounds. The soundside was considered the front of the islands, and the ocean beach, where the fury of storms hit hardest, was thought of as the back. It was the jumping-off point, the place where swimmers could venture from the encircling arms of a continent into an ocean of uncertainty and terror. Islanders spoke of their homeland as if they were intent on keeping their backs, figuratively speaking, to the wind.

The cattle that ranged freely across the Outer Banks in the late nineteenth and early twentieth centuries seemed to know when a weather shift was imminent, and they anticipated changes in the wind to escape biting flies. If they moved to the "back of the beach," east wind was on the way. If they migrated to the marshes, the easterly breeze would swing west. Most of the time the range stock stayed in open grasslands and dunes. When they wandered into the villages, residents began boarding windows for a hurricane.

The intensity of the weather always depends on the wind, and Outer Banks saws impart more homespun knowledge about gales and breezes than any other facet of life. A heavy dew in the morning means heavy wind by afternoon. If a swarm of biting flies shows up on a fishing boat far offshore, a land breeze is bound to shift to an ocean breeze. When the wind swings hard to the northeast, it will most likely blow itself out in a day:

A Saturday shift, come late or soon,
It seldom stands till Sunday noon.

Once or twice a winter, however, a northeaster lasts for most of a week. No matter how it begins or ends, local wisdom holds that the blow will always diminish on the third, or fifth, or seventh day, never on an even-numbered day. Normally the wind migrates slowly from northeast to east to southeast to southwest, moving clockwise in the anticyclonic pattern typical of high-pressure systems.

There are exceptions, of course, when the wind moves backwards or counterclockwise. For generations native islanders have known such shifts to be harbingers of the most violent storms. The weather change might come as a localized thunderstorm or a devastating hurricane, but a backing wind is always to be feared. As an old saying suggests, "I'd rather look at Grandma's drawers than see a backing wind."

Wind is culture and heritage on the Outer Banks; wind shapes earth, plant, animal, human. It toughens us. It moves mountains of sand as we watch. It makes it difficult to sleepwalk through life.

The spring I moved to the islands I lived in a house beset by wind. Air seeped easily through the decayed siding and whistled through the roof. The constant clatter made me lonely and chafed my nerves, but I gladly sought the shelter of those rooms rather than stand exposed to the chilling breeze. I developed a ritual for going out: Before opening the door I pulled on my coat and gloves, yanked down my hat, and braced myself for an onslaught.

I conditioned myself slowly, taking walks in steady wind for twenty minutes at first, with the hope of working up to forty-five. An appreciation for wind was not in my nature; I had to learn to like the feel of air pummeling my chest and roaring across my skin. "Light" wind, I learned, blew less than fifteen miles an hour. Anything less than ten miles an hour was not worth mention.

Walking with my hood pulled hard against my scalp, I began to notice how animals coped with wind. Terns, the kamikazes of the bird world, seemed oblivious even to hard gales. I remember watching them one spring afternoon at Oregon Inlet as air howled down on us from the north and waves sloshed against each other. Together wind and tide made a mess of the landscape; with the frothing water and the whipping branches of oceanside shrubs, it seemed like the world was being shaken at its foundations. Yet the terns hung steady in midair, flapping their wings quickly and chittering to each other, their beaks pointed downward as they scanned the ocean for fish.

Not many animals come out in such wind. Those that do may find the normal parameters of earth redrawn. In a sustained east wind the water in the sounds is pushed toward the mainland, so that vast stretches of bottom are exposed. Islanders refer to this as the tide running out, and indeed it is the only kind of falling tide to be seen on the banks' western shore. The water level in the estuaries here does not respond to the pull of the moon. All sound tides are erratic and driven strictly by wind; they ebb in northeasters and flow during westerly blows.

Soon after I moved here I learned that water swept east by wind for twenty miles has a way of suddenly spilling over its normal banks, like a bowl tipped sloppily to one side. One morning after several days of hard west wind I parked in a lot near a fish house on Pamlico Sound. An islander casually warned me, "You might ought to move your car, 'case we get some tide." Translated this meant, "Move it or lose it." I parked on higher ground. Within an hour three feet of briny water filled the fish house lot.

Water ripples like a washboard in heavy wind. Its malleable surface shows approaching gusts long before they can be felt. Riding in a sailboat, trying to safely harness the Outer Banks breeze, you can watch the front edge of a gust push across the water as it sweeps toward you, takes hold of your sail, and keels your boat hard to the side.

Even the more docile winds affect the shape of the water and the distribution of creatures within it. East winds send the surf pounding against the beach; west winds slow the shoreward roll of breakers and make them stand erect. The best surfing waves are sculpted by a northeast blow that shifts cleanly to the west. But if the west wind blows too long, the breakers are knocked flat. Surfers disappear, replaced by commercial beach fishermen who row dories just offshore to set their nets for bluefish.

We all have our favorite winds. Outer Banks surf casters like a land breeze because, as they say,

Wind from the east, fish bite the least.
Wind from the west, fish bite the best.

A westerly breeze draws bluefish, trout, mullet, and other species to the calm waters in the lee of shore. During duck hunting season it also pushes waterfowl from the middle of Pamlico Sound toward the islands, putting them in easy range of hunting blinds. A friend of mine, an avid hunter and fisherman who lives on Hatteras Island, grew so enamored of the soundside breeze that he threatened to name his first-born son West Wind. His wife's wisdom prevailed; they named the child Teal.

Good fishing or poor, the light summer easterlies are dearest to my heart. West winds muddy the ocean waters, but east winds clear them. West winds bring biting flies to the beach, but east winds banish them to the marsh. The most pleasant summer days are those with an ocean breeze strong enough to set up a little surf but not too strong to make swimming dangerous. Waves roll lazily ashore as wind gently fills my lungs, caresses my skin, and sweeps cobwebs from my brain. I lie in the sun, hot but cool enough for reading. I slip noiselessly into the clear green surf and float on top, watching as sparkling grains of sand tumble out to sea between waves.

I live in an island forest now, where tree trunks slash the winter wind before it can hit the house full force. At night I listen to the loblolly pines pitching back and forth, high overhead, and wonder how many more years the cottages on the ocean will be able to stand against the forces that batter them. I do not bundle up as carefully when I go out; to tell the truth, I have come to look forward to the cleansing power of heavy blows. But unlike the old-timers I will never think of the ocean as the back side of the islands. It is the front line of battle, the front line against the wind.

In eight years I have been in more gales than I can count. A few have stayed in my thoughts. One of my clearest memories is of an August day when I stood on the back porch of my little wind-haunted house and waited for a hurricane to blow through.

It was 1986, the year of Hurricane Charley—a runt, as hurricanes go, but with gusts to eighty-five. A friend had come over to visit my husband and me with his dog, a Chesapeake Bay retriever. The storm, passing offshore, was throwing off east wind and was not expected to do much damage. Even so, no one wanted to be out in it. It was enough to stand on the leeward side of the house and watch the myrtle bushes being shaken like rag mops.

That summer a pair of Carolina wrens had built a nest in the pump house and raised several broods. There were still chicks in the nest when the storm hit. In the excitement I had forgotten about the wrens when I saw a quick movement under the dilapidated table we used to clean fish.

An old beach chair was folded and stashed beneath the table. Leaning over, I could see an adult wren clinging to the chair. He was soaked from rain and, judging from his hunched posture, too exhausted to move even as far as the pump house. We had caught him off his home base and he knew it but did not seem to care.

The others noticed the wren the same second I did. Nobody moved, not even the retriever, although he eyed the wren with a lazy spark of interest. Nobody did anything except look out at the wind and rain. We stood on the back porch, an unlikely alliance—two men, a woman, a dog, a bird—each of us snagged, momentarily, from the flow of our normal lives, refugees from the wind.

Bob Shacochis

Greetings from the Big Pineapple

from *Outside*

Beyond the rooftops of the mansions of Miramar—once an aristocratic neighborhood and still an elite address—storm clouds scrape low over Havana. Columns of purple rain march through silenced barrios. Banks of steam erupt from the streets, wisps like puffs of smoke snagging in the treetops. It's the end of May, Cuba's rainy season has begun, and the ribs are showing on the emaciated body of the island's not-yet-middle-aged revolution. From the balcony of my hotel room, the first impression is hard to shake: Havana is a city at war, a city on a dire countdown, a city that understands it's about to be invaded.

Of course, it isn't, and won't be, not really—armed conflict is a chimera employed to focus the attention of revolution's children. But there are other kinds of invasions. Forsaken by his sugar daddy, the Soviet Union, Fidel Castro has singled out tourism for no-holds-barred development, dispatching a fun-in-the-sun strike force to bandage Cuba's hemorrhaging economy with hard currency stripped from a relatively toxic source: Western consumerist culture. WE DEFEND SOCIALISM BY DEVELOPING TOURISM, say the billboards. We need a miracle, says *el jefe,* but what is he thinking, rolling out the red carpet for the capitalist hordes?

Even before we boarded the Ilyushin-18 in Cancún, I was experiencing a mild case of apprehension not entirely associated with being lifted into the air by a Soviet hand-me-down. Miami's Cuban-expatriate community had led us to expect the very worst: a cowed and sullen population, suspicious of one another, their lips glued by fear. An infrastructure in accelerating collapse. Overt loathing for *yanqui* imperialists, who had used the Gulf War as a dress rehearsal for satisfying Washington's longest-running grudge, the Cuba problem. Since the first of January, more than 600 men and women had flung themselves into the Gulf Stream off Cuba's northern coast on inner tubes and makeshift rafts, the largest exodus of refugees since the Mariel boatlift in 1980. Word on the street in Havana had it that only one out of every hundred who attempted this desperate adventure made it to the shopping malls of southern Florida alive. The Cuban word for these people was *escoria,* "scum."

Cuba, always forced by its two-crop economy of sugar and tobacco to export everything it produced, could no longer afford to import the basics. The 28-year-old U.S. trade embargo was squeezing the island harder than ever, causing already short supplies of food and medicine to dwindle. In Miami, scholars who had traveled to Havana for an academic conference advised me to pack soap and coffee as gifts. Don't plan on renting a car, they warned—the gas pumps had run dry, and Fidel had proclaimed 1991 the Year of the Bicycle. As dictated by the U.S. State Department in its paradoxical wisdom, American tourists were free to travel to Cuba, but spending money while there was illegal, good for a $250,000 fine and up to 12 repentant years in jail.

Cuba, the Big Pineapple, seemed a Dantesque hellhole, and I couldn't imagine what sort of reception awaited us at Havana's José Martí International Airport, especially considering that we—the Professor, Caputo the paparazzo, and I—had tired of waiting for Havana to grant us proper visas and decided to slip into the country by way of the back door, Mexico. The State Department would no doubt have taken exception to our plan, but there was no time to waste. We were on our way to observe the 41st Ernest Hemingway International Classic Billfish Tournament—one of the oldest billfishing competitions in the world. North American anglers, for the first time in years, had found a way to participate in this most prestigious event, dropping bait into the socialist sea. We figured to wet a line, then travel the length of the island from Havana eastward to the beaches and freshly painted facades of the *turista* archipelago of the north coast, then to the mountains, the Sierra Maestra, where it all had started, where a young university student/gang member/lawyer/baseball pitcher had decided that it was time to take paradise off the market, choosing instead the course of ultimate adventure, the Everest of political endeavor, revolution.

So it was that the day before the tournament was to end, we boarded an Air Cubana flight out of Cancún, sobered by the caveat of the agent behind the counter. Protect yourself from your government, she advised; don't have your passports stamped in Havana. After a seemingly endless delay our flight was called, and we were bused to an isolated corner of the tarmac to board an ancient Soviet-made flying steam-bath. The cabin thundered with the noise of the Ilyushin's four propellers. Minutes later we listened in dread as the engines were cut one by one, delivering us into a terrible silence. The flight crew abandoned the cockpit, mopping cascades of sweat from their brows, muttering about electrical failure.

Sitting in front of us, a trio of extremely merry Mexicans, undaunted by the drama, appointed themselves social directors. "Don't worry," the most extroverted muchacho declared grandiosely. "Everything's under control." They passed around a calming bottle of tequila. "We are making a study of Cuban girls," explained their point man. His two companions nodded wolfishly. "We are very concerned about our addiction to these girls, and have decided to analyze the situation further." This news cheered the Professor, who admired their academic spirit. By and by the electrical failure was repaired, the brave pilots returned, the engines cranked over, and we began to lumber down the runway. "Go, go, go," chanted the muchachos, rocking in their seats as if we were puttering up a hill in a Volkswagen.

"Well," observed the Professor, plumbing the bright side of the delay, "at least we got a sauna out of it." As we reached altitude, it began to snow inside the plane, icy flakes blowing out of the air vent onto Caputo, who took the change of weather in stride. Cuba, after all, was the home of magical realism.

Once on the ground, we queued in front of the immigration booths, anxious and humble, and advanced together like three lost lambs. The official who examined our passports unsettled us profoundly: I can't say we ever quite recovered. She was young and lovely, and she flirted with us—sweet chat and welcoming smiles. We cleared customs without the agents displaying the slightest interest in our gear.

"This siege mentality," said the Professor, "is going to wear us down fast."

How clever of these die-hard Marxist-Leninists, I thought, to lull us like that, but surely the charade would end once they were confronted with the boys from Mexico City, three horny, half-drunk, and totally irreverent specimens of the type border guards love to turn away. If Cuba accepted the muchachos, then the place was wide open.

We pushed through the terminal doors into a muggy, overcast afternoon. There were the Mexicans. Their leader ambled over to us, all mischievous eyes and conspiratorial grin, wagging his finger as if *we* were the naughty ones.

"Sooner or later," he crowed, "we knew you were going to come." Someone had just told him we were North American tourists.

In the beginning was the word, and the word was Ernesto himself, the progenitor of the marlin tournament, and an honorary god in the Cuban pantheon of machismo. Off and on throughout the 1930s, Hemingway leased Room 511 at the Hotel Ambos Mundos, conveniently around the corner from La Bodeguita del Medio—a bar crazy enough to let writers drink on credit—and a ten-minute wobble from a more sophisticated watering hole, El Floridita. Papa found Cuba a resourceful environment in which to pursue his three addictions, writing, billfishing, and boozing, and he immortalized each pursuit. His alcohol-infused wisdom still adorns the wall above the bar in La B del M—MY MOJITO [a rum-based mint julep] IN LA BODEGUITA, MY DAIQUIRI IN EL FLORIDITA.

In 1934 Hemingway commissioned a Brooklyn boatyard to build the *Pilar,* his legendary 38-foot marlin hunter. Five years later, a 15-acre farm south of Havana caught the eye of Hemingway's third wife; they rented Finca Vigía, and Hemingway spent much of the next two decades there, purchasing the place in 1940 with his first royalty check from *For Whom the Bell Tolls.* By 1950 Hemingway's own ascent to fame paralleled Havana's burgeoning notoriety as the New World's most decadent amusement park, a saturnalia orchestrated by Cuba's corrupt military dictator, Fulgencio Batista. Batista's Babylon offered a standard buffet of sin—prostitutes, drugs, gambling at Mafia-owned casinos, live sex shows at the seedier nightclubs, and a more restrained extravaganza of tits and ass at the dazzling Tropicana—and well-heeled tourists poured onto the island to be thrilled by the wicked ambiance. Down at the Finca Vigía, Hemingway finally figured out what to do with all his wealthy friends, the celebrities and playboys, the hunting buddies and would-be heroes who kept circling through Havana. He herded them into a bona fide fishing tournament.

There's a fascinating photograph, shot from the bridge of a sportfishing boat on the event's tenth anniversary in May 1960: A young Fidel Castro is hunkered over Che Guevara, who sits in the fighting chair; two lines are in the water, but Che's legs are stretched out, his booted feet rest on the transom, and he's reading a book. As judge and sponsor of the competition, Hemingway had invited Castro as his guest of honor, hoping to convince the charismatic warrior, who seemed permanently attired in olive fatigues and combat boots, to present the winner's trophy. But Castro himself, the luckiest man in

Cuban history, won the tournament, hooking and boating the largest marlin.

There's a second photograph: Hemingway and Fidel, *macho a macho,* beaming, Papa surrendering the trophy: two men who helped define their times. They had never met before and never would again. That day Hemingway rode the *Pilar* out into the Gulf Stream for the last time; soon he would leave Cuba for good and go to Idaho, where a year later he would commit suicide. That same year, 1961, his tournament disappeared behind an iron curtain of ill will manufactured by uncompromising ideologies. There were far worse casualties, to be sure, but once Hemingway came ashore off the *Pilar,* no other North American boat would participate in his tournament for three decades. Not until a good-natured, tenacious, fish-crazed, egomaniacal heart surgeon from New Jersey chutzpahed his way onto the scene.

"The Americans are in a position to win this tournament," Dr. David Bregman proclaims as we breakfast with him on Saturday, the final day of the competition. The Cubans at the table suppress laughter. The U.S. team—three boats from New Jersey, two from Florida, one from Baltimore—have managed a paltry two fish between them even though the action has been hot thus far. Naturally, since the Cubans know the fishing grounds, a Cuban boat is in first place, and two Mexican boats are not far behind. But in the end the Hemingway tournament is no more Cuban than an international bankers' convention in Miami Beach. The theme is Cuban, the stage set is neo-Floridian, and far below the surface creak the worn-down gears of everyday Cuban life. But the tournament unravels somewhere else.

Over eggs, the Professor, Caputo, and I receive our sailing orders. The three of us will ride out with Doc aboard his 48-foot Viking, the *Heart Mender.* We will observe to our hearts' content, but Doc will attend to any fishing—after all, he reminds us, it's his boat. As the last Cubans drift out of the dining room, Doc snatches a platter of sliced pineapple off the serving table and foists it upon the Professor.

"Quick," Doc urges, "don't let them see you." He requisitions two more platters—cold cuts and watermelon—and, chuckling, he and the Professor make a mad dash for the rental car. Clearly, Doc and his crew are having a splendid time.

"My Spanish is great," explains Doc as we rocket past the police checkpoint at the landward entrance to the marina, barreling toward a gas pump at the back of a gravel lot. We slide to a halt just before we hit the attendant. "I took a couple of years in school and—it's amazing—it's all coming back to me. "*Dónde is el gasoline?*" he queries the pump jockey, who shrugs his shoulders, and off we speed at an alarming velocity toward the *Heart Mender,* the first U.S.-registered vessel to enter Cuban waters legally (except for the Mariel boatlift, which doesn't count) since the early years of the revolution. It's almost 9 A.M.—starting time—and Doc is in the mood for battle.

On the way out the channel, we split a flotilla of kayakers, the Cuban Olympic team in training. At the marina's headland, the captain opens up the engines, but no sooner does the boat plane, it seems, than he throttles back to trolling speed. The mates ease six lines into the water. We're only a quarter-mile offshore and the depth-sounder reaches a thousand feet; another 400 yards out and the bottom drops to 6,000 feet. And yet we can see people walking on shore. It's like hunting elk in the suburbs.

I retire with our host and the Professor into the boat's swank, air-conditioned salon, and without much prodding Doc launches into a soliloquy on the two subjects he finds most praiseworthy: himself and fishing. It so happens that after he co-invented the intra-aortic balloon pump in 1969, he became a brain in demand, addressing international medical conferences and training surgeons in the Soviet Union and China. In 1989 the Cuban government wanted to enroll his expertise and asked him to be one of the headliners at a national medical conference. Doc said he would if he could bring his boat from Key West and fish. The Cubans thought about it and said, why not? The U.S. State Department said no. But Doc had once operated on Armand Hammer's brother, and . . .

"Doc!" both mates holler simultaneously—the divine interruption. Doc bolts from his seat. It's 9:15, and the *Heart Mender* is hooked up, the unlikely champion Dr. Bregman on center stage, a fighting belt strapped around his sizable waist.

The first mate spikes the rod into the holder above Doc's groin, creating a literal connection between the fisherman's masculinity and the furious instinct of the unseen beast. "Tip up," coaches the captain from the bridge. "Let him dive." This is a kill tournament; there'll be no cavalier tag and release. Sweat pours down Doc's torso as he bows forward and reels back, bows and reels. After five or six minutes the beast rises, blasting through the indigo surface, its bill parrying the lethal air. It's a marlin, a stand-up blue big enough to take the trophy, and it dances with magnificent rage for 50 feet or more, the iron-black sword of its bill slashing the Havana skyline.

After 20 minutes, the fish is just off the transom, ready to boat, panting as it lies twisted on its side in the transparent seas, one fierce eye condemning the world above. The mate extends the gaff over the side, maneuvering for the right mark, the perfect moment. Then the marlin spits the hook. With cool contempt he throws the line into Doc's face and is gone, leaving us a silenced, awestruck crew. Doc hands the rod to the mate, accepting the loss with grace.

"A brave fish," he declares in fluent Hemingwayese. He unbuckles the plastic belt, tosses his baseball cap aside, and retreats to the comfort of the chilly salon, dismissing his crew's efforts to console him. He plops down on the couch, the good sport, reflective, storing away the memory.

"Did I have on my red hat or my orange one?" he asks. "I'm a very colorful figure." With a tiny smile of satisfaction, he speculates that a year's maintenance on the *Heart Mender* comes to about twice the Professor's salary.

From the beginning, the professor offers a dissenting viewpoint to our initial impression of Havana. "No, no, no, señor," he says, which is the extent of his involvement with the Spanish language. What he sees from the balcony is not the city's imminent disassemblage but something on the order of an exotic passion permanently flaunting the edges of self-destruction, semiferal but with a hip intensity, sidling up to disaster and then fluttering away, a city like a Latin woman, beautiful but exhausted, dancing through the perfumed night with a gun in her hand.

We mobilize for an assault on the city's ambiguous appearances, walking first to the Plaza de la Revolución, a vast open space resembling The Mall in D.C. but dropped into the middle of a massive empty parking lot in a tropical Newark. To one side sits a reviewing stand made of white stone, with a marble podium facing out on a macadam lot, its field of telephone poles wired with spotlights and loudspeakers. Here Fidel enacted, in the early days of the revolution, his "democracy of the people," tutoring the masses for hours on end, haranguing them like a fire-and-brimstone preacher, making them laugh like a stand-up comic, building them up to whatever emotional pitch the day's challenges required, until—and this is the vital and democratic part of the ritual—they shouted back to the Maximum Leader in unison: OK, have it your way, *jefe,* we want to go home. If you've seen televangelists browbeating an audience, you won't be shocked to learn that this system works, more or less, nor will you be thunderstruck to hear that all domiciles throughout Cuba's cities and countryside, even the humblest shacks—especially the humblest shacks—have antennas on their roofs and, down below, old black-and-whites burning blue through the evening hours.

We stroll into Old Havana down narrow cobbled alleys eerily Neopolitan, though Havana's streets are by far the most tranquil and nonthreatening of any I have walked in the Latin diaspora. Urchins flutter around us hoping for Chiclets, but by Monday they'll be uniformed and back in school. In the stone-paved Plaza de la Catedral, a man approaches me, asking for a cigarette. He is white-haired and constitutionally thin, dressed in immaculate khaki work clothes. He wants a light, then the lighter, and though I give it to him I take it back, since I have no other and Cuba is out of matches. He gasps when I tell him we are from the States. North Americans, rare as pots of gold—he loves them, hates Castro.

"Life is very bad in Cuba."

"If you say so," I say, but in truth he looks no worse off than his blue-collar counterpart in Miami. If he had been in Mexico City, or Port-au-Prince, or Lima, or Kingston, if he had a context in which to place his misery, perhaps he wouldn't be so quick to claim it. What is absent in his denunciation, what is absent throughout Havana, is the dead tone that marks deep suffering and despair.

Like so many others, my new friend wants to change money, my dollars for his useless pesos. With dollars, a *habanero* can supplement his government rations—one shirt, one pair of pants, one pair of shoes a year; one pound of meat, five pounds of rice each month—with goods from the astronomically expensive black market. Illegal, of course, but Cubans are being forced by shortages and the government's rigidity to turn themselves into hustlers and sneaks.

Undaunted by my refusal, the fellow offers to sell me cigars—Cohibas, the best—at half the price of the tourist shops. When I don't say no, he suggests we walk down Empedrado, a street as old as the New World, to La Bodeguita del Medio, and negotiate over a drink. The Bodeguita is just opening its doors, but already a crowd has assembled outside the establishment, a joint instantly recognizable as one of the solar system's last repositories of cool, a neighborhood hangout with global traffic, a place where dialectics and rum fuse into a collective, joyous, cacophonous blur. Behind the counter two bartenders manufacture endless *mojitos,* 20 at a time, for the relentless tide of thirsty *turistas* that churn through, sweeping in and sweeping out, glancing cross-eyed at the ubiquitous graffiti and taking deep dizzying whiffs of the proletarian smells of bohemian Cuba. Across the street, three plainclothes police officers stand like statuary, arms folded, glowering at the escalating euphoria.

My new friend displays a tremendous appreciation for both rum and drama. "Let's get the cigars," he stage-whispers repeatedly, peering anxiously toward the door. The bartender has adopted Caputo, channeling him free *mojitos* in exchange for baseball updates. The Professor sponsors English lessons for two saucy dreamettes who are instructing him in a language of their own: Cognac, they say; champagne. "The cigars, let's go," my friend mumbles. I nod and we're out the door, he walking a half-block in front, broadcasting guilt, cringing in posture, the worst blackmarketeer I've ever encountered. I feel like arresting him myself.

Down Old Havana's strange and marvelous streets I follow him until he ducks into a made-to-order shadowy portal, the arched entrance to a decrepit palace divided long ago into apartments. We ascend a marble staircase, right-angling up through medieval space, musty and decomposing. Sensing our arrival, an old woman, his mother, opens the door. Only a television set places the apartment in any world I know; otherwise, the precise honey-colored shafts of light, the glassless windows, the crumbling textures and bare furniture, the provisional quality of its humanity are, in their extremeness, too unfamiliar for me to recognize except as Hollywood augury.

The deal takes less than a minute. The seller needs dollars; as a skilled tradesman he earns 200 pesos a month—the price of shoes on the black market. The buyer—well, the buyer doesn't need, doesn't even like cigars. The buyer is simply seduced. The buyer finds official Cuba enigmatic, the image formulaic, but how easily and swiftly the rhetorical veneer is scratched and another secret revealed. Bedding Cuba: The historical precedents are countless, large scale and small; it's a North American tradition. Scruples barely make it as a footnote, a tiresome annotation. I zip the wooden box of cigars into my knapsack and, warned by the dealer's mother to be careful, we return to La Bodeguita, where silence and fear are obsolete.

The question of whether or not we will be able to drive the 780-mile length of this apparently gasless island is resolved the following morning, thanks to Abraham Maciques, the president of Cubanacan, to whom Dr. Bregman had introduced us at the tournament. Cubanacan is the muscle behind Castro's tourist trade, an autonomous government agency not unlike a corporation, free to engage in multinational commerce, free to invest, free to be profitable, free to construct a second society—albeit a ravenously capitalistic and exclusive society—on to but separate from the old system, all in hopes of keeping the revolution solvent. When I inquired if there might be a way to help us secure fuel in the hinterlands, Maciques said not to worry, that he'd have someone take care of us.

By noon we've been provided with a van, a burly middle-aged driver named Eric, and Roberto, a young mustachioed rake of a guide whose services we at first decline, not wanting to be chained to some ideologically rabid government minder.

"Give me a chance," Roberto says with pained sincerity. "You're my first Americans." I ask him if he thinks his country will survive what Castro is calling this "special period."

Who knows? he says with body language, looking untroubled. "The future is the future."

"And right around the corner," I add, "seeing as you're catching onto capitalism so nicely."

"Ah!" says Roberto, touching my elbow lightly, and again with each of his exclamations. "Karl Marx says to take what you can of your enemy's good points and use them for yourself."

"That's not how my mom told me to run a revolution."

"What—your mother?"

"It's a little joke."

"OK, good, I like the North American sense of humor. But listen," he says, tapping my arm in a brotherly way, "we are very aware of the dangers of tourism and how careful we must be to maintain the principles of the Triumph of the Revolution."

Our van is appointed with a cooler full of juice, cola, and Hatuey beer on ice, with several cases of beverages packed in reserve, including a crate of seven-year-old Havana Club rum, "if we need a little drink," says Eric. With his thick book of gas coupons, we appear adequately outfitted for a Homeric ten-day binge, if nothing else.

As we head east out of Havana I ask Eric to sidetrack off the main highway to the fishing village of Cojimar, home port of Gregorio Fuentes, the now-ancient captain of Hemingway's *Pilar.* As we draw close, the land begins to roll a bit, its soft hills lined with cottages not unlike the conch houses and art-deco bungalows of the Florida Keys. We stop at the turquoise cove where once the *Pilar* was the undisputed queen of the fleet. A small, austere park pays tribute to Cojimar's most illustrious friend and patron. After the village heard of Hemingway's death, every fisherman donated a brass fitting off his boat, and the collection was melted down to create the bust of the writer that stands watch over the quay.

We locate Gregorio's modest house, and he invites us to crowd into his living room. Throughout the last 30 years, he has been harassed by curiosity seekers and schemers, but now it seems everyone believes he is dead, and he lives in the isolation he has always sought. Still, he appears pleased for the chance to unscroll the past once more, remarking that it might be his last opportunity, and he talks for hours in firm and measured speech, the incarnation of Hemingway's protagonist in *The Old Man and the Sea,* though the writer couldn't have had any idea back in 1951 that one day his true subject would be Gregorio himself, stepping transcendently into the portrait:

> The old man was thin and gaunt with deep wrinkles in the back of his neck. The brown blotches of the benevolent skin cancer the sun brings from its reflection on the tropic sea were on his cheeks. . . . Everything about him was old except his eyes and they were the same color as the sea and were cheerful and undefeated.

From 1935 to 1960 the two men were in many ways inseparable. During World War II they patrolled the coast for German U-boats; during the struggle against Batista, Gregorio tells us, he and Hemingway kept an eye on the local waters to assist Castro and his rebel armies. Hemingway even took Gregorio to Africa to hunt lions.

"Hemingway is the only North American in the world for me," Gregorio says, sitting erect in his chair. He wears a wristwatch with a marlin on its face, though he hasn't fished since saying good-bye to the man he still refers to as Papa.

"Before he died," says Gregorio, "he made his last will and left me a document to hand to Fidel Castro. I was called by Fidel to read the testament, and everything, all Hemingway's property, was for the revolution, but the yacht and the fishing equipment were for me. Fidel said to me, 'When you get tired of the yacht, bring it to me.' And I answered, 'I'll never be tired of it.' After that, many bullshitters came to this house to try to get the *Pilar,* and they left the house in silence. That's why Hemingway chose me to work with him, because I understand things. I want to avoid people who think I should get money from my relationship with Hemingway. I can walk anywhere."

In six weeks Gregorio will be 93 years old, and Hemingway, were he alive, would turn 92 eleven days later. They used to celebrate their birthdays together, sharing dinner and a bottle of whiskey on both dates.

"After Hemingway died," Gregorio says, "I maintained the tradition on his birthday. I would go down to his statue by the harbor. I would have one drink of whiskey for myself, and Hemingway's I pour on his head. But I haven't done it for years, because you can't find whiskey anymore in Cuba."

I say I will bring him a bottle—the tourist shops are well stocked. He gives me an *abrazo,* an embrace, and we leave the old captain to puff on his cigar in solitude, bound to the myths he had helped create.

The afternoon wanes; the light on the sea is harsh and tiring as we motor along the pastoral coastal highway toward the resort beaches of the narrow peninsula called Varadero. We pass a coastline too plain for a postcard, strung with clusters of plebian bungalows or dreary cement-block hotels, catering to the domestic trade mostly by means of work bonuses and incentives. Then the shore turns ugly, carpeted with spiky sisal plantations, shelved with razor-sharp ironrock at the water's edge and punctured by filthy oil wells, Cuba's very own Saudi

Arabia. Whatever riches lie underground, Cuba seems desperate to suck them forth.

Varadero, meanwhile, is presiding over its own oil boom, the kind associated with suntans. On one of the longest (12 miles), most user-friendly beaches in the Caribbean, every business conglomerate in the industrialized world (except the United States) is vying to see which can build the plushest hotel fastest and cheapest. The French, the Germans, the Spanish, the Italians, even the Jamaicans are building here.

We pull into the drive of a swank, four-star compound. Hotel Tuxpan, a bewildering temple to the gods of generic pleasures. The price is peanuts—half what it would cost elsewhere for identical accommodations adjoining similar splendors—but it's too expensive in concept, too immoderate in sensibility, for yeoman travelers like us, so tropo-cosmo it has inflated itself right off the map, out of the Cuban landscape and into an artificial capsule of brochures and charter jet packages, its character now as universally digestible as baby formula.

Over the lobby's pipes, Sinatra sings "I did it my way" as we check in. I feel hostile, an agent provocateur, more so when Roberto and Eric say that they will be leaving us for the night, since as Cubans they are barred from staying at a Varadero resort. "Tourism apartheid" is what the people call it. Roberto reasons with us to understand, but the fact remains: They are, in theory and in practice, second-class citizens in Cuba's new order.

The Tuxpan is owned 50/50 by Cubanacan and a group of Spanish investors, was constructed by Mexicans, and is operated by Germans: Cubanacan retains the supply contract for itself. Five of its staff of 213 are foreigners, and except for a Belgian entertainment director, each foreigner has trained a Cuban understudy who will someday inherit his or her respective position: manager, chef, housekeeper, bookkeeper. The system works: Cuban tourism has one of the best reputations on the European market, and the Tuxpan is humming along at

95 percent occupancy. "In Varadero," Roberto notes ingenuously, "you see new things every day. You might ask yourself, 'Is it Cuba?' " The answer is unfortunately obvious.

The night sparkles with the gas flares of the oil-drilling platforms across the water. We venture to the disco, where we find the hotel manager, an ebullient, shock-haired Irishman named Eamonn Donnelly, hunkered down in the blast, a giant music video projected above a dismally empty dance floor. "You can't really get a discotheque off the ground with only 28 German guests," Eamonn shouts through the music. He's pressing to have Cuban locals authorized to come in on weekends, because they're the only ones who could breathe life into the place.

"I can't take any more irony," Caputo screams over the music. "The Cubans are trying to keep the Cubans out. The Irish are trying to get them in."

Cuba has 289 beaches set like diamonds in its 2,500 miles of coastline, and three rugged mountain ranges utterly compelling in their beauty. But unless you're near the shore or around the sierras, Cuba's topography is dominated by its *llanos,* its flatlands, which seem to stretch forever, level as a gridiron and just as parceled out, one agricultural co-op after another. Mile after mile on our way south to Bahía de Cochinos, Bay of Pigs, we watch sugarcane fields and malanga farms pass like continuous yawns, the geography as monotonously fecund as South Florida's, the distant ridges sentineled by royal palms.

From the tourist town of Guama, where Fidel headquartered himself in an old sugar mill and commanded the counterattack during the Bay of Pigs invasion, the road arrows through mangrove swamp and thick palmetto-scrub forest, the pavement in fluid motion with thousands of insect-size land crabs, their shells black and their legs vermilion, crunching under the tires. As we near Playa Larga, the beach at the top of the bay, solemn concrete monuments rise from the bush, intermittently at first, then with greater density. They honor Castro's troops, 161 killed in action, and they stand where the soldiers fell during the three-day battle in April 1961. Some 1,500 Cuban exiles, sponsored by the CIA, were defeated in their attempt to invade the island, and that was the end of diplomatic relations between Cuba and the United States.

"This is a most beautiful place, yes?" Eric observes, with such serene feeling that I turn to look at him. His opinion can only be echoed. The bay, rectangular like an Olympic swimming pool, its waters equally blue, is majestic, and Castro was correct, I think, to turn a place so rich in nature yet so polluted with bitterness into a tourist haven. "Yes, I love the beaches here. I love the water—it's very pretty," Eric continues, something peculiar in his tone.

We drive on toward Playa Girón at the mouth of the bay, where some of the worst fighting took place. We park beneath a billboard: PLAYA GIRÓN—THE FIRST ROUT OF IMPERIALISM IN LATIN AMERICA.

"I was with them," Eric reveals matter-of-factly: We stop. "I was a 19-year-old student when the invasion happened. I came with the militia brought by Fidel to the final battle. Here, right here." Afterward he had helped guard the captured men. "Yes," he laughs softly, without malice or regret. "I became a major in the air force, but I'm retired now." He fishes out his wallet to show us his identity card—a younger Eric in an officer's uniform, someone who has found 30 years sufficient to quell the hatred, if not the sorrow, no matter what his allegiance.

Eric decides to remain in the van while we tour the museum of the battle with Roberto, whose own father had been tortured by Batista's army before escaping to fight in the Sierra del Escambray. We stroll quietly among the photographs and dioramas, the flags and 30-year-old weapons, the carefully preserved detritus of the revolutionary process. Eric, meanwhile, has lowered his seat back and is relaxing to the radio, an old warrior listening to new music.

As fast as possible, we speed through the visually tedious province of Ciego de Avila, numbed by its unbroken succession of cane plantations, pineapple farms, banana groves, and citrus orchards, though the air is fresh with Cuba's omnipresent smell of jasmine. We cross into the province of Camagüey, Cuba's largest, where sugar remains king but cows and cowboys register a more poignant effect on lifestyle. Daily flights from Havana bring *turistas* to the city of Camagüey; from there the pale hordes are bused to the encampments at Playa Santa Lucia, and our own destination for the day, three miles of secluded sand and a staging area for access to Cuba's northern archipelago—thousands of keys and sandbars spread over hundreds of miles, most deserted, many unexplored, connected by an underwater system of reefs dwarfing its counterpart to the north and second in size, we are told, only to Australia's Great Barrier Reef. No one, however, has to tell us that those translucent waters provide some of the last unspoiled snorkeling and diving in the hemisphere. At least we could bless the revolution for that, the gift of obscurity to a utopia of coral.

The following day, after a morning dive through coral fields prolific with gamefish and lobsters, we leave Santa Lucia pronto to make it to Santiago de Cuba, on the southeast coast, before nightfall. As twilight paints the countryside, we begin to carve our way through the valleys of the Sierra Maestra, the birthplace of Cuban independence and, in the following century, revolution. In 1956, returning from a one-year exile in Mexico, Castro, his brother Raúl, and the young asthmatic Argentinian doctor Che Guevara, with 79 other men, were shipwrecked west of Santiago de Cuba and battled their way up into the seemingly impenetrable peaks of the Sierra.

"We identified so completely with the natural surroundings of the mountains," Fidel later recalled to biographer Tad Szulc. "We adapted so well that we felt in our natural habitat. It was not easy, but I think we identified with the forest as much as the wild animals that live there."

Castro's strategy, to nibble away at and demoralize his foes, triumphed, but the one enduring mistake he made was to allow himself to become obsessed with the United States. After Batista's aircraft raided a rebel base in the mountains, dropping U.S.-supplied bombs, Castro wrote to a friend:

> I have sworn that the Americans will pay very dearly for what they are doing. When this war has ended, a much bigger and greater war will start for me, a war I shall launch against them. I realize that this will be my true destiny.

It was. Four years later, Kennedy positioned a naval blockade around the island, and Castro brought the world to the brink of nuclear holocaust during the Cuban Missile Crisis, securing his nation's place as one of the pariahs of modern times.

We reach the end of the line, Santiago de Cuba, after nightfall, yet even in darkness it's clear that this is a city surviving on finesse and brinkmanship. The municipality is plagued by a breakdown in its water service; when we check into the Hotel Versalles the taps run, more or less, but stop for good by midnight. The hotel's extensive menu has been reduced to three stewy dishes, and there's no bottled water, although you can drink Miller beer out of the can. There are no cigarettes, no cigars, no medicine, few buses, yet despite the comprehensive crunch, Santiago, Cuba's Hero City, "the cradle of the revolution," is not brittle, but resilient. Most of the citizenry appears to be in the streets, celebrating the annual Caribbean Music Festival.

The day's journey has turned into a grueling marathon, and we have become slap-happy, proposing to our Cuban friends a revolutionary theme park—Fidel Land—in the Sierra Maestra, a roadside attraction for the charter-package hordes that would one day overrun the island. It's a blasphemous tease, and after we stop howling, we apologize, because you don't have to respect a government to respect or fall in love with a country and its people.

Our plan is to spend the night in Santiago de Cuba and then to have the eternally amenable Eric haul our penitent *yanqui* selves 60 miles toward the western coast and 6,476-foot Pico Turquino, Cuba's highest mountain and a revolutionary shrine. We ask Roberto about the possibility of procuring supplies—food and water—for the climb.

"No problem," he says, which in a country that has so many problems is the phrase most spoken. Soon, however, we're ensnared by the hotel's cabaret, the canopy of trees above sprinkling us with flowers knocked off their stems by the vibrations of M.C. Hammer on the sound system, and Roberto, a third rum collins in his hand, seems to be smitten by one of the women in the chorus line. I retire around midnight in the sobering knowledge that tomorrow we'll be ill prepared to climb anything higher than a porch stoop.

In the morning, as we load the van, squalls bruise the southern horizon. Roberto, bleary-eyed and disheveled, shuffles from his room to the parking lot, an expression of relief brightening his sleepy face.

"Hey, what'd I tell you *locos,* you can't climb El Pico during the rainy season."

We'll do the drive anyway, I tell him, and maybe the weather will clear by the time we get to the mountain's base. We're Heroes of Tourism, I say, we have to try, even though Roberto has not kept his promise and we will be hiking all day on empty stomachs.

The coastline is a geologic symphony, the 1812 Overture: the mountains crescendoing with spectacular force into cushiony mulberry clouds; the muscular flanks of the range, thickly wooded and sheer, diving straight into a booming sea; bolts of lightning punctuating the drama off in the direction of Haiti, 200 miles to the southeast. The road snakes around paradisiacal bays and harbors, each with its rustic fishing village. On occasion the pavement ends where the interface of mountain and sea is too radical to prevent the roadway from washing out during tempests.

We reach the trailhead, finally, after endless delays manufactured by Roberto, who seems to be stalling, unwilling to confront the mountain. Into his water bottle the Professor pours a nauseating mix of Tropi-cola and energy crystals. I fill mine with all the juice remaining in the cooler and stuff it into my daypack alongside my raincoat and a half-liter of bottled water. Caputo is married to his 60 pounds of camera gear, but there's nothing else to carry anyway. Behind us, the sea thunders; in front of us, so do the mountains, their tops swaddled in ominous clouds. Suddenly, there's a crack in the overcast and sunlight shoots through. "I'm coming with you," says Roberto. "I'm a Cuban. It's my duty."

We file out of the van and up the first foothill, where we wait for Roberto to catch up. He's sweating and puffing and looks ready to be taken away on a gurney.

"OK, I'm not Che, " he says. "I cannot be a guerrilla. Well, maybe in the city." He walks back down to sleep in the van.

On we push, through the low pastures and scrub. Horses gallop away from us along forest paths; the bells of goats chime in the distance. The sun blazes down on us now, and after an hour we've consumed most of our liquids and the crows have begun to laugh at us.

A few years before the revolution, Celia Sánchez, one of Castro's original confidantes, hiked up Turquino with her liberal-minded father to install a bust of José Martí, the father of Cuban independence. They dreamed that one day his spirit would inspire Cuban patriots to fight the shameful injustices that plagued the nation. If Martí was Cuba's George Washington, few people outside of the country were willing to grant that Fidel Castro was its Abraham Lincoln, but there he was anyway, by 1957 in control of an ever-expanding area in the sierra the guerrillas called the "Free Territory." In April of that same year, Celia Sánchez guided a CBS News crew up Pico Turquino to film an interview with Castro in front of the bust. Though he lived in the sierra, Castro had never climbed El Pico, and Che Guevara recalled later that Fidel took a pocket altimeter with him and checked it on the summit to verify that the peak was as high as the maps indicated. The point being, wrote Tad Szulc, that Castro never trusted anybody or anything. I, on the other hand, am willing to believe that the motivation that brought us three Americans to this mountain had something vaguely to do with trust. Then again, maybe this is a misguided and naive notion, maybe this is why we are doomed not to make it to the top, although our parched throats, our hunger, our late start, and the cold rain that has transformed the footpath into a river have contributed to our failure as well. After five hours of rugged climbing, we're above 4,000 feet and tuckered out, sucking raindrops off broad jungle leaves.

Ahead of us we can see a faint indentation in the tree line on the mountain's flank, implying a path that cuts a merciless diagonal through woodlands as dense as Borneo's. And beyond, still impacted in clouds and still higher, looms the summit and the bust of José Martí.

It is time to turn back, we all agree, to head down to repose with rebel daiquiris in our hands and make our pal Roberto Cuba's first Martyr of Tourism.

Back in Santiago we walk toward the plaza through a gauntlet of hospitality, deciding to have our dinner on the terrace of the Casagrande Hotel, an establishment so magnificent in its squalor that it seems born out of an opium smoker's vision, real only by virtue of a technicality. It will soon be closed for renovation.

A guy at the door checks credentials, but the cream of the Cuban crop circulates at will, and we take the last table among a noisy scene of TV crews, politicians, poets, musicians, foreigners, and apparatchiks. Roberto and Eric, delayed by the quest for gasoline, aren't here yet. Again, as before, Cubans initiate the conversations. Here is a trumpet player who has toured the United States but isn't interested in defecting; here is a baseball player who says he snubbed a lucrative invitation to head north to the Show. Here is a 24-year-old black woman who says with passion, "Where is the sugar of Cuba? Where is the rice of Cuba? My feelings are not political, but economic. I ask myself, what is the problem with my country? Why is it so worse off than other countries? And my answer is, I don't know, I don't know, but things must change before we can go on."

And here is a young black man dressed up in snappy suspenders and wire-rimmed glasses who informs us that the lyric by Grand Funk Railroad—"I don't need a whole lot of money, I just need someone to love"—is an anthem for Cuba's youth. A teenager tells us of a growing split between the people who made the revolution—Eric's generation—and those born into it—Roberto's generation.

Caputo and the Professor, in wonderland, are having an epiphany. The photographer has never before been in a country where it is so easy to take pictures of the people. "It's like they're *pleased,*" he marvels.

"That doesn't happen in an unhappy culture," replies the Professor. Which seems true enough. Other than the scarcity of material goods and the thinning effectiveness of services, the everyday culture, away from the resorts, has none of the earmarks of a totalitarian system. No one hesitates to talk with us about any subject. There is an astonishing lack of visible military presence throughout the land. "When the colossus to the north has its heel over your head," the Professor opines, "and the people are this way, you have to say the problems are out of the people's control."

I record the conversation in my notebook, and when Roberto arrives with Eric at the table, I show it to them. "You damn American guys are trying to make me cry," says Roberto, his throat constricting. We all draw deep, sorrow-filled breaths. I excuse myself to the bathroom, where I would have, on principle and out of outrage over the tragedy of U.S.-Cuban relations, kicked everything apart, but everything is already broken.

All that's left is to get the bottle of whiskey back to Gregorio in Cojimar, because he said he trusted the word of a friend, because some rituals are worth keeping alive, and because after all, we are neighbors.

Annick Smith

The Rites of Snow

from *Outside*

Who can explain the euphoria of snow lovers? Our black lab puppy Shy Moon came new with us to our Montana homestead in the winter of 1970, and she'd leap and roll and burrow into snowbanks like a wag-tailed otter. Shy Moon's run of mongrels—Bagel, Mocha, Goatee—and the two shepherd dogs who live with me now, Rasta and Betty Boop, are no different. Snow falls and they dance into it. They open their mouths to catch snowflakes on their tongues, chase snowballs, dive into drifts and come up white-nosed, hoary, tingling. The dogs are laughing, like me. Like my sons.

The boys come home for Christmas if they can. All four are grown now and living in Maryland, San Francisco, Kalispell. I never go out on a Christmas tree hunt until the twins, Alex and Andrew, arrive. It's a ritual that began twenty-one years ago when they were four years old, our first winter on the ranch. We headed into the woods on snowshoes through four-foot drifts. My husband, David, was short of breath from the heart disease that would kill him a couple of years later, but he led the way, an axe slung over his shoulder. Eric and Steve, gangling, long-haired, and hip at fifteen and thirteen, pulled the little ones on our new toboggan, a gift from the grandparents.

Every winter we search for the perfect, full-limbed fir or pine that must touch the beams of the living room in our recycled, hand-built, hewn-log house. We do not worry about conserving young trees, for they are abundant in our forest, third growth. It's the old ones we prize and protect, the few ancient survivors of a century of logging. These winters my sons are nearly as tall as the trees they chop down and they carry the fragrant, snow-damp load a quarter-mile down the logging road to home.

The ritual continues with bluegrass on the tape deck, the trimming of boughs, stringing of lights (my job), and a life's accumulation of ornaments to hang. Each ornament has a history. There's a painted Santa nearly fifty years old from my childhood in Chicago; enameled Mexican tin fruit—purple grapes, red cherries, yellow bananas—from a trip to Oaxaca; handmade yarn bells from the country school my boys attended in the hamlet of Potomac; Hmong hangings from Missoula fairs; a ceramic Flathead angel; imitation birds; clusters of miniature felt oranges.

As I stand precariously on a stepladder to hang a candy cane, I remember decorating a tree in Seattle when I was as young as the twins, already a mother of two and dead broke. David was in graduate school and we lived on Magnolia Bluff in a tilting house overlooking Puget Sound. I gathered white shells from our beach, and bits of blue and amber sea-rounded glass, and fastened them to the tree with wire. I strung red holly berries stolen from a neighbor's bushes with popcorn to garland the tree. We lit it with birthday candles bedded safely in aluminum foil. Two-year-old Steve in his red pajamas was so flushed with the excitement of his new tricycle that we didn't realize until late in the afternoon that he'd run up a fever of nearly 104 degrees. Christmas fever can turn dangerous on you anytime, which is what the gray-haired woman hanging her candy canes knows only too well.

Snow ended the dog days of August this year, two inches on my deck, the violet and fuchsia petunias fringed with white, white frosting on the strawberries and squash blossoms, and in the evergreen hills young firs and ponderosas drooped like weeping willows with their burdens of untimely snow. It is called the August singularity—a sudden cold front from Canada, which signals the end of summer.

On August 21 my meadow was baked brown; the pine hills that circle our homestead were crackling dry from a month of blue-sky days in the 90s. On August 22 the temperature dropped into the 30s, snow fell, and that night we began the rites of winter. My son Andrew and a niece and a few young visitors clustered around the brick fireplace. Gin gave way to Jim Beam, white wine to red. We wrapped ourselves in afghans, dug sweaters out of mothballs, and threw logs on the fire. I shed the torpor of summer like a snake sheds her skin and rejoiced in the buzz of energy, the excitement that comes with first snow in any season.

Living at four thousand feet in the foothills of the northern Rockies, I've seen snow on the Fourth of July, snow in September, but only this once in August. Perhaps it's a sign from the weather gods, for snow has become a dwindling commodity. We've suffered a ten-year drought, open winters, the boring gray sky over mud and leafless trees. Mountain snowpacks are down, stream flows are lower than ever, forests burn, and ranchers battle fishermen for what water remains. Maybe it's the dreaded greenhouse effect, maybe El Niño currents, maybe the snow will come back—the sweet snows of yesteryear.

Twenty years ago we shovelled paths through waist-high drifts to feed chickens or to reach the outhouse. We were building the big house and lived in a one-room log bunkhouse with a loft: four boys, two dogs, two cats, and hippie parents. We melted snow for water, cooked on a Coleman gas stove, and could not see over the snow-fat road banks thrown high as a car by the snowplow. In February, the county quit plowing our drive and the Land Rover was stuck in the middle of the road for a month. We snowshoed half a mile from the end of the county road to our cabin carrying coal and groceries in backpacks.

Friends in town pitied us, but David and I were happy with our chosen burden. The work of day-to-day living in accommodation to backcountry winter turned our energies outward. Cutting wood, feeding stock, keeping vehicles running; these were physical chores that bound the family into a unit. The mental beasts of fear—fear of fatal illness, fear of fracture and separation—had to linger in the cold starlight beyond the fires we built to keep ourselves warm.

Life is easier these days, and we have exchanged the necessity of snowshoes for the sport of skis. I learned to cross-country ski in deep snow, and taught my kids to follow in my tracks. When they come home for Christmas the yard is thick with skis and poles. We've been lucky even in these dry years, for what snow has come has fallen in December.

Our meadow is a natural bowl sloping down from wooded cliffs. I get into shape by cutting trails up the meadow and through the trees. I've wrecked my right knee by shussing down an icy track into a barbed wire fence. Years earlier I tore the ligaments in both knees by trying to brake a runaway toboggan loaded with little boys by sticking my feet into the hard-crusted snow. It was a tough lesson in the art of sliding. Limp for two months and you will learn to go with the terrain, turn into it, but don't force a stop.

After a Christmas morning of opening presents in front of the fire, drinking mimosas, munching on croissants and the bittersweet chocolate-dipped orange peels that are my holiday specialty, we head for the skis. If we are lucky, the meadow is sparkling in the sun, hoarfrost gilding tall grass and the wild hawthorn. We are blessed with a field of snow out every door. The two-story log house with its steeply pitched shake roof stands like an ocean liner in its rolling white sea.

Bill Kittredge, my companion of fourteen years, learned to ski in Oregon, but he has given up snow sport for the green precision of golf (too many years spent feeding cows in a blizzard), and prefers to sit in his armchair browsing the new Christmas books. The standing roast of prime rib he has bought is in the oven. Old friends will arrive soon to join our traditional feast of rare beef and Yorkshire pudding, cream whipped with horseradish, red cranberries, green broccoli, fresh-baked bread, and at least two kinds of pie made by the boys—apple and pecan, or pumpkin, sometimes mincemeat.

Our first great feast on the ranch was Thanksgiving of 1971. There was not enough room in the cabin for all of us and our out-of-town guests, along with our carpenter/writer friends who were helping us build the big house. We'd been making doors and windows in a cavernous cement-block garage built to house the former owner's logging rig and stock truck. It was just barely heated by two woodstoves, but we set up trestle tables, borrowed a second Coleman stove, and cooked.

The menu centered on wild foods hunted, fished, and gathered in our new abode: trout from the Blackfoot River; grouse from the woods; meadow mushrooms and shaggy manes. I improvised a juniper berry sauce for the game and baked apple pies made with the fruit of the tree gone wild on our meadow. We sweetened our bread with fresh huckleberry preserves. We ate in mittens and wool caps. We gave thanks as the first blizzard of the year covered our small world with six inches of white.

We moved into the new house on Christmas Day the next year. It wasn't finished. A wool blanket covered the door to the living room where we had spread our mattresses. We had electric heat and a telephone, but no fireplace. The kitchen was open to winter winds, no plumbing in yet, no maple floor laid over the plywood. The tree we had cut down stood gaily in the corner, lights blinking, and the table was spread with goodies. I missed the intimate warmth of our one-room cabin, but this new house would be beautiful, spacious, solid as rock. Although David would live for two more years, it was the last Christmas we would all be together in the house we'd made by hand.

Only one Smith is religious in any conventional sense. Stephen is a devout Catholic, saved by the church from troubles too deep to bear without faith. He goes to midnight mass, and sometimes the twins and I go with him. It's a beautiful way to praise rebirth and salvation, the families gathered in their finest, incense and candles, a choir singing like angels. My parents are Jewish by birth and in culture, but never practiced the religion except to honor their Old Country parents. David was a failed Baptist, and the rest of us worship God or whatever we call sacred in our private and personal ways.

To thank the old year and welcome the new we throw a great party during the week between Christmas and New Year's Eve. We invite old friends and new ones, graduate students who aspire to be writers, faculty from the University of Montana where Dave taught, and where Bill still teaches. There are old folks and teenagers, young adults with toddlers, those of us in middle age. Someone always brings strangers from Japan or France, England, Australia, Hollywood.

I prepare vats of chili made with pinto beans. When Steve was home we'd have venison in the pot, for he is the large-game hunter in the family. Other times we make do with short ribs of beef and ground meat. The rest is pot luck: cornbread, salads of every variety, chips and dips, veggies and pies. I'll buy a keg of beer and gallon jugs of wine. Sometimes there's rum for hot drinks, always hot cider for kids and teetotalers. Coffee and cocoa will send folks home somewhat sober and belly-warmed.

Before we get down to chow, we must earn our hunger with winter sports. As the sun dips over a western ridge, partygoers take to the meadow and logging roads on skis. Children slide down the gentle slopes in sleds, black rubber inner tubes, snowboards. One year when the snow barely covered rocks and grass so we couldn't ski, the boys set up their net and we had a raucous game of snow volleyball, people sliding, leaping, collapsing in laughter in the freezing dusk.

Serious tobogganing happens only after dark. Our twenty-year-old sled is missing boards and it's time for Santa Claus ("Sanity Clause" as Eric used to say—he's a devotee of Groucho Marx) to grace the family with a new toboggan. Often the twins, Eric and his wife Becca, and Steve have prepared a track in advance. In a good snow year the run will begin on the upper meadow near the stone pile, jump the road, and continue on a steep pitch until the course levels out at the barbed wire fence that arbitrarily splits our ground from the neighbor's.

The two places were one a century ago, when the Swedish immigrants who homesteaded our land celebrated their first Christmas. The fires they built were the only lights in a forest full of wild animals that circled for miles and miles. Christ Tandborg and Anders Anderson and their families cleared a rectangle in the virgin woods to make hay meadows and grain fields, and began the endless task of picking rocks from the clay soil that runs one hundred feet deep. Left to itself the meadow is beginning its return to forest, but the work of human hands calls out for respect, so I have made a bargain with ghosts. We'll allow patches of brush and young pines to form islands of cover for bluebirds, coyotes, chipmunks, and the rabbits and mice whose trails cross ours in the snow. The pine, fir, and larch forest will remain untouched except as a place to collect firewood and Christmas trees. Elk, white tails and mule deer, black bears, and the occasional moose or mountain lion will find these woods a refuge from hunters and loggers. But we will continue to clear the meadow, graze summer cattle and our two old mares on it, harvest our twenty fenced acres of hay, and cling to a tradition that values nurture over greed.

Such clinging isn't easy when alien seeds are germinating under the pristine white. Knapweed, leafy spurge, Russian thistle, and a sulphur-yellow cinquefoil have been brought in on the wheels of logging trucks that cross my land winter and summer. You might think it's a pretty sight—acres of lavender knapweed, acres of yellow petals—but the roots of these plants poison grass. They have no natural enemies, for they too are immigrants from Yugoslavia, Iran, the Siberian steppes.

As I ski among the seed heads, I decide to do what I have never done. When the weeds bolt in July, I'm going to attack them with herbicide. No one, not even a determined environmentalist gentlewoman homesteader, wants to see her land go sterile.

One evening a couple of years ago during our holiday party, when the meadow was laced with lavender shadows from the setting sun, I skiied with a friend across the rose-tinted snowfields. We could hear the whoops of young tobogganers preparing for the night's sport. My two shepherd dogs and my friend's bird dog followed in our tracks. My friend is a professor of linguistics.

"Annick," he called from the top of the ridge, "it's worth three thousand dollars."

"What's worth three thousand dollars?"

"This," he said, pointing his pole toward the setting sun and sweeping it forward to encompass the meadow, the woods, the high peaks of the Bob Marshall Wilderness on the eastern horizon.

"One run on this place—this view, these friends—it's worth the three thousand more I'd be making in any other university."

My friend was being modest; the difference would be ten thousand dollars, for the pleasures of snow carry a high price. Montana has always been a natural resource colony for coupon clippers in New York, Chicago, Los Angeles, Tokyo, Berlin. They take our timber, our coal, our copper, our gold, our water. They hunt elk, fish for native trout, overrun our wilderness. We are left with boom-and-bust work in the woods and mines, servant jobs like making beds for tourists, bottom dollar for professionals. There is no future for our children, no prosperity.

What remains is the joy. We walk in space—a state six hundred miles across with fewer than 850,000 inhabitants. People recognize us on the streets. When we call our one congressman, our senators, our governor, they know our names. Our children want to come home, like the Native Americans who are returning to reservations to make a better life in a place that has always been theirs and sacred.

Those who take the chance may not be able to buy land if they're coming home to the Flathead, the Bitterroot, or the Gallatin valleys. Retirees from overpopulated and polluted shores, and Hollywood stars seeking hideaways from the neon world, have driven real estate so high there that locals can't afford to move. We writers and artists who have let the cat out of the bag are complicit. So we try to discourage would-be immigrants by talking about winter.

"You don't understand what winter means," we say, hoping they'll take their baggage to the Sunbelt. "It snows in August. It snows on the Fourth of July."

When summer ends and the tourists ride off in their motorhomes and the highways are slick with black ice, we hard-core Montanans begin our six-month winter dances. Bars fill up with blue-lipped men and women in parkas and boots. We drink too much, eat red meat, smoke any weed. We collect unemployment and spend hours jump-starting stalled rigs. We swear we'll move to Arizona. We pray for snow.

It is this mix of festivity and danger, sparkle and dread that draws me so close to winter, to mountains, to Montana. When you can see your breath, you know you are alive.

David Petersen

Where Phantoms Come to Brood and Mourn

A Remembrance of Edward Abbey

from *Backpacker*

There is a valley in the West where phantoms come to brood and mourn, pale phantoms dying of nostalgia and bitterness. You can hear them, shivering, chattering, among the leaves of the old dry mortal cottonwoods down by the river—whispering and moaning and hissing with the wind . . . whining their past away with the wild dove and the mockingbird—and you may see one, touch one, in the silences and space and mute terror of the desert.

Edward Abbey, from *The Brave Cowboy,* Prologue

It is March 14, 1992, the third anniversary of Edward Abbey's death. He was a writer, of course, a damned good one, and the godfather of so-called radical environmentalism. But this isn't about either of those things.

I am sitting in the desert sand beside Abbey's hidden grave, talking and joking and weeping with him, and smoking a cheap cigar—not the kind he preferred, but the kind he smoked a lot of; even for the

"Thoreau of the American West" (actually, he was better than that), life was often a compromise. It has been a pilgrimage, or as close to one as I'll likely ever come, this visit to the last refuge of the man I respected and loved more than any other. And befitting a true pilgrimage, the way here has not been entirely easy.

After a tiring road trip, my guide and I veer off the blacktop back road. I lock in my old truck's 4×4 hubs and we go grinding down a sandy desert two-track. A long time later, we reach the end of the jeep trail, where we will make camp. The rest of the way will be afoot.

As I swig water and otherwise prepare for a desert hike, my guide kneels and scratches a map in the sun-warmed sand, points westward, speaks a few soft words. From here, by choice, I am on my own. It's at least an hour's fast hike over prickly, unfamiliar terrain, she says. With little more than two hours of daylight left, I step out briskly.

I must be vague in this narrative. The shrine I am seeking is on public land and no burial permit was applied for; nor, most likely, would one have been granted. Ed needs his privacy. I am sworn, therefore, to a pact of secrecy.

And it's really best this way. By being nowhere in particular, Edward Abbey, whose writing and personal example have meant so much to so many, is now everywhere in spirit, happily haunting every slickrock promontory, every slot canyon, every cedar-scented mesa, every hidden valley, every wild place remaining in the American Southwest. If you know about Abbey, if you've read *Desert Solitaire, The Monkey Wrench Gang* or any other of Ed's almost two dozen books, then you know the sort of place I'm so carefully not describing here. Abbey Country.

I stride on, dividing my attention between the ground approaching my boots and the rocky, ragged western horizon. It is warm but not hot; maybe eighty in the sun. Perfect.

Half an hour out, a shadow like a B-52 slips across the ground ahead of me, crossing from right to left. I stop and look up. Between me and a blinding sun, a huge dark form glides in easy spirals on a thermal whirlpool. I look down for a moment, then squint my eyes and glance again at the indistinct, haloed silhouette. An eagle, possibly. Too big for hawk, raven or falcon. Nor is it likely a turkey buzzard; the wings lack sufficient dihedral, the tail is too broadly fanned. Too bad. How appropriate it would be just now if that *were* a scuzzy old vulture circling up there—Abbey's afterlife alter ego.

"Given a choice," he wrote in the essay "Watching the Birds," "I plan to be a long-winged fantailed bird next time around. Which one? Vulture, eagle, hawk, falcon, crane, heron, wood ibis? Well, I believe I was a wood ibis once, back in the good old days of the Pleistocene epoch. And from what I already know of passion, violence, the intensity of the blood, I think I'll pass on eagle, hawk or falcon this time. For a lifetime or two, or maybe three, I think I'll settle for the sedate career, serene and soaring, of the humble turkey buzzard. . . . And contemplate this world we love from a silent and considerable height."

Alas, the long-winged fantailed bird up there contemplating this particular bit of the world from a silent and considerable height is no vulture. And just as well. Like Ed himself acknowledged toward the end of his "Windhover" musings, "As appealing as I find the idea of reincarnation, I must confess that it has a flaw: to wit, there is not a shred of evidence suggesting it might be true."

Anyhow, my big bird, of whatever feather, is deserting me, fading fast into the glaring west, chasing the sun down the afternoon sky.

And I had best get back to my own chase. My feet pick up the pace until the rough-and-tumble terrain is flowing past in a soft blur. Flat to gently rolling, this is hiking heaven compared to the uphill-both-ways San Juan Mountains of southwest Colorado, my home stomping grounds. Even so, hiking here is complicated by a litter of sharp-edged rocks and a plague of cacti and other prickly desert vegetation, necessitating constant vigilance and frequent dodging, providing plenty of opportunity to stub a toe, twist an ankle, stumble and fall, maybe trod upon an indolent rattler. Hiking out across here with just a light pack, as I am now, is one thing, but toting a six-foot-three, 180-pound man any distance over this natural obstacle course would be something else entirely.

But a fistful of good and loyal friends did exactly that, honoring Ed's wishes to be "transported in the bed of a pickup truck and buried as soon as possible after death. No undertakers wanted, no embalming (for godsake!), no coffin. Just an old sleeping bag. . . . I want my body to help fertilize the growth of a cactus, or cliffrose, or sagebrush, or tree."

While he was about it, Ed had a little fun arranging his own wake, calling for bagpipes, a bonfire, "a flood of beer and booze! Lots of singing, dancing, talking, hollering, laughing and love-making. No formal speeches desired, though if someone feels the urge, the deceased will not interfere."

Ed got all of that and more at what was surely the biggest party Saguaro National Monument has ever hosted. I spent most of the day prostrate in the stingy shade of a paloverde tree—stoned in the morning, drunk in the afternoon—trying my best, like the other hundred or so mourners there, to smile and laugh and deny the tragedy that had brought us together. No matter that Ed had assured us that "it is not death or dying which is tragic, but rather to have existed without fully participating in life—that is the deepest personal tragedy."

Certainly, Edward Abbey suffered his share of life's tragedies. But lack of active participation was not among them. He had fun.

I'm occasionally asked what the "real" Edward Abbey was like: Did the laughing, farting, animate *man* bear any resemblance to "Cactus Ed," the eloquently gruff, gloriously ornery literary persona of his autobiographical prose?

I'd say the two were essentially identical. Not even Abbey the writer could invent a character as colorful and complex as Abbey the man. The Edward Abbey I knew was joyful and easygoing most of the time but fierce in argument, alternately sensitive and crass as dictated by company and circumstance, the perfect gentleman if he thought you deserved it, a loving husband and father, a loyal and generous friend, impossible to pigeonhole.

Of course, I came into the picture rather late, and there had been an Edward Abbey I *didn't* know—the young, restless, quixotic version.

That Abbey, along the way to becoming the Ed I knew, had experienced his share of troubles, most of them of the flirty-skirty variety. "How can I be true to just one woman," he would feign to ponder, grinning shyly, "without being untrue to all the rest?"

Good question.

Edward Abbey was no saint, thank God.

Lost in these musings, time and distance pass quickly and after about an hour of speed-hiking I am standing atop the promontory near where I've been told Ed is holed up these days, relaxing in his favorite sleeping bag. I survey the scene—a large, flat-topped expanse of rock, sand, cactus—then walk to a place that looks more or less right. And there I find . . . rock, sand, cactus. The perfection of nothingness.

Discouraging.

Pure hunch having failed me, I decide to try a pinch of method, and spend the next several minutes pacing back and forth across the promontory in something loosely approximating a grid search.

Nada.

Time grows short. Fifteen minutes more and I'll be wandering around here like Moses when the lights went off. Just me and the bats and the spooky hooters. And somewhere . . .

I'm admiring a sunset as beautiful and improbable as life itself, pondering where to search next, darkness creeping over the land and shadowing my hopes, when I hear the lonesome cooing of a male mourning dove. The melancholy music rises from somewhere beyond the promontory's rim, down a slope that drops off toward a desert valley spreading south and west beyond sight—broad, barren, eerie as hell beneath the deep-purple twilight. No roads, no buildings, no lights down there. Only a pure, clean, peaceful emptiness—the way I imagine death.

Without questioning the impulse, I go skidding and sliding down the slope, homing in on the calling dove. And why not? At this point, one direction seems as good as another, and the valley view from down there should be superb. As I draw noisily near, the mourner falls silent and wings away, a ghostly gray shadow dissolving into the gloaming.

Fighting back creeping despair, determined to search through the night if necessary—I have water, fruit, matches, compass, a windbreaker and flashlight in my pack, and the weather is sublime—I turn and start back up the slope, bumbling blindly through the dying minutes of the day . . . and bumble hard into a low-lying cactus, kicking a trident of nettlesome spines through the thin nylon of my boot top and deep into my left foot.

After breaking off all three brittle shafts in a clumsy, half-panicked attempt to quickly rid myself of their searing pain, I am forced to sit down and unlace and delicately remove the boot, peel back the sock and use the pliers on my tool belt to extract the hot-barbed tips. Damn.

Somewhere off in the shadows, a coyote laughs at my predicament.

Only now—throbbing with self-inflicted pain, one shoe off and one shoe on like some dippy nursery rhyme character, mumbling disparagements at myself for not paying more attention to where my feet were landing, cursing the coyote for his arrogant and insensitive scorn—only now do I look up and see, no more than six feet from my sunburned nose, a native rock the size and shape of a badger and bearing a neatly chiseled inscription, which I squint to read in the failing light:

EDWARD PAUL ABBEY
1927–1989
NO COMMENT

Well.

So and at last it has come to pass that I am sitting here in the desert sand beside an old friend's hidden grave, talking and joking and weeping with him, and smoking a cheap cigar. What's left of it.

"No Comment." That was Ed's reply when asked by a friend if he had any last words for posterity. A joker to the end, that Abbey.

Life sure can be strange. I like to think of myself as a practical man; no dreamy-eyed nature mystic here. Nor the other kind. One life at a time is plenty enough for me. Yet, here I sit in a remote sundown desert, alone but not entirely, dumbfounded by the double coincidence of dove call and cactus spine that would seem to have pointed me here—which *did* point me here—to this place I've wanted and needed for so long to be. And the timing of the coyote's laugh. It would be easy, almost tempting, to *not* dismiss it all as mere coincidence, given the circumstances.

"Do you believe in ghosts?" Ed once asked himself in his journals, answering, "Those that haunt the human soul, yes." In that respect, at least, I am truly haunted. Beyond that, it's hard to know *what* to think just now.

But I do know what Ed would think, what he'd say about the eerie coincidence of events and this superstitious line of thought (I almost said, "were he here"). He'd grin that wicked lupine grin of his, shrug, and offer, "Who knows? Who cares? And what difference does it make anyhow?"

Good questions.

I mouth the stump of my deceased cigar, stare at the modest headstone—perfect—and fall again to musing, casting back across the precious little time I was privileged to spend with Edward Paul Abbey, the man whose fellow writers (he had no peers) have called "brash, irresponsibly satiric, happily excessive . . . a full-blooded man . . . a man 'still with the bark on' . . . man of character and courage . . . the original fly in the ointment . . . a gadfly with a stinger like a scorpion . . . a rebel and an eloquent loner . . . a national treasure" . . . and occasionally, by those lacking the open-minded intelligence to stay with him, things far less generous.

The last time I saw Edward Abbey was just after Thanksgiving, 1988. He, his young wife Clarke and their lap-sized children Rebecca and Benjamin had sardined themselves into the cab of Ed's old pickup truck and driven the five hundred miles from Tucson up to my hometown of Durango in southwestern Colorado.

They had come for a book signing at Maria's, an elegant (Ed's term) little Southwest-flavored bookshop owned by Dusty Teal, an old river-ratting pal of Ed's. It was a favor typical of Abbey's generosity to friends, and the last stop, an addendum actually, to a murderous four-week, coast-to-coast tour for *The Fool's Progress.* Ed was frankly relieved to have that particular job behind him, swearing it was "absolutely the *last* time" he'd ever tour. (Suggesting there more than I could know.)

Ed seemed to enjoy himself immensely on that final visit, elated to be back in the rural Southwest, back home. Cheery and chipper, he.

For instance: at a restaurant one evening, Ed complained to our waiter about the size of his dinner napkin, pretending outrage, calling it "a damn postage stamp!" The waiter was game, taking away the offending napkin and returning momentarily with a checkered tablecloth. Not to be one-upped, Ed accepted the sail-sized replacement with a serious, deep-voiced "Now *that's* more like it." Unfurling the prize, he tucked a fat corner into his collar and resumed his meal. Only after the waiter had left did he break into a huge, triumphant grin.

The next day, we drove up onto a piñon-juniper mesa a few miles above town and hiked for an hour into a biting late-November wind, walking and talking the cold away. Despite the unfriendly weather, Ed had insisted on a hike.

Abbey was a compulsive walker, doing a mile or two most every morning, again in the cool of evening, and finding the time for frequent days-long backpack treks. Once, pushing sixty, equipped with an old Kelty pack, aspirin and Demerol, he hiked 115 miles in six days, alone, across perhaps the truest desert wilderness North America has left. Each night's hike (he rested through the blistering middays) was a life-or-death race to reach another water source before the morning sun attacked him. (Ed would later suggest that the rivers of highly alkaline desert water he'd drunk in his long career of desert ratting might have contributed to the esophageal bleeding that was slowly killing him.)

Though we always walked when we got together—up and down the desert wash that meanders close behind *chez* Abbey on the west edge of Tucson, among the sandstone hobgoblins of southeast Utah, amongst the cool aspen forests surrounding my mountain cabin—I'd never gotten to join Ed on a *real* hike. During that last little stroll together above Durango, we laid plans to remedy that. There was a place, he told me, a magical desert valley. We'd go there soon . . . Ed, our good friend Jack Loeffler and I would rendezvous in March for a week of wilderness camping and hiking and companionable bull-shooting. Perfect.

At visit's end, as the Abbeys were preparing to leave, Ed handed me a copy of *The Fool's Progress,* held open to an inscription scrawled large on the title page: "For my good friend Dave Petersen and his great wife Caroline—companions on this fool's journey out of the dark, through the light, into the unknown."

I knew that Ed had been sick, off and on, for quite some time, but I was unaware of just how *very* sick. I had no idea, certainly, that he was dying, nor did many others; I guess he didn't want to burden anyone unnecessarily. (Now, how I wish he'd burdened me.) But even in my ignorance, that haunting *Fool's Progress* inscription foreshadowed the dark side. Standing there with that huge heavy book in my hand, I recalled . . .

. . . My first nervous meeting with Edward Abbey, famous writer and (I'd been warned) curmudgeon extraordinaire. I had traveled to Tucson to conduct a magazine interview—a meeting it had taken me weeks of letter writing and uneasy telephone conversations to win. We met on the plaza at the venerable and elegant (Ed's term) Arizona Inn and talked through a lovely Sonoran January day, nursing *Cerveza Coronas* to ease the tension between strangers. It worked. ("Beer for breakfast," Ed observed, loosening up, "is one of the good things in life.") Our conversation ranged late into the night and was the longest and most detailed interview Ed would ever give. It was also the beginning of a friendship destined to die even as it flowered.

. . . The time I asked Ed to write an essay for a magazine I was helping to launch—it would impress my employer and gain the fledgling publication instant attention—and Ed politely, reluctantly declining, explaining that he was already swamped with writing commitments. Then, a week or so later, "River Solitaire" arrived, accompanied by a note saying "I found this story in my journals and typed it up. It's fairly loose writing, but it's yours if you want it." Loose writing it certainly was not, and I knew that Ed had taken time he didn't have in order to help a friend.

. . . That awkward time Ed spontaneously offered to loan me a thousand dollars, no conditions, when I carelessly grumbled that times were a little hard.

. . . His generous mentorship, repeatedly offering to sponsor me, and other struggling writer-friends, with his agent and publishers.

. . . And, most vividly, I recalled the experience that had introduced me to Cactus Ed—my first reading of *Desert Solitaire.* It was that book, more than any other stimulus, that had opened my sleepy eyes to the heartbreaking beauty of the natural world, to the bittersweet mystery of life on this miraculous earth, our one true home. "The only home," Ed had written, "we will ever know."

It is not hyperbole to say that *Desert Solitaire* changed my life.

We shook hands, exchanged *abrazos,* said our so-longs—"*Adios, amigo.* See you in March for that camping trip." Then Ed bent into the truck alongside his family—and was gone.

On March 4, the day before I was to leave for our desert rendezvous, complications at home forced me to phone Ed and beg off. Graciously, he concurred with my excuses. "Don't worry about it," he said. "There'll always be another day."

Ten days later, Ed Abbey was dead. He was only sixty-two.

Thinking back on that last phone conversation now, Ed had been right, after a fashion—there *would* be another day, and this is it.

I inhale deeply the light desert air, wondering at the mysterious spicy fragrances rising from the blackness of the valley below—the selfsame valley, ironically, that Ed had wanted to share with me three years ago. It is a place, I am learning, where phantoms come to brood and mourn.

If you go there you must hear them . . . where the air is cool and sweet with the odor of juniper and lightning, where the mockingbird and the canyon wren and the mourning dove join with the phantoms in their useless keening.

It is Abbey Country.

I squat beside the crude headstone and say to Ed the things I've come all the long way here to say, then lace boot loosely over injured foot, pull on my pack, stand and tip my cap to this good, wise man I was so very fortunate to have known. As a parting gesture—there's nobody here to call me maudlin—I place a good cigar, the kind Ed preferred but rarely indulged in, on the sand in front of his headstone. Then I turn and limp out into the star-spangled night, resuming my own fool's journey through the dark, into the unknown.

Annie Dillard

On Bellingham Bay

from "The Living"

Author's note: The setting for this piece is Bellingham Bay, on Puget Sound, 80 miles north of Seattle. The date is January 6, 1892. It is the dead of winter. The hero, Clare Fishburn, has received a death threat. He walks by the water, as darkness falls.

Chapter XLI

Clare walked south by the beach. The sky was dimming already, subtly, as though someone were slowly lowering the wick of a lamp. Far offshore gulls were crying into the southwest wind over a herring ball in the water and diving into it, and rising blown with more cries, while the dark water churned as if the sea's floor had broken beneath it and let loose . . .

Why had he possessed such an unwarranted confidence in himself? His shoes ground on the stones.

He could see a bird's tracks below the tideline, where the line of black and red gravel gave way to sandy mud. The tracks appeared out of nowhere, as if God had formed a creature and set it down. Three toe claws poked holes in the mud, and a wide web connected them. The bird had walked, manlike, along the shore with a steady, firm tread. Clare followed the line of tracks, his neck forward.

The webbed tracks looked witless, as if the bird lacked a head.

Abruptly now, the tracks stopped—with the two feet pushed deep at the claws. The tracks ended for no reason, and the sandy mud in their path was blank; the bird had flown up. Clare turned and saw that his own passage had made blunt tracks, too, in the gravel; he was trailing himself, and his tracks ended under his shoes.

He was, in his entirety, a spool of footprints, starting north of here in the settlement beach cabin where he learned to pull himself up on his mother's black skirt. His trail vanished and resumed as he walked and rode through his days and years; he lived twelve years in Goshen and moved back to Whatcom, walked to and from the high school and office. Now on this beach his track went winding behind him like a peel, as though time were a knife peeling him like an apple and would continue through him till he was gone. His tracks, his lifetime tracks, would end abruptly, also—but he would have gone not up, like a bird into the sky, but down, into the ground.

"I shall go to the gates of the grave," Clare thought. It was a passage from Isaiah, in which dying King Hezekiah turned his face to the wall. "I shall go to the gates of the grave: I am deprived of the residue of my years. I said, I shall not see the Lord, even the Lord, in the land of the living: I shall behold man no more with the inhabitants of the world."

A man would not know which step was his last, to pay heed to it. Where on the face of the earth would his footprints be fresh when the trapper tracked him down? The boys would have to carry his body along its last few routes.

He needed to learn how to die. He had learned everything else as it came along—how to read, drive a team, scythe a field and winnow grain, fell a tree, miter a corner, how to use and fix a lathe and a steam saw, demonstrate electromagnetism, set purlins for a roof, cut pipe to plumb a sink, machine an axle bearing, price a section, and sell a lot—and he excelled at what he learned, and now he had to learn this next thing, to release it all. Was it not important? How does a man learn to die when the experts are mum?

Old Conrad Grogan, the surveyor, nearly died, was all but dead, and came back to life and stood up still thin and erect—his black mustaches combed over his lip, his yellow hair in thin strands, potbellied, competent—and lived another six years. To Clare it looked like Conrad Grogan threw himself into those years: he started the debating society, married a hard-favored widow down on Whidbey Island, brought her back, whacked up a treehouse for her grandchildren, built himself a little sailing dory painted red, and strode the streets of the town right lively, his face creased and shining. Then he took to bed screaming for a few days, and panted for a few days, turned purple, and died. Clare did not know if Conrad Grogan died well, either the first time or the last, or what it took when a man had only general warning, or if he could work himself around to where something was required which he could then produce on the spot, such as, for example, courage—which would not loosen the tight situation, but would please him and cap all he had learned. He imagined June's voice adding, "Hurrah, boys."

Chunks of tan foam spume blew over the beach stones; when one chunk tumbled into another, their stiff suds stuck together, and they trembled.

Clare had not seen much sunshine lately. The needle on John Ireland's aneroid lay pinned to the left, as if the wind held it down. The mercury in John Ireland's thermometer stayed in the forties day and night. Clare had seen colored engravings in the weeklies, and read stories, which suggested to him that winters, in other places, were both colder and sunnier . . .

The tide was coming in, and Clare moved up off the gravel. He climbed over the black shark carcass that Glee had dragged in—an enormous, irregular rind. He rounded the pitted sandstone ledges of the headland, sea ledges awash and sharp with barnacles, and crossed a beach, stepping on massed logs that storm waves stranded. The logs' old dried roots stuck up higher than his head, tall as he was. It would be melancholy to break a leg coming back in the dark of night. He presented a good target now, raised against the pale sea and walking straight on logs five feet down from the brush cover. He glanced into the dense woods, but had to look back at once to mind his footing.

He was finding—now, in his forties—adult life unexpectedly meaningful and grave; the path was widening and deepening before him. Tragedy is a possiblity only for adults; so is heroism . . .

Clare walked bent, his long neck down and his chin up. He could still see, on the freezing water, the dark dumb ducks floating in rafts that tipped and rode swells. The overpowering, slushy sky was closing down. He should go back, he knew, but he went on, and his thighs itched and tingled as they always did when he walked in the cold. He made for a stretch of sand ahead. When he reached it he stopped and drove his hands into his pockets. Torn seaweed littered the sand, and wet fir cones, bottles, and twigs.

Naturally society cherished itself alone; it prized what everyone agreed was precious, despised what everyone agreed was despicable, and ignored what no one mentioned—all to its own enhancement, and with the loud view that these bubbles and vapors were eternal and universal. If [his wife] June had stressed to [their daughter] Mabel that she was going to die, would she have learned to eat with a fork? Society's loyal members, having sacrificed their only lives to its caprices, hastened to entrap the next generation into agreement, so their follies would not have been vain and they could all go down together, blind and well turned out. The company, the club, and the party had offered him a position like bait, and he bit. He had embedded himself in the company like a man bricked into a wall, and whirled with the building's maps, files, and desks, senselessly, as the planet spun and death pooled on the cold basement floors. Who could blame him?—when people have always lived so. Now, however, he saw the city lifted away, and the bricks and files vaporized; he saw the preenings of men laid low, and the comforts of family scattered. He was free and loosed on the black beach.

Clare sat on a log, shaved strands of a plug into his palm, ground them to powder using his knife handle as a pestle, and loaded and lighted his pipe. "As a lion, so will he break all my bones . . ." Having felt his freedom, must he now die? Conversely, could he endure this freedom, when it burned in his stomach and smoked in his throat?

In the match's flare he could see a swollen line of sand grains trailing over the hard beach in scallops. The back swash of the last high tide dropped sand grains there. It was in the summer of '83 that Krakatoa exploded. Clare was in his fruit-grafting enthusiasm then, and did not remark the famously sublime sunsets the ash caused around the world, because sunsets here were routinely sublime. He did notice what the newspapers proclaimed in the following months: that the explosion caused one wave to travel the sea, wash over Java and Sumatra, and drown thirty-six thousand people. Those thirty-six thousand people reproached him, as he read the paper and sipped his tea on the puncheon porch, for he was a good democrat, and believed that any man was as good as any other, roughly.

He had asked his mother if she thought God punished those thirty-six thousand people for living wrong, and visibly shocked her. She replied that they were all going to die anyway, which shocked him, and she added that it was time he got married, which he knew.

His eye sought the line of forest on the headland, but its black silhouette was lost in the black sky, as if the sky had abolished it. To the south he could see no fires from Finn Beach. Out over the water, in three directions, distance sputtered out. The wind had fallen; the tide made a small approaching noise like gibberish.

The dark was now thick, flannel. Its blackness had texture and depth, like that of a charcoaled page, in which dark clouds billowed.

Here, in all the world, there shone only his own light—his red burning tobacco, and the glowing dottle beneath it, and the black unburnt bits above. There was no other light, human or inhuman, up or down the beach, or out on the invisible islands, or back in the woods, or anywhere on earth or in heaven, except the chill and fantastical sheen on the sea, whose cause was unfathomable. Before him extended the visible universe: an unstable, thick darkness almost met the silver line of the sea. A long crack had opened between the thick darkness and the water. The crack, half the apparent height of a man, gave out upon a thin darkness, black without substance or stars. He looked out upon the thin darkness, and seemed to hear the souls of the dead whir and slip in its deep fastness. They wanted back. Their bodies in the graveyard on the cliff could not see to steer their sleeping course, their sleeping heels in the air.

It was nearing five o'clock now. When Clare stood, his shoes on the beach rolled stones. He smelled the chill on the rising water. Inside his gabardine jacket, under his vest and collarless shirt, and inside his long-legged underwear, his flesh was losing its heat. By the time he rounded again the headland towards the town, his fingers felt to one another like pipe lengths. He wanted back, too. Obenchain's stump stood on the cliff between him and the town; he had gone too far. He heard his own footsteps. He inhaled and exhaled tensely, as if he might topple; he seemed to taste mineral darkness on his tongue, or ash, like the moon. It was too late to walk on logs; he felt with his feet for the narrowing beach. Ahead, a dim light smudged the cloud cover over the town, as its dwellings and streetlights cast up into the muffling blackness their lamps. He was not yet home.

He came up on Pearl Street by the town wharf. There he saw, in the frail light of the warehouse lamp, an orange sea star wrapped round the wharf piling. It was a starfish with many thick, short arms. It looked like a swollen medallion the size of a dinner tray, and alive. Clare had seen a sea star's thorny hole of a mouth; the mouth was at its thick center, on the underside, on the piling. Oystermen knifed starfish on sight, for a starfish humped its suckers around an oyster, forced open its shell with its contracting arms, vomited its stomach out of its own mouth, inside out, insinuated it between the oyster's parted shells, and dissolved and digested the oyster's soft parts directly. Now, as Clare passed, the black tide was wetting the beast, and it detached itself, one orange edge at a time. Its crusty nubs moved thickly. Their tubes loosened their grip on the piling, and the animal dropped into the water.

"Thus saith the Lord," Clare thought, climbing past the town to Golden Street, "Set thine house in order; for thou shalt die, and not live."

Kenneth Brower

Island Beaches

from *Islands*

In the Virgin Islands this winter, snorkeling in toward the beach at Watermelon Bay, I met a green turtle heading in the same direction. We were off in thirty feet of clear water, under a bright subtropical sun, passing over that ambiguous zone of sand that is either the end of the sea floor or the beginning of the beach. The turtle had come, I suppose, to graze on the turtle grass growing here. I dove and detoured to swim alongside her.

For several lazy strokes of the great oars of her foreflippers, she suffered my company. I studied the lovely imbricate pattern of her carapace, the scratch marks there, the green sea-patina and the muted colors underneath. Pulling on the near oar, the turtle made a slow and dignified turn out to sea. I followed, digressing from my original destination and from the subject of this essay.

The turtle grew tired of me. Pulling on both oars—three double strokes, four—she left me behind and dematerialized in the blue. I head for the beach again. In ten feet of water I passed a small barracuda. It circled landward to look me over. Barracuda are among the most low-browed of creatures, and are said to be stupid, even for fish, yet every barracuda I have ever met has displayed a fine curiosity. The barracuda was so close to beach-colored that I lost it on looking away. I found it again only by the thin, dark line of shadow it cast on the sand.

In three feet of water, a luminous blue wall of schooling fry appeared ahead. The tiny, translucent fish were big-eyed and iridescent, each one jewellike, wrought in lapis lazuli and silver and gold. The wall accelerated, thinned, shied from me, its colors changing with each shift of angle to the sun. Parting ahead of me, the school reassembled behind.

In fourteen inches of water, I let the small waves take me in to the beach. I was pleased and slightly surprised, as always, how shallow my draft was. In ten inches of water, I watched the sand ripples shaping themselves just under my nose. With each incoming wavelet, a blizzard of grains blew inland. The blizzard hugged the curve of the ripple, just as windblown sand hugs the curve of a dune. Then came the backwash, and the blizzard blew back the other way. The beaches of this planet are forever reforming, taking new shapes according to old patterns. Here, six inches below my faceplate, the ocean was applying finishing touches that would never be quite complete. I sat up in shallow water, pulled off my fins, and thought of the island beaches I have known.

There were cold, high-latitude beaches. The pitiful little beach at Barter Island, at 70° north, just off Alaska, is just a few inches of sand between the island's tundra and the Arctic Ocean. It is hardly a beach at all, but it marked the end of five weeks of walking across the Brooks Range. My two companions and I were thin and hungry. We were all walked out. An Eskimo hunter ferried us across to the island. When his prow furrowed the sand, I could have jumped out, dropped to my knees, and kissed each grain.

There were the beaches of Chichagof, Baranof, Kupreanof, Admiralty, Kuiu, and Prince of Wales islands, in southeast Alaska. Those big islands, together with a host of smaller ones, all glacier-carved, with shorelines convoluted, form the maze of the Inside Passage. A friend and I once paddled that maze in a kayak, traveling from Glacier Bay in

Alaska south to Canadian waters. The beaches were our havens. On tiring of paddling, in the twilight of Alaskan midnight, we would turn the prow in toward them. Some were white sand, some dark shingle. On both sorts of beach lay enormous, bleached logs of Sitka spruce and yellow cedar. Along high-tide line the beaches were bounded by driftwood tangles of giant roots, pale and twisted, like the limbs of Greek statuary after a raid by barbarians. Inland, just beyond the pallor of the statuary, was a wall of living forest, dense, tall, and dark as night.

The gently shelving, white-sand beach—that staple of the Caribbean travel poster—was our nightmare. Hauling the heavy-laden kayak beyond the tide's reach, on such a beach, meant covering great horizontal distances, much sweat and toil. The hard, steep shingle beach was what we wanted. The steeper the better. We used small driftwood logs as rollers to ease the kayak up the slope. In the mornings, by first light, the rollers were invisible and the kayak seemed to levitate above the stones of the beach.

If the beaches were our havens, then for local predators they were salvation itself. The natural economy of the North is boom-and-bust, and in deep recessions Northern predators fall back upon the resources of the shore. Wolves are not too proud, when they are hungry, to beachcomb. They come down from the high country to hunt the intertidal zone for shellfish and any carrion washed ashore. The year of our kayak trip was a bust year. In one Alaskan fiord we watched a lone wolf trot the shoreline toward us. He was so preoccupied with the cobbles of the beach, or with the pangs in his stomach, that he stumbled across the kayak before realizing that humans were here. He was a black wolf with fine yellow eyes. Those eyes were full at first of a blank surprise, and then, I think, embarrassment. He stared at us a moment before walking slowly into the trees.

Another time I saw a fox poke its slim nose under beach stones, foraging for amphipods. Inspired by the fox, I tried amphipods myself, collecting them from under beach stones and boiling them on a driftwood fire until they were a promising red, like tiny lobsters. I bit in boldly. Amphipods are gritty, taste awful, and I spit them out again.

But most of the beaches of my memory were warmer.

There were beaches at 0° latitude, in the Galápagos Islands, an archipelago divided by the equator. Beaches in the Galápagos come in all sorts: olivine, red cinder, black volcanic sand, white coral sand, and a wide range of hybrids. The long beach at James Bay, on the uninhabited island of San Salvador, is one of the brighter sort, dazzling in the equatorial sun. Behind the beach, screened thinly by salt-tolerant vegetation, runs a long, brackish lagoon in which flamingos parade in slow motion, shocking pink against the green of the mangroves beyond.

There were the beaches of Hood and Isabella islands, where the bulls of Galápagos sea lions haul out to doze amidst their harems. In my first stay in the Galápagos, which lasted four months and came before Galápagos National Park had established rules, we played a sea lion game—a game that now would be illegal. The contest was simple: Who could snatch the fish-float or other piece of flotsam that lay closest to the bull?

The bulls chased us up Galápagos sands, and we in turn chased ghost crabs.

If the beaches of the warm latitudes have a totem animal, it is that ethereal crab. Pale as a ghost and quick as one, the ghost crab is capable—it seems—of passing abruptly and ectoplasmically through the surface of the sand. The ghost crab wears its eyes on tall stalks and is impossible to surprise from behind. The fastest of all crustaceans, it has been clocked at 1.825 meters per second on hard sand. It is a master of sudden changes of direction, besides. We hadn't a prayer of catching one before it reached its hole.

The damp sands low on Galápagos beaches are marked everywhere by the hieroglyphics that ghost crabs leave in feeding. The crabs employ the simplest sort of orthography; no letters really, just punctuation. First there is the long scrape mark their maxillipeds leave in gathering sand—a dash. Then there is the round sand pellet rolled by the mandibles in extracting particles of food—a period. Finally, and most commonly, there is the exclamation mark of the dash and period together. The commentary of ghost crabs can cover a whole beach, between each erasure of the tide. The messages are all exclamatory, like those notes fifth-grade girls pass among themselves in class.

There were the beaches of Little Cumberland Island, in the Sea Isles of Georgia. The white dunes of the Little Cumberland beach are broken by oases of palmetto, oak, and Spanish moss. Alligators hunt the marshes behind the dunes, and wild pigs forage there. Ghost crabs write their excitable commentary down low on the beach slope. In summer twilight, on breezy days, it is easy to mistake the ghost crabs for white foam skittering inland, or to mistake the foam for ghost crabs. Foam vanishes more gradually, rolling itself smaller and smaller until the last bubbles pop. Ghost crabs disappear suddenly, vanishing into their holes.

There were the beaches of San Benitos, San Martin, and Cedros, off the Baja California coast. On certain beaches of those desert islands, Mexican fishermen have built multicolored shacks of cardboard and flotsam. Whatever junk the fishermen are unable to recycle into their walls, they entrust to the sea wind. Inland of each shack is a cone of windblown garbage. Beyond the last rusted can, impaled on its cactus, the island is pristine again. On certain other beaches of those Baja islands, elephant seals haul out. The elephants doze, colossal, in the Baja sun, warming themselves after half-mile dives into black and frigid mesopelagic ocean.

There was Lee Marvin Beach, on Babeldaob Island in the Palau Archipelago of Micronesia. It was on this narrow white-sand beach, under a sheer, jungle-covered, coral-limestone cliff, that the odd movie *Hell in the Pacific* was filmed. The Palau Islanders did not name the beach for Toshiro Mifune, the other actor in that two-character drama. They did not name it Hell Beach, or Hollywood, or Malibu, as Palauan humor might have permitted. They named it Lee Marvin Beach because, of all the film folk, they liked Marvin best. Lee Marvin did not take himself too seriously, and he was fond of closing the bars each night—both traits that Palau Islanders find admirable. *Hell in the Pacific* was a collaboration between American and Japanese film crews. War nearly broke out again, the Palauans say, as the two factions began to relive the old one.

There was a beach at Santubong, in Malaysian Borneo, where Alfred Russel Wallace composed his famous letter to Darwin. Wallace had arrived independently at a theory of natural selection. His letter jogged Darwin, who had spent twenty years fussing over small details in *Origin of Species,* into hurriedly publishing that great book. I arrived somewhat more than a century after this correspondence. For several days I lived in a bungalow where the jungle met the beach. My bed had a fine mosquito net, and my window looked out on the South China Sea. One day, strolling the sands at Santubong, I watched a Malay fisherman cast his net. He wore a conical coolie hat of straw. He strode slowly, then froze in midstep, like a heron. (Convergent evolution, a Darwinist would call this.) At long intervals he uncoiled, sending his weighted circle of mesh out toward sardines. Wallace, uncoiling on this same beach, had cast his net of speculation into a sea of possibilities. I contemplated Wallace and Darwin, two men whose insights transformed the world. I had no great, epochal ideas of my own. If I had any ideas at all, in fact, I cannot recall them.

There was the beach at Cay Chapel, on the barrier reef off the coast of Belize. It is a beach caught between worlds. British soldiers stationed in Belize vacation at Cay Chapel on weekends. The beach is populated by brown-skinned men tattooed like the old Polynesians, but speaking Cockney.

There were the white-sand dunes of Barking Sands on Kauai, at the northern end of the main Hawaiian chain. With each step on Barking Sands, the beach squeaks and protests under your feet.

There were the new black-sand beaches that have followed the present series of eruptions on the Big Island, at the southern end of the same chain. Incandescent lava, on reaching the sea, shatters to fragments in great steam explosions, blackens, and washes ashore as pebbles or sand. The black beaches are sudden, appearing sometimes overnight. They are often ephemeral, disappearing as quickly. I walked out on several of them. The black sands should have been exhilarating. They are testimony to the geophysical vitality of the planet. Earth is not a dead sphere, like the moon. But those steep, coal-chute beaches made me uneasy, all the same. They lay where my recollections insisted on other landscapes. They engaged a certain sense of wonder, maybe, but in my heart I didn't like them.

There was the old black-sand beach at the mouth of Waipi'o Valley, on the opposite end of the same island. Somewhere in the black sands of Waipi'o, the story goes, lies the entrance to Lua O Milu, the Hawaiian Underworld. Once a year, a long procession of ghosts wends its way down the valley floor and disappears into the blackness of the sand. Afterward, no one can find the place.

The first thing on Raine Island that my binoculars raised, from my station on the foredeck, was the ruined stone tower that stands on that sandy cay. The tower was built by convict masons in 1844. It was the first navigational aid on the Great Barrier Reef. Sixty-four feet tall, it shows above the sea well before any land appears. A cloud of dots floating above the tower resolved themselves, as we drew closer, into frigate birds. The frigates faced into the wind, trimming their great wings, holding position over the crenellations of the tower. Then the base of the tower rose, and then the white beach below. Soon I could discern turtle tracks everywhere on the sand.

Raine, like the other sand cays of the Great Barrier Reef, is *all* beach, really. Its center is beachrock, its entire circumference white coral sand.

Raine is the most important breeding island for sea birds in Australia. It is Australia's most important turtle-nesting ground as well. By day, dense clouds of terns, frigates, gulls, and boobies rotate above the island. By night, green turtles come ashore to lie, then return. Every inch of sand is furrowed by the tractor marks of turtles. In a single night, scientists once counted 11,000 of them on the beach.

The beachrock of the island's interior ends in miniature cliffs about three feet tall. The nesting urge of the turtles sends some of them, with dumbfounding persistence, past the dunes and up to the cliffs. The cliffs are insurmountable, for turtles. Often the females, after long and fruitless struggles, end up tipping themselves over backward. They lie helpless on their backs for days or weeks, dying finally in the heat of the sun. The shallow dunes below the cliffs are a graveyard of empty shells. I spent two mornings on Raine righting inverted turtles. Each one was an engineering project. I would study her a moment—an armored reptile the size of a steamer trunk—then I would scoop sand away on the downhill side, perhaps, before finding a driftwood pole for leverage in prying the creature over.

The flippers of an inverted turtle are thick-skinned and horny except where they enter the shell, and there the skin is a dry, white, crinkly parchment. When I touched the turtles intimately there, their big dark eyes came open, bleary with thick turtle tears. They exhaled the sighing grunt of an overweight matron. It was a sound halfway between worry and resignation, yet somehow dignified.

Raine was our northernmost landfall on the Great Barrier Reef. From there my partner and I worked our way south. Our assignment was a book chapter on the reef, we had six weeks to spend, and we dove on as many reefs as we could. The cays of the reef grew progressively simpler as we moved south. Our voyage, it seemed to me, was like a lesson in cay formation run backward.

One morning we passed a white-sand cay upon which storms had rolled a line of dark coral boulders. That afternoon we passed two more boulder-strewn cays like that one. The Great Barrier Reef was like some endless sea serpent. The cays were where its back showed above the waves, and those serrate lines of boulders were the vertebrae. The next day we passed a smaller cay, fifty feet long, perhaps, and featureless except for twenty noddy terns in a file along its imperceptible crest. "Land!" my colleague shouted, jokingly.

Some hours later we passed a cay nearly identical, except that it had no noddies.

In passing this last cay—a spit of sand and nothing else—I realized what it is about beaches. The beach is the simplest possible landscape.

Sand, sea, sky, and no more. There is a lovely, perfect reductionism in a beach. It was a beach that God was contemplating, I would bet, when He called the dry land Earth and saw that it was good. The beach is a beginning. Walking the good simplicity of the sand, in the sea wind, lets us begin again ourselves from scratch.

Peggy Shumaker

Poems

from *Ploughshares*

The Day the Leaves Came

For so long the hillside shone white,
the white of white branches laden, the sky
more white, the river unmoved.

And when the first stirrings started
underneath, the hollowing subtle,
unpredictable, rotten crust gave way—

ice water up to the ankle! She
turned from her work and shook
her wet foot. The buds had broken.

Not the green of birches in full leaf.
Not meadow, tundra, berry patch, tussock.
For this moment only, this green—

the touch of one loved
in secret, a gasp held in,
let go.

from *Alaska Quarterly Review*

Exit Glacier

When we got close enough
we could hear

rivers inside the ice
heaving splits

the groaning of a ledge
about to

calve. Strewn in the moraine
fresh moose sign—

tawny oblong pellets
breaking up

sharp black shale. In one breath
ice and air—

history, the record
of breaking

prophecy, the warning
of what's yet to break

out from under
four stories

of bone-crushing turquoise,
retreating.

from *Northern Lights*

Birch Syrup

As I turned off Spinach Creek Road, I wondered about walking in. In early May, the driveway, a fairly steep quarter-mile dogleg, ran as two small streams split by a mossbacked middle ridge. Caribou lettuce edged the roadway like dusty lace.

The last car in (or out) hadn't sunk too far, so I decided to chance it. First gear—my nimble Honda shinnied up the wet slope, no problem. Sharp left, and I pulled into the turnaround behind the house. Steam rose from an ancient campstove set up by the cold-storage shed. Glen lifted a hand in greeting, then turned shyly back to his work.

I stretched over the seat for the two fresh baguettes I'd brought from town. Noses exposed, they pointed toward the tall stainless bucket and the steam polishing Glen's ruddy face. Wet spruce and peeling birch stood by, murmuring. A thick sponge of leaves gave softly underfoot.

"Birch syrup," Glen said, adjusting the flame under the clear fluid. He and Melissa had snowshoed to a stand of good-sized white barks, peeled back a loose flap, and bored past the heartwood to draw sap from the whole core. They tapped in an inch or so of hose, fastened on a pail, and let the warm days and cold nights do their work. In a few clear days, the trees gave seventeen gallons, clean and cold as spring water, with a touch of the tree taste still lingering.

Melissa called us in to mince the garlic she'd sprinkle over burbot Glen had pulled up through the ice on the Tanana. We fed each other over thin bites of smoked cheese, caught a glimpse of the season's first waxwing, hesitating by the feeder.

Last season a moose offered himself just out the back door.

Some people laughed at Glen for taking him—too easy, they said, not sporting. But Glen's Athabaskan relatives told him if the animal leads you on a long chase over hard ground, something's not right in your relationship with the animal. He said thank you, shot it, and forced his kid to stay home that night to help butcher.

A strange dog, cocoa brown and bounding, tagged along on our after-dinner walk, running ahead to bite the snow, running back when we moseyed too slowly. Perfect ovals of stone caught Melissa's quilter's eye. She chose a smooth black one to hand to me.

The whole watershed—mountain, hillside, valley, flatland. Each rise balanced with a hollow, and everything alive, connected.

The sap had boiled down to dark amber. We strained it into boiled jars, hand-tightened the lids. I stayed too long, almost till dark in a time when darkness almost doesn't come. They gave me a jar to take home.

Harry Middleton

Baja

from "Rivers of Memory"

It is curious what stirs the memory, brings it to a boil. Often, it takes only the play of light and shadow to send me into a dream, into some fit of remembrance. The mind seems to have an unquenchable passion for the possibilities evoked by details. Every stimulus is strip-searched, gobbled up, or discarded. One mind's boredom is another's wonder.

Even the most common sights and sounds can carry me away, deposit me along some fine stretch of mountain river, sunlight warming my face and neck and arms, blue shadows drifting across the face of bright, moving water, dissipating among shoals of warm black stones, or transport me to some wild wood or saltwater flat, the water an endless shimmer of perfect greens and blues under a brutal tropical sun and cloudless skies where the fish seem more illusion than hard, muscled fact.

Recently I caught a glimpse of myself in a full-length mirror. The mirror's merciless reflection seemed so strange, so unlike the image of how I see myself, that I found myself regarding it suspiciously, creeping up on it from the side to test its truth. Life marks and shapes the land, just as the earth inexorably marks and contours those who share the land's history, get mixed up with its fortunes and fates. The heartbreaking beauty of the wild country I have known, spent time in, sought out, has not been kind, considerate, understanding. Deep leathery lines crisscross the back of my neck. I seem to have developed a permanent squint, even when wearing sunglasses. My fingers look disfigured. So thick are the callouses on my fingers and palms that I have noticed of late that my sense of touch in my hands has dulled, so that pleasure feels only slightly different than pain. My hands and arms are a trellis of thick, pinched purple scars, each one a signpost, a totem of my horrible addiction to wild country, wild rivers, and wild fish.

A scorpion sting left the deep round scar on the soft flesh of my right forearm. The scorpion got me as I was reading a Kurt Vonnegut novel in an abandoned adobe hut on the rocky burnt hills of Trelingua, in the Big Bend country of west Texas. The whole thing was my fault, not the scorpion's. After all, the desert night belongs to the scorpion and its kind. I saw it as it scurried away, glowing a deep neon blue under a vast dome of desert night sky, a sky so clear that I could see Andromeda. Five minutes after I was stung, Andromeda seemed to be wheeling madly through the blue-black starry desert night, and so did I.

Kurt Vonnegut's fiction has always has a curious impact on me. I had a novel of his in hand the night I crawled into my sleeping bag in Honduras. I hadn't gotten past the first paragraph when I felt the tarantulas on my left arm. Three of them. I was staying on a small cay of the Hog Islands, off the Honduran coast. William Marley Bubo, a native of the islands, had invited me to share his hut, fish with him in his handmade canoe. We fished with hand lines at night, fished deep for big tuna and kingfish. Bubo was the most prestigious fisherman in his village because his canoe had a sail. The sail was a yellow plastic shower curtain Bubo pulled from the indigo sea one night after it was jettisoned from a passing American boat full of vacationing divers.

A tarantula's bite, by the way, is no worse than a wasp's sting. I hardly had time to notice the bites, anyway, since the malaria that was probably deposited in my blood a week before began to take hold, filling my brain with bubbling fevers that felt like someone was scraping the soft walls of my skull with sandpaper. Vonnegut was involved with the malaria too, now that I think about it. I used the novel to crush the mosquito hunkered over a vein on the top of my right hand. Who says good fiction has lost its usefulness?

Vonnegut's fiction, however, had absolutely nothing to do with the great, deep gash on my right arm running in a wide salmon-colored crease across the forearm, near the elbow. Unlike so many of its neighbors, this scar is surgical in nature and is marked by a noticeable aesthetic neatness, a quiet elegance.

What I thought was a persistent tropical ulcer turned out to be something called marine tuberculosis. Like beauty and awe, the bacteria that cause the condition can sometimes be passed from fish to man. A month after my sojourn among the Honduran Hog Islands, an emergency room doctor in Salt Lake City enlarged the wound, scraped the tendons and muscles, sewed me up, gave me heavy doses of antibiotics, sent me on my way.

I got out of Salt Lake City. I should have known I was in for trouble the night before, when, after finishing a splendid meal at a local Chinese restaurant, I cracked open the obligatory fortune cookie to find no fortune at all, just bits of hard, tasteless cookie in my hand.

I had been in Mexico, fishing the rich waters off the Pacific coast of Baja, when I scratched my arm when a modest-sized striped marlin threw a big orange-and-blue rooster-tail lure. The lure caught my arm as it ricocheted about the stern of the big white boat. And for days afterward I handled fish, many fish, especially marlin and dorado. Perhaps that's how the transfer was made, the opportunistic bacterium that causes marine tuberculosis slipping into the scratch on my arm, setting in and settling down in a new and undiscovered universe of warm blood.

I stayed in Cabo San Lucas for a week, arriving by small plane from La Paz. I have not been back to Cabo San Lucas since. I understand that over the years it has mutated from a lazy fishing village to a sparkling destination crowded with tourists and a chaos of anglers, trophy hunters, and dream-seekers alike.

As I say, I had to hire a small plane from La Paz. It was a bargain. I was able to rent plane and pilot for less than fifty dollars, American.

Having never seen such a plane before, I cannot tell you the make or name or model, only that it had only one wheel, no windshield, no radio, and the flap on the left wing was operated by the pilot by way of a long piece of chicken wire. Pablo was the plane's pilot and copilot, all five feet of him. He told me proudly, as he coaxed the plane into the air, that he would be fifteen by summer's end and that he was looking forward to getting his license, buying a brand new Ford taxi in La Paz. The plane with no windshield and one wheel carried four seats and on this trip seven passengers, not including Pablo. Pablo, smiling confidently, told me that he often made the trip with as many as ten passengers. Looking slightly menacing, like some odd bundle or ordnance, my fly-rod tubes were tied snugly above the plane's one wheel. The plane's dark shadow against the burnt Baja badlands below reminded me of ominous World War II newsreel films always being shown on public television channels, neat squadrons of dive-bombers suddenly dropping out of the sky.

I never saw Cabo San Lucas from the air. Somewhere near town, Pablo suddenly decreased airspeed, let the plane drop several hundred feet, and began buzzing a nondescript piece of desert. After a few passes, a small gathering of indifferent goats finally wandered off, the bells about their throats tolling loudly, tolling, I thought, more than once, for Pablo and the one-wheeled plane and its passengers, including me.

Pablo landed near where the disinterested goats had been. A pale blue Chevy Nova suddenly appeared, almost shyly, from behind a nearby tangled motte of brush and stones bleached beyond red by the unforgiving Baja sun.

The shirtless driver mopped his head and neck constantly with a red bandana. "Taxi," he said. "Two dollars American. It's a hard walk to town, señor."

I unloaded my stuff at the hotel, found a table on the terrace nestled in shade, cooled by the constant breeze off the ocean, and drank bottle after bottle of warm Mexican soda pop: a dash of flavor, a touch of water, and the rest pure, teeth-grinding, pulse-pounding sugar.

The room had a one-speed three-speed fan and a great window facing the ocean, a window I kept open wide, letting the sea's ancient mournful sighs fill the room. Morning came as a capillary of light between land and sky, as though one had been torn from the other. The sky above the ocean was laced with delicate blue-green clouds drifting to the west. From the docks, looking out over the ocean's smooth, glistening surface, a wild chorus of gulls circled above Los Arcos, a magnificent arch carved out of stone by the press of ocean and tide and weather.

Los Arcos separates the Pacific from the haunting blue waters of the Sea of Cortez. Later, as the light edged across sea and land, as morning spread, the boat, the *San Lucas,* passed close to Los Arcos. Its warming ledges and galleries of stone were crowded with sea lions.

A young Mexican boy, dressed only in a ragged pair of brown shorts, busily prepared the heavy rods. Some he fixed with artificial lures. The hooks of the others were sunk deep into thick white slabs of fresh baitfish.

Past Los Arcos, the captain turned the *San Lucas* toward open water, deep water, the Pacific rising and falling on the backs of dark swells flashing blue and green in the soft morning sunlight. In the distance, landward, behind the sharp contours of the Arch, every surface etched with sunlight, the violet shadows of low-slung mountains seemed to drift beyond the village, slouched across the edge of the sky, through a pitiless landscape of gnarled, sun-blasted brush, sand, and cacti, a landscape that, in the morning light, seemed one more of shapes and forms than of substance. By midmorning, the sun already high and full, the temperature rising, the land's details are lost in the desert's intense heat, which is forever ruthless. Even the wind coming off the ocean was hot and unforgiving, coating the skin with a crusty film of salt, stinging the face.

The ocean's dark waters were cool, though, and heavy with life, fecund. Here, both the Pacific and the nearby Sea of Cortez are immense, rich protein factories, their waters crowded with fish, fish of every size and evolutionary temperament, fish gorgeous and mysterious, as wild and arcane as the waters that sustain them. For years and years, sport fishermen have come to these waters desperate not just for the company of fish, but for the false glory of big fish, trophy fish, fish as prize, mounted mementos—grand sailfish and broadbills, giant marlin and roosterfish, dorados, cabrilla, wahoo, and yellowfish. Such anglers yearn not so much for the beauty of this place, or the wild sea, but for the fish that might put them in the record books. The quest for such fish takes its toll. A fisherman at the hotel bar boasted that the waters off Cabo San Lucas coughed up more than two thousand marlin a year. "It's like gathering up sardines," he laughed, "almost too easy. Anyone, I mean anyone, can come here and take a big fish, a real wall-hanger, and go home a sea-conquering, marlin-busting hero, and never have to touch a hook or piece of bait." And he bought the bar another round of drinks and another and another, celebrating the 555-pound marlin he had killed that morning and was shipping back to the wall in his den in Lima, Ohio.

I was thinking about the man at the bar as the *San Lucas* cut her speed, as the Mexican boy stacked the rods, let out bait and line, as large pools of orange morning sunlight glistened off the ocean's roiling surface, as the ocean's water went easily from ebony to jade in color.

The captain joined me in the twin swivel chairs at the boat's stern and we talked of fish, of the sea, of the village. He told me that lately his luck had been good, very good, and that just last week his boat took a great marlin for a book editor from New York City who loved the fight but would not touch the great fish once he and his Mexican boy had killed it and strapped it securely up against the stern of the boat where the sharks would not attack it, tear gigantic holes in its flesh before they had a chance to get it back to the dock where the New York editor had hired the town's only photographer to take a picture of the marlin strung up high by its wide black tail, the editor dwarfed beside it, careful not to look at it, rod in hand, smiling wildly. The captain told me that the book editor had him saw off the fish's bill, which the book editor wiped clean, wrapped in newspaper, and carried back to New York with him.

All morning we sat in the swivel chairs thinking of fish, dreaming of fish, watching the big colorful plastic lures dance temptingly in the swells behind the boat. The captain told me that today he would go as far as eight miles beyond the Arch looking for big fish. We had not even covered half that distance before the young Mexican boy began to shout *Strike! Strike!*

The heavy line came off the big Diawa reel fast, clicking and buzzing, sounding like the amplified scratching and clawing of countless insects. One powerful jerk of the rod across the body and to the side and the fish and angler are well hooked. It is a dorado. I can tell by the weight of it and its fight. I bring it in quickly, trying to preserve its strength rather than mine. Often, releasing an exhausted fish, one that has been spent in a long struggle, is no different than killing it. The outcome is the same. Alongside the boat, at the surface, sunlight on its blunt head and smooth back, the dorado is a shock of neon colors, bluish yellows and greens and silvers. It had taken the hook well but had not swallowed it. Released, a single shudder moved across its flanks and the fish vanished into the deep water, leaving only a momentary white tear in the surface as evidence that it existed at all.

There had been many dorado and a roosterfish and yellowfish, but, as yet, no marlin. The sun was high now and so intense that you could not look directly at the light coming off the water. The Mexican boy was drinking soda pop and telling me of the big marlin the boat had found last week, the one that had surely weighed almost a thousand pounds, the one that they had been hooked to for more than ten hours, before the fish finally went so deep they could not haul it up, and it broke the line. The Mexican boy kept showing me the palms of his hands, the deep, purple bruises and open cuts the rod had made as the fish hauled the boat farther and farther out into the deep water. The Mexican boy showed me his hands proudly, told me he would tell his own children someday of that fish and show them his hands as evidence and testimony of the fish's greatness. And there was more soda pop and cold chicken and fresh bananas and stolen moments in the shade under the white canvas top spread over the bridge of the boat.

I had just looked at my watch when the Mexican boy's wailing screams began. Seven minutes after four in the afternoon. *Mar-lean!* he shouted. *Mar-lean!* Instantly I grabbed the terribly bent rod while the captain used the boat to try and set the hook, slowing, then gunning the big diesel engine. The marlin broke the surface of the ocean, leaped into the hot sun-drenched afternoon air, throwing its massive head toward the boat, arching its blue-black back above the sea, then twisting at once sideways and back, its turquoise flanks and bone white belly suddenly flashing in the sun. I threw it slack, trying to keep it from throwing the hook, and I could feel its great weight as it went deep, deeper, the reel clicking rhythmically, giving the marlin more and more line, which connected us, bound in that mix of ocean and sunlight. It did not come again to the surface for almost an hour and during that time burned its power and grace into my senses, into the flesh and muscles of my hands and arms, my back and legs. It rose quickly, exploding out of the dark green ocean, hung in the cooling afternoon air for a great long moment, and it seemed to me that in its cold blue eyes flashed the earth's measureless wildness and mystery.

It was a beautiful striped marlin of modest size and it threw the hook on its third magnificent jump and I was not sorry, really, or disappointed, angry, bitter. It was a wonderful fish and I was glad just to have had the good fortune to spend the last hours of a warm Baja afternoon in its company, hooked not to my world but to its.

There were four more dorado as sun and sky and sea slowly joined, mingled with the darkening shadows and gray winds of dusk. I stood at the bow, warmed by sunburn and simple joy, that rarest and most bewildering of emotions, and watched the silhouettes of birds circling the dark stones of Los Arcos. Near the dock children laughed loudly as they played in the cool green waters along the beaches.

The dock was crowded with the curious, with children, with the hungry and poor, with fish merchants, a handful of young men who offered to mount my fish cheaply yet beautifully, perfectly on the best artificial fish forms in Baja, and the town photographer who was eager to snap my picture with my catch, validate my moment of fishing glory.

I had kept two big dorado and gave them to the little crowd of villagers who had gathered to meet the boat at the dock. The young Mexican boy had told me, shyly, that such a gesture would not only feed many who had not eaten that day but might bring luck to the boat, to him, and to the captain.

I walked slowly back to the hotel from the dock, enjoying the cool night wind coming off the Pacific and the sounds coming from the hotel's terrace, laughter and clinking glasses, the sweet rhythms of Mexican guitars, and above it all the low roar of the ocean as it pressed endlessly against the shore all the while, absentmindedly rubbing the worsening cut on my right arm and thinking of the young Mexican boy's hands and knowing that the marlin and the ocean had left its mark both in flesh and muscle and deep in the folds of memory.

Brenda Peterson

Bread Upon the Waters

from *Sierra*

"Seagulls memorize your face," the old man called out to me as he strode past on his daily walk. I stood on the seawall feeding the flock of gray-and-white gulls who also make this Puget Sound beach their home. "They know their neighbors." He tipped his rather rakish tweed motoring cap and kept walking fast. "Can't let the heartbeat stop," he explained.

I meet this man many days on the beach. We rarely talk; we perform our simple chores: I feed the seagulls and say prayers, he keeps his legs and his heart moving. But between us there is an understanding that these tasks are as important as anything else in our lives; maybe they even keep us alive. Certainly our relationship with each other and with this windswept Northwest beach is more than a habit. It is a bond, an unspoken treaty we've made with the territory we call home.

For ten years I have migrated from beach shack to cabin, moving along the shore like the Native tribes that once encircled all of Puget Sound. But unlike the first people who loved this wild, serpentine body of cold water, my encampments have changed with the whim of my landlords rather than with the seasons. Somehow mixed up in my blood of Seminole, Swede, and French-Canadian Indian is my belief that I may never own land even if one day I might be able to afford it.

Ownership implies possession; as much as I revere this inland sea, she will never belong to me. Why not, then, belong to her?

Belong. As a child the word mesmerized me. Because my father's forestry work moved us every other year—from southern piney woods to soaring Montana spruce to High Sierra fir—the landscape seemed in motion. To *be long* in one place was to take deep root like other settled folk, or like the trees themselves. After I have lived a long life on this beach, I hope that someone might someday say, "She belonged here," as much as the purple starfish that cling to rock crevices covered in algae fur.

The Hopi Indians of Arizona believe that our daily rituals and prayers literally keep this world spinning on its axis. For me, feeding the seagulls is one of those everyday prayers. When I walk out of my front door and cross the street to the seawall, they caw welcome, their wings almost touching me as they sail low over my shoulders, then hover overhead, midair. Sometimes if it's been raining, their feathers flick water droplets onto my face like sprinklings of holy water. The brave fliers swoop over the sea and back to catch the bread in their beaks inches above my hand. Then the cacophonic choir—gulls crying and crows *kak-kak*-ing as my special sidearm pitch sends tortillas whizzing through the air, a few of them skipping across the waves like flour frisbees.

I am not the only neighbor who feeds these gulls. For the past three years, two afternoons a week a green taxi pulled alongside the beach. From inside, an ancient woman, her back bent like the taut arch of a crossbow, leaned out of the car window and called in a clear, tremulous soprano. The seagulls recognized the sun-wrinkled, almost blind face she raised to them. She smiled and said to the taxi driver, "They *know* I'm here."

It was always the same driver, the same ritual—a shopping bag full of day-old bread donated by a local baker. "She told me she used to live by the sea," the driver explained to me once. "She don't remember much else about her life . . . not her children, not her husband." Carefully the driver tore each bread slice into four squares the way the woman requested. "Now she can't hardly see these birds. But she hears them and she smells the sea. Calls this taking her medicine."

Strong medicine, the healing salt and mineral sea this old woman took into her body and soul twice a week. She lived in the nursing home at the top of our hill, and every time I saw the familiar ambulance go by I prayed it was not for Our Lady of the Gulls.

This fall, when wild hurricanes shook the South and drought seized the Northwest, the old woman stopped coming to our beach. I waited for her all autumn, but the green taxi with its delighted passenger never came again. I took to adding two weekly afternoon feedings to my own morning schedule. These beach meetings are more mournful, in memory of the old woman who didn't remember her name, whose name I never knew, who remembered only the gulls.

Not long afterward my landlady called with the dreaded refrain: "House sold, must move on." I walked down to the beach and opened my arms to the gulls. With each bread slice I said a prayer that Puget Sound would keep me near her. One afternoon I got the sudden notion to drive down the sound. There I found a cozy white cottage for rent, a little beach house that belongs to an old man who's lived on this promontory since the 1940s. A stroke had sent him to a nursing home, and the rent from his cottage will pay for his care.

Before I moved one stick of furniture into the house, I stood on the beach and fed the gulls in thanksgiving. They floated above my head; I felt surrounded by little angels. Then I realized that these were the very same gulls from two miles down the beach near my old home—there was that bit of fishline wrapped around a familiar webbed foot, that wounded wing, and the distinct markings of a young gray gull, one of my favorite high fliers.

Who knows whether the old man was right? The seagulls may have memorized my face and followed me—but I had also, quite without realizing it, memorized them. And I knew then that I was no newcomer here, not a nomad blown by changeable autumn winds. It is not to any house, but to this beach I have bonded. I belong alongside this rocky inlet with its salt tides, its pine-tiered, green islands, its gulls who remember us even when we've forgotten ourselves.

Michael McPherson

Poems

from *Manoa*

Maalaea Bay

These waves have kept their same shape
for who knows how long, rising over
shallow reef and heaving white crests
toward blue recesses of the inner bay.
There are little differences now,
like this backwash off the seawall
guarding a string of condominiums
sprung from parched red dust ashore.
The kiawes were cut back to border
windblown acres of green sugar cane.
Small boats motor out, bound for deep
fishing grounds beyond Kahoolawe.
Across from the harbor the old store
still sells its famous hot dogs,
but the quiet in this evening sky
whispers of a coming dark, expansion
and rock groins to block new waves
from reaching the gentle arc of reef.
This bay is a haven for endangered

green sea turtles, their leathery
heads bobbing along inshore currents,
their flippers extended like wings.
A surfer watches blue waves advance
from the breakwall, feels the first
lift him as it passes under his board,
remembers when he first paddled out
into this bay thirty years before.
He pushes into a wave and feels wind
sear his face as he leans to keep
from falling, holding his edge high
in the wave as he rides to calm water.
His legs feel like taut springs again,
they absorb the quick chatter of offshore
wind dimples under his speeding board.
He guides a line sliding to the blue bay,
climbing in steep pockets of water,
the white crest closing on his shoulder
as he rides beyond aging, past changes
indelibly etched and yet to come,
hurtling toward a place without time.

Water

It springs miraculous from this cliff,
filters clear passing high black rock
and cascades into green waving acres of cane,
pooling where invisible chemical residue
leaches undetected from moist red clay,
and mingling in torrents and trickling streams
it follows this land never to reach the sea,
carried through pipes and flumes and ditches
toward hotels and golf courses of southern shores
and underground into mill drains of the central plain,
into showerheads and faucets and freezers,
into skin, hair, eyes and bones,
chains of causation too remote to trace
altering silent time while life dreams,
faces lifted into warm blustery summer rain.

Pat Matsueda

Poems

from *Manoa*

Samurai

ICHI

Over time your heart
gets you nowhere
bursting like a severed vein
as if you cut yourself
with your own blade

NI

Travelling through
the humid forest
you hallucinate:
your mind shimmers in the air
like a medusa;
the mottled ground breathes
like a leopard
But you know
these are illusions

SAN

The wind pounds lightly
upon the water
The smell from a
warm stand of trees
enfolds you

No matter where you are
your profile is that
of a stranger

SHI

You will cleanse your brow

Gulls are screeching
in the salt sprays
as you walk down a path
of white sand
You have come
to surrender at the temple
of red claws, gold teeth
and black wings

Wave of Cereus

The black stone wall around the school
climbs the hills like an old tortoise,
its back mottled with sunlight and shadow
falling like butterflies through the monkey pods,
the shower trees.
By day it's an ugly barricade
smelling of generations of leaves and children,
overgrown with cactus planted half a century before.
But on certain nights of the year
        the cacti bloom,
and a wave of flowers breaks
over the wall.
        Moonlight falling on the petals turns to wine,
and unknowing passersby wonder what light
low and cool
draws such a flame
out of the wall.

Two friends stop to rest against the cool stone,
speaking gingerly of her lover, his friend.
For the first time they disclose
the few incidents of violence,
the long suffering.
Then wordlessly he takes her hand
and unfolds the slender fingers against the wall.
Words of sympathy, her surprise
displace the dark and quiet.

        The cereus glows like a hundred torches
along the wall:
the large spiked petals,
the deep white hearts.

David Rains Wallace

The Bones from Gracias

from *ZYZZYVA*

The Honduran National University was a contrast with the colonial warren of downtown Tegucigalpa. It stood on a plain a few miles out, a cluster of stone high-rises with a ceremonial air, like the pre-Columbian sites outside Mexican cities. The biology building was at the cluster's edge, where the plain dropped into ravines. The *Museo de Fauna* was shut up when I got there, but an attractive young woman soon appeared, also wanting to get in. Somehow this conjured up the *dueño,* a friendly young man who opened the steel door.

I found so much more than I'd expected inside the museum (I'd had no idea what to expect, I'd simply heard there was a biology museum at the university) that I felt a little numbed, a little reluctant at the prospect of edification. I'd thought there were very few collections of vertebrate fossils from Central America, and none to speak of from Honduras. The museum was tiny, an ordinary-sized lab room, but glass cabinets right inside the door were crammed with big blackish and yellowish fossils. There were llama and horse bones from the Miocene, toxodon and ground-sloth bones from the Pleistocene, honey-colored slabs of petrified wood. When I asked the dueño about them, he told me most of them had been dug up a few miles outside the town of Gracias in western Honduras. An expedition from the University of Chicago had gone there in the 1930s, and had found not only bones of llamas and horses, but of mastodons, dogs, and rhinos.

Gracias already interested me. It looked remote on the map, buried in the subcontinent's mountain spine below Honduras's highest peak, Celaque—a good place to look for evolutionary relics like the fir and yew trees said to grow on Central American mountaintops. The dueño didn't know the exact location of the Gracias fossil beds, but I thought somebody there might tell me. When I got back from the museum, I asked a couple of Peace Corps volunteers about it. Neither had been to Gracias, although one, a geologist, had heard of fossils there. He was assigned to explore Honduras's still-little-known geology, and asked me to bring back a rock from Celaque. He'd heard it was volcanic, but wasn't sure.

No bus ran all the way to Gracias, so I took one to La Esperanza in the mountains south of it. The bus left early, and when I got to the station in the low-rent Comayaguela District, it was still dark. An elderly man was already waiting. He said he was an opal miner in a town near Gracias, and carefully unwrapped some small, dark rocks suffused with red and green flecks so iridescent they seemed unnatural. He knew nothing about fossils near Gracias.

We spent the morning heading north on the Pan American Highway, over rolling pine plateaus and past the sprawling U.S. Army base at Comayagua. At noon, the bus turned off the pavement and followed a rugged dirt road west over a series of valleys and ridges that seemed more antique the farther we went. We passed no conveyances except oxcarts and the occasional truck. Pines, oaks, and bright green *Liquidambar* trees covered the ridges. As we made one hairpin turn, a flock of band-tailed pigeons flew past, an ordinary sight in California. Remnants of tropical dry deciduous forest dotted the valley's fields and pastures—spreading, dark green guanacaste trees, and *Tabebuias* and poro-poros with orange and yellow flowers.

The last valley of the day was higher than the others, with oaks and swampy meadows instead of dry forest. La Esperanza was a few cobbled streets, a market that was breaking up as the bus pulled in, and a cordoned-off garrison beside a huge blooming jacaranda in the square. I stayed the night in a *pensión* that had a color television in the dining room, but that served for breakfast, lunch, and dinner the same *comida* of eggs, beans, and tortillas John Lloyd Stephens had described eating three times a day during his search for Mayan relics in the 1830s. I walked outside town at sunset. Pine and oak woodland surrounded a reservoir and public baths built by a general in 1932. Smilax, ragwort, wintergreen, and maidenhair fern grew on the ground as they would have in southern Ohio, but big floppy *Monstera* vines covered flowering trees by a stream. Walking back through town, I heard monastic chanting from a church, so loud and accomplished that I wondered if they were playing a tape cassette.

The next morning was cloudy and chilly. Nobody knew of a bus to Gracias, so I walked west out of town and stood in a dusty wind, hitch-hiking. A man in a pickup full of corn sacks gave me a ride, first up a steep, heavily wooded ridge, then down a hair-raising succession of turns to a river where the bridge was out and we had to ford. On one steep slope, we passed a La Esperanza–bound minibus so packed with passengers that it reminded me of a toy bus I'd had as a boy with passengers painted on its windows. A couple in back was locked in a Hollywood smooch, as though driven to it by the pressure of humanity. The truckdriver dropped me in a strange little savanna valley overhung with white bluffs eroded from volcanic ash. Red orchids and orange sunflowers grew in the dry *Andropogon* grass.

Another ride brought me to San Juan, a windswept straggle of cinder-block houses farther down the savanna valley. I drank a Coke in a *pulpería* where two teenage travelling salesmen were pushing cosmetics ("from Paris") and patent medicines to some women. A dog emerged from the kitchen with a stack of cold tortillas and sat down gravely in the street to eat them, then barked sternly at something and charged off. Nobody knew about a bus, so I started walking through more pine woods and pasture. When I stopped to rest, a man came along and we talked a while. I asked him about fossils, and he thought I meant *fusiles*—firearms. I hastened to clarify, and he seemed impressed at the idea of ten-million-year-old bones in the vicinity, but didn't know of any.

A rickety bus finally came along, and I crammed myself in the last available space, beside the driver and facing the other passengers, mostly campesinos in cowboy hats. A blond woman nursed a baby under my nose. The cowboy hats bounced up and down in unison as the bus banged over rocks, and the bored driver swung the wheels past the sheer drops from which only a windshield cracked in three places separated me. The road descended through a series of small valleys where dry forest plants again appeared. A very large mountain loomed to the west—a rambling, blocky spine crowned with silhouetted trees, evidently very tall trees. Two dark blue birds arrowed across the road. They were Steller's jays, another common California sight, but the first I'd seen in Central America.

Gracias is one of the oldest colonial towns in the Americas, temporarily the capital of Central America in 1544, but it didn't seem particularly antique, typical rows of cobbled streets with shadowy shops and dwellings behind worn wooden doors. It was certainly no tourist town. Except for a fatigued Australian on a park bench, I was the only one in evidence. The park was a nationalist antique instead of a colonial one, with dusty but dignified old trees, a bandstand, and a polychrome, life-size, cigar-store Indian statue of Lempira, who led a revolt of the Lenca peoples against the conquistadores in 1537.

I got a room and started asking around about fossils. The local forest ranger knew of petrified wood in the hills, and a Peace Corps volunteer assigned to help develop a national park on Celaque showed me a piece a local schoolteacher had given him. It was black and translucent yellow. I wondered if the yellow was amber—petrified resin. The volunteer didn't know, and suggested I ask the teacher, Don Antonio, who taught in the nearby community of El Pinal.

Nobody knew anything about the 1937 University of Chicago expedition. I seemed to have exhausted the available information sources, so I decided to walk to El Pinal in the hope I might stumble on a fossil site or learn something from Don Antonio. The road ascended a plateau covered with live oaks, then dropped into broken country studded with pines and deep gulches. I didn't see any fossils, and the day rapidly grew so hot that the road blistered my feet. I'd caught a cold in La Esperanza, and I felt so bad I climbed into a stream bottom and spent the afternoon there.

Silvery livebearers (the tropical fish group that includes mollies and guppies) disported in a sandy pool, and a shy cichlid darted among black tadpoles. A bird flew down to drink—an acorn woodpecker, another California commonplace. I realized I'd been hearing them calling all morning. Three brilliant orange orioles chuckled and squawked, and cicadas said "feedeedeefeedeedee, feeeeedeeeeeee-eeeeeeeeeeeeee" in the higuerons and nancites.

The traveling sun kept shining through the treetops, and I moved downstream to escape it. Invisible things plopped into the water, and a distant buzzing roar grew to frightening intensity as it passed over—an Africanized bee swarm, a big one. (Africanized bees are the "killer bees" that U.S. authorities are trying to keep south of the Rio Grande.) I heard another plop, and a baseball-sized brown head protruded from the creek. It was a marine toad, so-called for reasons unclear to me.

I came to a place where the creekbed dropped away in a cliff that msut have been an impressive waterfall in the rainy season. A pile of leaves had accumulated in a rocky basin, and I saw stirrings in it. I pulled a few leaves aside cautiously, and something sinuous and yellow flashed out of sight. I dug further, but instead of the sinuous thing, I found an ordinary-looking brown-and-green frog at the bottom. It was comatose, as though sleeping through the heat. I piled the leaves back. A flock of green parakeets flailed overhead, squawking with abandon.

That night I visited Don Antonio's house in Gracias. On an unlit back street, the house seemed silent and dark, but a woman answered my knock and led me into a dim, cluttered study. Don Antonio came in, a curly-haired, thickset man in his forties, quiet and amiable. He said he knew nothing about the 1937 expedition, or where his fossils came from. He'd bought them from the people who found them. Then he brought out an intricately cusped mastodon molar that barely fit into my hand, although a third of it was broken off, and a piece of leg bone with the honeycomb pattern of marrow. He said he had petrified wood of other semi-precious stones as well as amber, but he didn't show it to me. Instead he brought out sleek stone hatchets and a crude limestone statue that he said were made by unknown people, people who came before the Lencas or the Mayas.

Don Antonio thought his molar and leg bone were from the dinosaur age. When I said they were much more recent mammal bones, he asked me if I believed "Darwin's theory of evolution." I equivocated, talking about the distinction between the overall concept of evolution, as evidenced by fossils, and Darwin's theory of natural selection. When I mentioned that Darwin had based natural selection partly on the way organisms can be changed by artificial selective breeding, Don Antonio said: "You mean crossing animals?" I said yes. He said he'd heard of a cat that was crossed with a rabbit recently. I expressed doubt, and he said it had been in a newspaper. When I said you can't believe everything in newspapers, Don Antonio laughed and said I was like Doubting Thomas.

The next day I went to Celaque, leaving before dawn to walk the several miles to the mountain's foot. The way ran gradually uphill through scrubby dry forest, then pines. About halfway, a raven lit in a pine by the road, another Central American first. It looked smaller than North American ravens, but its croak when another appeared was the same. They flew off northward together.

A steep ravine opened at the foot of the mountain, and the forest in it looked and smelled North American, so that the little patches of plantain and cassava that someone had planted seemed incongruous. Hornbeams and madrones grew among pines and oaks. A little *Sceloporus* lizard, like the fence lizards everywhere in California, did "push-up" threat-displays at me, flashing a blue belly. The trail crossed a boulder-strewn cascade and swung upward through columnar *Liquidambar* trunks among which another Steller's jay procession glided. A pair of woodpeckers beat on a pine, and a Wilson's warbler sang. The cascade looked like a trout stream, but contained only small, whitish crabs.

After a half hour of steep switchbacks, the forest strangely began looking more tropical than it had lower down. There the oaks and pines had been bare of epiphytes, up here bromeliads and *Monsteras* covered branches. Moist coves were full of tree ferns and of the biggest begonias I'd ever seen, with leaves eight to ten inches across and rose-sized pink flowers. These were cloud forest plants: evidently there was increased precipitation at this elevation.

The trail entered an abandoned clearing with two tumbledown log cabins. A small reddish viper slipped unhurriedly into the brush, in which grew deciduous saplings that looked familiar. I realized they were alders, the trees that grow in Pacific Northwest clearcuts. The clearing was full of alders, but the forest above it was even more tropical, with massive trees so festooned in vines and epiphytes I couldn't identify them. Leathery-leaved *Clusias,* small palms, and red-and-yellow flowered bromeliads grew on branches and the ground. Pines grew here too, but different species than lower down (the ranger had told me there were six species on Celaque). Some had five-foot-diameter trunks.

The trail grew increasingly steep and faint. I was close enough to the mountain's spine to see the silhouetted trees I'd glimpsed from the rickety bus in detail now, weather-beaten conifers with ragged branches flung out as though in loneliness at their isolation from the North American forests they'd evolved in. Conifers are very conservative. Alders and oaks migrated south into South America after the Isthmus of Panama opened about five million years ago, but the pines and firs never got further south than Nicaragua.

The trail entered another vegetation zone where conifers replaced broadleaf trees. Spiky yuccas grew on the ground instead of succulent bromeliads. Here the trail was even steeper and fainter, and it was getting late. Mean dogs seemed a fixture on the road from Gracias, and I didn't want to meet them again after dark. I sat and looked at the valley for a while. White buttes and river terraces rose from the dry forest past Gracias's toy towers like bones in a thicket. Then I started down. When I got back to town, the streets were eerily empty, although it was only around 8 P.M. Walking past the church, I heard a great echoing of song from its closed doors. Everybody was at evening mass.

I had to leave next day, and as I rode down the valley to Santa Rosa de Copán, where the paved road begins, I caught glimpses of the white bluffs I'd seen from Celaque. In places, the river had carved what might have been giant versions of Don Antonio's molar and femur in the porous volcanic stone. Back in Tegucigalpa, I gave the rocks I'd picked up on Celaque to the geologist. They were volcanic as he'd expected, but he was surprised that they were rhyolitic instead of basaltic. Rhyolitic stone is associated with volcanoes that explode, which seemed to go along with the white ash deposits everywhere around Gracias. The geologist wasn't surprised at my failure to find fossils. He'd just spent two months in the Mosquitia rain forest, including areas so unpeopled that the brocket deer and great currasows had no fear of him and his Tawaka guides. The only fossil he'd found had been a small ammonite (a shelled relative of the octopus, extinct since the dinosaur age). He showed it to me, a whorled nubbin in a limestone slab.

I learned no more about the Gracias fossils in Honduras. At the Instituto de Arqueología e Historia, they knew of only one paleontologist, and he was only reachable through a bank in San Pedro Sula. But after I returned to the U.S., I found a paper on the 1937 expedition in the 1941 bulletin of the Geological Society of America. The expedition had spent two months digging in the winter of 1937–38, and had found most of the bones in "one small area of badlands" called Rancho Lobo, three miles north of Gracias. Perhaps it was near the bony-looking bluffs I'd glimpsed.

The expedition must have been worthy of Indiana Jones, but I didn't get any sense of that from the article, which concentrated on geological technicalities. I couldn't find any more about the expedition on the University of California library computer. Most of the participants seemed to have become inactive after the early forties, perhaps killed in the War. Their discovery seemed to have fallen through a paleontological crack.

Yet the Gracias fossils were highly significant, because they included no animals of South American origin. The mastodons, rhinos, llamas, dogs, and several species of small, toed horses were largely the same as those that inhabited North American prairies in the same geological epoch, the Miocene. This strongly suggested that the Isthmus of Panama hadn't risen above the sea yet, and that Central America hadn't yet become a land bridge for organisms migrating between the continents.

The Gracias animals' world wasn't like the North American prairies, however. Plant fossils found with the animal bones were tropical, including palms, acacia-like trees, and two tree genera still common in South and Central American rain forest. The Geological Society bulletin article speculated that the mastodons and dogs had inhabited a swampy alluvial plain of savanna and gallery forest in the shadow of volcanoes of which Celaque is the remnant. It sounded more like Africa than South America.

The Gracias fossils were a glimpse of something I've wondered about. For tens of millions of years before the Isthmus of Panama linked North and South America, the southern part of North America, from present-day Mexico to Nicaragua, had a tropical climate. Yet most of the organisms characteristic of New World tropics today—parrots, monkeys, anteaters, sloths, agoutis—come from South America, and didn't reach Central America until the land bridge formed.

What lived and evolved in those North American tropics during the sixty or so million years between the dionsaurs' extinction and the Panamanian isthmus? A tropics without parrots and monkeys seems strange, but there's no evidence they lived in Honduras before the land bridge. Were there North American counterparts of parrots and monkeys that became extinct after South American parrots and monkeys moved in? Parrot and monkey bones are too frail to fossilize well, so we may never know. The Gracias fossils are among the only known relics of one of evolution's most thoroughly lost worlds.

Sherry Simpson

Where Bears Walk

First publication

LaVern Beier is not afraid of bears. The Alaska Department of Fish and Game calls him a technician for his proficiency in finding, trapping, and tranquilizing mountain goats, wolves, wolverines, and all manner of creatures that do not wish to be found, including the drugged brown bear slumped on the patch of stale snow before us. Vern is not just a technician, though. Something in Vern Beier makes me imagine he is part bear himself, the offspring of one of those mythic matings between bear and woman that never led to any good for the bear. (As for the woman, who can say?) Perhaps it is Vern's wiry hair, the shagginess of his black beard, the economy and purpose in his stocky frame that make me think such things. More likely it is the steady brown eyes that see more than he ever says. But I detect the resemblance also in the rough but loving way he runs his hands through the thin spring pelt of this half-conscious bear, as if he knows her. Pretty bony, is all he says. Must have been a hard winter.

I am not looking at the bear's coffee-colored fur. I am looking at her teeth. My, what big teeth she has. Slobber webs canines the shade of scrimshaw and the size of a man's thumb. This bear galloped for more than ten minutes from the pursuing helicopter, her legs pistoning her over ridges and up slopes, driving her across the alpine reaches of Admiralty Island. She did not hide; she ran. Even after Vern leaned through the copter's open door and sighted his rifle on her bounding rump, darting her twice with a tranquilizer potent enough to down an elephant, she ran and ran until the drug slammed into her and she did not get up. I make a promise to myself when I see that. I promise never again to fool myself into thinking a human can run from a bear.

Because I am in no danger at the moment, my sympathies lie entirely with the bear, though as a newspaper reporter writing an article about bear research, my job is to take notes, not to sympathize with anybody or anything. I understand the scientific rationale that volunteered this bear to be chased, prodded, poked, tagged, plucked, measured, and collared with a radio transmitter that by a steady beep will describe her movements but never convey the true power of her motion. I have no trouble reconciling a personal fear of bears with a distant appreciation of them. But I don't tell anybody the real reason I asked for this story: so I can touch with my own hands what frightens me most.

Vern and his partner, wildlife biologist Kim Titus, are here on this early July evening because they need data. It is not enough to know that a silver mine on Admiralty Island, or too much clear-cut logging on neighboring Chichagof Island, harms bears. You must say it in a tangled dialect of science and bureaucracy, the way Kim says it in his cramped office at the Department of Fish and Game: "In theory the model will predict the capability of the habitat to support some given population of brown bears, or some reduced population of bears, given certain developmental impacts." Out here under the naked sky, in the world of fish and game, he says it this way: "We're documenting the demise of the bears."

I have never been this close to a living bear. Her eyes flicker under half-closed lids. Does she see me? Does she dream of being scented out by strange and roaring creatures? Does her heart lunge in her chest? With each shuddering breath, she groans deeply, a sound laced with menace to my ear. "Is she snoring or growling?" I ask Vern, hoping my voice reveals nothing of the dizzy way blood spins through me. "Probably both," he says without concern. Three times he has killed a charging bear in self-defense. He never sets his short-handled rifle with the custom walnut stock out of reach. He is not afraid of bears, but he is not stupid.

Neither is Kim Titus. He is more than a number-cruncher muttering incantations of science and reason, though that is what his job requires of him. Fresh to Alaska from Maryland, he is a falconer and has spent several summers studying merlins in Denali National Park. He knows something of wild animals. But he is new to this particular project, and his lanky boyishness and his eagerness only reinforce the quiet authority Vern wields here on this mountaintop. Kim holds the degree, but Vern holds practical knowledge.

Vern rearranges the bear, stretching out her legs and tilting her head so she can breathe more easily. He estimates her age at about six years old, a teenager in bear years, and her weight at about 280 pounds. "They come a lot bigger than this," he remarks. "They come a lot smaller than this. But she's big enough to kill you." Perhaps by the way I circle the sedated bear, leaning close, but not too close, he senses my nervous thrill. "Ever held a bear's leg before?" he asks. I'm not sure if he's provoking me or soothing me. He moves to her haunches and shifts a hind leg into my hands. I struggle to heft it as he draws blood from the tender groin. Each dark hair is ticked with white; skin shines palely through the sparse fur.

"Feel how warm her paws are," Vern says, laying the blood-filled syringe in the snow. I press my palm against the leathery pad. The curving ebony claws stretch longer than my little finger. Heat radiates into my skin. When I was eight, one of the fathers in our neighborhood killed a bear and stripped away its hide. His son showed me a naked bear paw that looked like a human hand with its bluish veins and knobby fingers. No wonder so many people regard the bear as a savage relation. The Inuit thought of bears as ancestors. The Lapps called the bear "old man with the fur garment." The Finns named him "golden friend." A Tlingit Indian who encountered a brown bear always spoke to it as if it were a person, addressing it in kinship terms. If a bear killed a Tlingit, the clan followed the social law of a life for a life; the Tlingit's family sent a hunting party to kill one of the bear's family.

Under my hands, this bear is a furnace, burning with life. Vern watches me, and when he sees the look on my face, he smiles a little.

When the helicopter lifts itself from the plain—*maybe no human has ever set foot here before,* I'm thinking—the bear lifts her groggy head for a moment and peers after us. She looks clownish with a yellow and a white tag punched into each ear and a white leather radio collar circling her neck. We have stolen something from her.

In the helicopter, we soar around peaks still dappled with snow, dip into valleys, coast over alpine meadows. The evening sun drifts toward the horizon, where soon it will snag on the Chilkat Mountains. The slanting rays illuminate tufts of grass, beds of heather, purple lupine drooping with tight blooms. Beyond Admiralty Island, golden light spills across the rumpled waters of Chatham Strait. There is something not quite real, something dreamlike, in the way we float through this stained-glass light.

We look for bears. Already this spring they have marched down to the tidelands to break their winter's fast with fresh sedges, savory horsetails, the stems of skunk cabbage still burrowed into wet, sucking earth. Once the alpine snowpack retreated, the bears trekked back to the mountain slopes to feast on another generation of greens. They mate here, in the open meadows. Just last week, as Vern and Kim collared a bear on Chichagof, a boar and sow delirious with lust accidently raced over a ridge directly at the men. In the confusion, as the men scrambled for their guns and the bears realized their mistake, no one was sure who yelled "Shit!" and who yelled "Shoot!" In the final moments, before a reckoning was required, the bears veered away, and everybody was happy.

Come midsummer, the bears of Admiralty will journey yet again to the coast to gorge on spawning salmon throwing themselves up streams. For dessert, the bears nibble blueberries growing in avalanche chutes, and then they return upcountry to den. A few bears never leave these elevations; they forego the meaty salmon and don't know what they're missing.

Admiralty Island is the Manhattan of bears. An average of one brown bear occupies each of the island's 1,700 square miles. In interior Alaska, where people call brown bears "grizzlies," though they are all of the same tribe, you will find an average of but a single bear in every 15 square miles or so. There are more bears on this island than in the entire continental United States. The Tlingit Indians call Admiralty by the name "Kootznoowoo," which means "Fortress of the Bears."

But Admiralty is not a haven, just a holdout. Trophy hunting, clear-cut logging, and the constant press of civilization threaten bears even here. You can kill bears quickly, by shooting them, or slowly, by moving in with them. When the American West was bored through by railroads and pocked with towns, it took just fifty years to eliminate nearly all grizzly bears in those parts. Today, people fight with each other in places like Idaho over whether bears should or should not be reintroduced to their former haunts, but I see little point in planting bears where they are not wanted. People will insist on seeing bears always as prey or predator. Life for a bear is more complex than that.

Flying high, swooping low, we spot several bears rummaging around the valleys and crowns of Mansfield Peninsula at the northern crook of Admiralty Island. Some escape with little more than a fright, for Kim and Vern seek females, especially sows with cubs. They want to know if Greens Creek Silver Mine pushes bear families into new ranges, rather like city families abandoning the neighborhood to a freeway. If the bears do strike out for more peaceful territory, who will they elbow out of the way? Or will they simply birth fewer young?

Near the head of Greens Creek Valley, the helicopter chases a three-year-old recently booted out on his own by his momma. The bear scrabbles up a slope and skids down the other side. He rams into a wall of ice and snow and caroms off, regaining his feet to race away again. I suck in my breath, and Kim, noticing, says, "They're tough animals." The bear tears up a slope, and the pilot swings the copter around a rocky spur and along the ridge to meet the bear, who skids to a stop almost comically and reels around. Vern has already targeted it; he shoots and says calmly, "Dart's in." A minute later the bear sits down, seemingly perplexed, and falls over into the scree.

After we land, Vern prods the bear with his rifle barrel to make sure it's out. "Beautiful coat," Kim says, admiring the golden fur. The researchers quickly complete their routine, though they decide not to collar this young male. By now, Vern has tagged nearly one hundred brown bears on Southeast's islands, so he is efficient and smooth at this work. Kim uses a wicked-looking punch to tattoo a number into its black lip, and he smears the marks with indelible, fluorescent green dye. It is a curious sort of ritual, echoing the way Tlingit hunters marked bear skins with red ochre. If a modern hunter kills this blonde bear in Gambier Bay, or at Oliver Inlet, or along the shores of Barlow Cove, the Department of Fish and Game will note the bear's fate in its big book of numbers.

It does not really bother Vern and Kim to think a hunter may kill the bears they mark. Theoretically, hunting regulations can always be changed to protect bear populations, although hunters and biologists will argue for hours about how to define a healthy bear population. One reason the researchers are studying bears on Admiralty and Chichagof is because the number of bears killed in this "game management unit" has doubled in the past thirty years to a mean of nearly one hundred bears per year. But much has changed since 1950, when *Alaska* magazine reported that a Juneau federal judge had recently returned from a hunt with the cream-colored pelt of his 129th bear.

What angers the biologists most is clear-cut logging, especially in places like northeast Chichagof Island, where large tracts of old-growth timber are systematically shaved from Tongass National Forest and private lands for Southeast Alaska's two pulp companies. By 1989, almost 17,000 acres had been logged—nearly 9 percent of land on the island's northeast peninsula. Bears rely on all kinds of terrain in their wandering lives, but a clear-cut is not one of them. The problem is not only that logging squeezes bears into shrinking habitats. Logging roads lead hunters easily into the dense forests; garbage dumps lure bears into villages and logging camps where they are sometimes shot for their bad habits.

Officially, Admiralty is considered a national wilderness area, as if words were ever enough to create such a thing. But even here, bear hunting is legal on most of the island, Native corporations log their lands as any other business would, and Greens Creek Mine has claimed a valley, a salmon stream, and a watershed. "The frontier is ending," Kim says. And Vern adds, more bitterly than I've ever heard him, "It stopped when they built the pipeline. We're not making brown bear habitat anymore. I don't know of any place where we're making it."

We descend into a wide bowl gemmed by a lake of melted snow. Six blacktailed deer, dainty as fairies, graze in line along the ridge. Two bears shamble through this basin, one breaking into a half-hearted trot around the lake when it hears the helicopter whining. Vern darts the other bear, the larger of the two, thinking it a female. When it shows no sign of slowing, Vern aims through the open helicopter door and shoots it again with a particularly effective drug called M99. One drop will kill a human, but it takes several cc's to down a bear.

With the tufted darts dangling from its hindquarters, the bear starts up a bluff knitted with twisted spruce and blueberry bushes. "All I can say is, you guys are going to have fun in here," the pilot says over the intercom. "Yeah, it'll be great," Kim replies, peering out the window. "She can roll a long way in here." He's worried that the bear will pass out and fall before it reaches the top. The helicopter rises about twenty feet from the bluff as the bear steadily climbs, its passage revealed only by trembling brush. Suddenly the animal lunges from an opening below the helicopter and swipes at the skids, so close that the pilot jerks the craft away to avoid the bear's reach. "Did you see that!" Kim exclaims, and we all look at each other, laughing nervously. But really, it seems only slightly amusing to reflect that if rescuers were to find our crumpled helicopter at the bluff's foot, they would never know a bear had clawed it from the sky.

The bear does indeed fall senseless ten feet below the clifftop, but the brush holds it fast. The pilot lands the copter on the plateau so Kim and Vern can hoist rifles and a cargo net over their shoulders and scramble down to the animal. The pilot maneuvers a hook over the net and hauls the limp bear out. A scale on the net weighs the animal at 480 pounds.

It turns out to be a male, but Kim and Vern work him over anyway. Kim straddles the boar with his long legs, then lies with his face buried in fur as he stretches a measuring tape around its girth and I resist making bear-hug jokes. A hunter sizing up the pelt would call this an eight-foot bear. Vern estimates it at about thirteen years old. A brown bear can live twenty years or more in the wild, if it avoids disease, starvation, bigger bears, men with guns, and unexpected tumbles down cliffs.

Vern asks me to hold the bear's head while he uses pliers to yank a small tooth that will reveal the bear's age as surely as my driver's license reports mine. I grasp the rounded ears and pull, straining to lift the massive skull and to ignore the half-open, reddened eyes. The long snout is scarred, gnarly with ridges and bumps. "Love bites," Vern calls them. You hear that bears smell terrible—people who have survived maulings remark on the awful stench—but this early in the season, these bears smell like clean dogs.

When Vern finishes, I lower the bear's head and then sit close, stroking the muzzle, admiring the nearness and smallness of my hand next to the range of yellowed teeth.

It is these teeth I dream about, when I dream about bears. Teeth, and blood. Some part of me connects the dreams to the dark passage from childhood to adulthood, through rites of blood and sex and love and loss, beyond that youthful time when we're attracted to dying because we don't believe in death. When I was a teenager, when my girlfriends and I camped in the forest, there always came a time of night when we told bear stories to scare ourselves, and then we told sex stories to scare ourselves. I was always the first to hear the bear's hoarse breath, to smell the rank presence, to imagine what waited in the dark. I was the one who worried that bears could smell us bleeding as only women bleed. I was the one who lay awake all night trembling, trying not to breathe, waiting to be rended, waiting to surrender.

I pass my hand over the bear's head, across thick, coarse hair. I can't help myself; I ask if a sedated bear has ever suddenly come to life. Vern tells about the time a biologist was nearly unmanned when a bear abruptly swung its head around and snapped. Everybody laughs, even me.

I smooth the black pelt, then ruffle it again. I'm taking liberties I haven't earned. I know that. Near the shoulder rests a tiny feather, creamy with tan stripes—from a grouse, I suppose. I lift it with my little finger and poke it into the coin pocket of my jeans. Tlingit hunters in Sitka once covered the heads of bear skins with eagle down to honor the bears' spirits. I don't know what to give, so I take.

As Vern and Kim finish collaring the boar, they notice a trio of bears rambling across a slope on the opposite curve of the basin. Through binoculars Vern sees a sow trailed by two tiny cubs—"cubs of the year," they're called. This is just the sort of family the researchers covet most for their mine study. Vern decides not to administer the antidote that would bring the drugged boar to its feet in minutes. The male is probably loitering in the basin with the darkest of intentions. Male bears are cannibalistic and will eat cubs, a fine reason for mothers to be so fierce. We leave the boar slumbering on the tundra and climb into the helicopter to hop across the valley.

As the copter begins tracking the sow, the cubs struggle to keep up, tumbling and falling, tripping over themselves. The mother slows to wait for them, then bursts into a gallop again. The cubs churn their short legs as fast as they can, but not fast enough. I clench my teeth together when I see the way they glance blindly at the sky, not sure what they're running from. We circle, looping, twisting, hovering overhead. The bears slide down a gully. Vern hangs out the door, hair blowing wildly, takes aim, darts the mother in the rump. In a few minutes, as she begins mounting a rocky chute, she sags and then falls, hind legs splayed behind her.

The helicopter lands behind a ridge, and we creep over to the bears, whispering so we don't frighten the young. The cubs cling to their mother and watch our approach; only as we draw close do they retreat, turning back to look at us every few steps. They bawl in a curious, wrenching croak. A hundred feet away they clamber onto a rocky shelf and peer over the edge at us, and I try not to stare too hard back at them.

The men work quickly so the cubs do not wander off. Vern has a hard time finding a blood vein on the inside of the sow's hind leg, so when he does feel it, he asks me to mark the pulse with my finger while he readies the needle. Her blood surges in hesitant throbs against my skin. I think of the bear in her winter den, this faint beat offering comfort to the cubs while they, still barely formed, burrowed against her fur. Aristotle believed the mother bear licked her cubs into being, shaped them for the world.

The clean air chills. It's nearly 10 p.m., and the sun fades in a painterly way, coloring the sky in shades of salmon. The nearness of the honey-colored bear, the occasional squall of her cubs, the panorama that draws my eye beyond this green basin, across the straits—I try to saturate my memory with these details. A feeling of beauty and loss pierces me as I struggle to tell myself something important, something lasting about this night, about how I have glimpsed the way bears live here, high above the world, and yet not nearly far enough away from roads, chainsaws, guns, helicopters. Here I stand, after all, wearing a silver ring, and trying to think of the right words to scribble in my paper notebook. If this mountaintop is wilderness, then it is wilderness that rubs so close to civilization that I can feel it fraying beneath my feet.

It is one of the oldest stories in the world, how the woman married the bear, and gave him half-human, half-bear young. In the Haida version, her brothers killed her bear lover, of course, but the offspring lived to teach the people, to help them hunt, before returning to the bear world. It's been said that we kill what we both revere and dread. That is what myths do, turn something greater than ourselves into something human. I'm doing it right now.

It's a hard thing to know, that our weakness is that we hate what is stronger than us. And yet, without bears roaming through forests, climbing down from mountains, frightening us, what will we respect on this earth? What is left to remind us that while we stand in a world shadowed by myth, wilderness, death, we cannot master it, nor can we deny it?

When Vern finishes collaring the bear, he injects her with an antidote so she will rouse quickly and gather her cubs. He stands for a moment, looking down at the sow. She should be stirring, but she's not. Kim gestures to me, and we pick our way back to the helicopter. I look back just once, to fix the still bear and those cubs in my mind. A few minutes later, Vern climbs into his seat. He doesn't say anything. I want to ask him about the bear, but I'm afraid to know. Sometimes, not often, but sometimes, things go wrong. Sometimes the drugs kill them, or hypothermia, or other bears. I'm afraid to know what could happen to the sow and her cubs. This is my weakness, that I'm afraid to know.

Sky translates itself into night as we fly homeward, across the peaks. We land on a mountain slope to recover the passenger door removed earlier so Vern could lean into the wind and track bears. Kim leads me to a nearby ridge and pauses at the edge of a trail. After a moment, I see what he wants me to see. Deep into the tundra, hollows dimple the path where, for centuries, bears have placed their feet in the same spot with every step. They wear their passage into the earth as they come down from the mountains and then return, season after season. I realize that there's another way to see bears—that a bear has nothing to do with us at all, that it lives wholly for itself and its kind, without any obligation to teach us a thing. The trail rises from the valley and disappears into dusk above us, and I feel no urge to step onto that trail myself.

When we return to the helicopter for the last short hop to Juneau, Kim and I look across Mansfield Peninsula, the major part of Admiralty not set aside as official wilderness. "This is beautiful, isn't it?"

Kim says, almost helplessly. A moment later, he adds, "This is all scheduled for timber harvest." He starts to say something else, but stops.

At home, in the dark, I hold my hands to my face. The smell of bear clings to me, not a stench, but a wild, pungent scent that I breathe again and again, as if I could draw it into myself. Perhaps those who are half-human, half-bear smell like this. Perhaps they look like everybody else, but they are cloaked by a feral spirit. Perhaps they see things they don't say.

The scent evaporates by morning. The scrap of feather I robbed from the bear's pelt disappears from my pocket. Anyway, it was so small. What remains is this: I still dream of bears, but in the dreams I watch. I don't run. I don't speak. The bears watch me, silent, waiting. I am not afraid of bears, I tell myself. I am not afraid.

Dan O'Brien

Life on the Myopian Frontier

from "Sacred Trusts"

When I sit on the steps of our ranch house at night I can see a single electric light somewhere near the top of the Black Hills. The light first appeared a couple months ago and it annoys me because it creates the sensation that humans have finally elbowed their way to the top of the mountains that are, in many ways, the central feature of my life. I can't help imagining that the Black Hills are filled with people to the point of overflowing.

For thirteen years after I started making payments on that little ranch there was no sign of civilization from the porch at night. I liked it that way, enjoyed the feeling that I was folded harmonically into the landscape of the Great Plains, that I belonged and that neither I nor any of my kind was disturbing the beauty and precision of the Hills in any significant way. I was profoundly thankful not to be living in the congestion I have seen in this country and around the world. I felt safe, remote from the deprivations of crowded cities and countryside.

Of course I knew the ranch was not a truly remote place. There are no such places anymore. It was mostly a quirk of geography that made the view from the porch seem pristine. Sitting in the exact right place on the top step, I didn't notice the light from the bedroom window above and I could feel totally alone. The yard lights of the neighbors and the small town ten miles south are mercifully hidden by ridges and buttes. But because this new light shines from somewhere high in the Black Hills, it is conspicuous. It draws my eyes every time I step from the house and reminds me that human population pressures have pushed people to even the marginal land of the Earth, resulting in tragic destruction of ecosystems and other species. The light is a symbol of that pressure and it drives me wild.

When I moved to the little ranch from an even smaller one in the southern Black Hills, I fell in love with the solitude that came with the night. As is the case with most people, the quiet and seclusion were restorative for me, and I have come to think of them as unprotected rights, like the right to free speech or worship in lesser countries. Some of us out here have learned to savor those qualities and feel they are part of what makes our lives special. But special as it may be, life in the shadow of the Black Hills has a severe economic reality, and we've also learned that you can't eat solitude. These ranches are often not able to sustain us through the hard times that seem to keep on coming out here. Four years ago I married a woman with a good job in the nearby town of Rapid City. Her job is economically more important to us than our little ranch could ever be and since she needs to be near her work, we moved to town. So even though I drive to the ranch every day, I don't get to spend many nights out there anymore. Now most of my nights are spent in the nice little midwestern-type town of Rapid City. It's a pleasant place and still part of the Black Hills that we love and need. But I greatly miss sitting on that porch and seeing nothing but bright, dancing stars above the dark reptilian spine of the Hills.

The new electric light in the Hills could be ten miles off or it could be forty. It's hard to say because, from our front porch, you can see a very long way. All of western South Dakota and the northern plains is a land where vision is still very important. The animals, and some of the people, depend on their eyes much more than any other sensory organ. There is a feeling that you need to see things coming from a long way off, so vision is primary out here. In the daytime the antelope and mule deer watch me from a mile away as I go about my daily routine.

The hawks, falcons, and eagles watch from somewhere too high for me to see. Even at night the distances one can see are amazing. On the moonlit nights I can see silvery ridge lines thousands of yards away, and the silhouette of Bear Butte six miles to the southeast.

Even though the electric light in the Hills is probably much farther away than Bear Butte I can see it clearly. But it does not aid my vision, it detracts from it. That light does not have the soft edges of the moon and stars. It takes the silver from the night and forces me to focus on a pinpoint. It's impossible to regard it as anything other than a foreign object in this landscape. It appears ostentatious and intrusive.

Unfortunately, ostentatious and intrusive objects are not that rare out here. In fact, the recent human history of the Black Hills might well be summarized as a string of reactions to things foreign, ostentatious, and intrusive. I say recent because the only written history we have is barely a hundred years old. To be sure, there were important events that took place in the Hills before 1874 when General George Custer directed the first significant white penetration. For centuries small groups of indigenous North Americans evicted each other from the Hills, but the first real changes to the land or people since the last ice age have come in the last two generations. Changes to the Black Hills came very late in the saga of North American settlement. But when they finally came, they came fast and brutally, with a lack of foresight that has been common throughout the world but is particularly acute in the conquest of North America. The pace of change, the coarseness of its application, and the indifference to what is lost has slackened only slightly in the Black Hills of South Dakota.

White men had been on this continent for nearly four hundred years before there was a European dwelling in the Black Hills. American independence had been fought for and won a century earlier. The United States had divided in a great civil war and was on the mend by the time the first white army laid eyes on the land that is believed, by some, to be the birthplace of humanity. It was only curious twists of fate that allowed the Hills to remain unsullied long after most of the continent had been overrun by European Christians. Lewis and Clark's path tracked several hundred miles north of the Black Hills when they inspected the newly purchased land in 1804. The Bozeman Trail led settlers south and west. Colorado, Oregon, California, and Nevada had earned their statehood years before Europeans cast their consumptive gaze toward the Black Hills. In addition to the discouraging label of "The Great American Desert," the Black Hills and a large portion of the present state of South Dakota were protected from encroachment by being designated a reservation for the indigenous Pantheists of the Great Plains in the famous Treaty of 1868. Of course when Custer found gold in the Black Hills in 1874 all bets were off. The government reneged on the treaty and the drive to civilize and Christianize the native Lakota people was intensified. The push to populate the "empty" land was begun in earnest and the nearsighted belief that there would always be room in the American West established itself firmly in the national dogma.

From that point in time the Black Hills raced to find their place in the jigsaw puzzle of manifest destiny. In eighteen months the brand new town of Custer went from a population of zero to eleven thousand. By 1876 the Black Hills boasted over fifteen thousand white souls, each with the dream of finding their fortune in the clear streams or black earth of America's latest promised land. Of course only a few found a fortune—to this day South Dakota remains one of the poorest states—but many found work in the mines and supporting businesses that sprang up around the boom towns. By 1910 the population of the Black Hills was over fifty-seven thousand and the night view from my front porch, had there been a house here then, was still uninterrupted, gray above when the moon was new and always solid black below, where the Hills were known to be.

Stories of the richness of the Black Hills fueled the fires of greed through an ongoing gold rush and an extended period of homesteading. Most of the stories were lies, but they brought thousands of people from Europe and the eastern states where the natural vitality of the land was already being sapped by the crush of human population. A huge percentage of those people were bitterly disappointed by their Dakota experience. They blamed the weather, the government, and just plain bad luck for the fact that they did not prosper. No one, until recently, seemed to realize that this land could actually be a paradise if humans were spread thinly among the other species instead of displacing them.

It's true that the majority of emigrants were poor, uneducated people who were only trying for a better life. They were simple people who had not read Malthus and did not have the time to consider that each ecosystem, according to its fertility, has a fairly rigid carrying capacity. There was no way for them to understand that each piece of land can only supply a given number of individuals with all they need for a happy existence. There was certainly no great plan to overtax the ecosystem. The reality, as in most places, is that things simply got out of hand. It would have taken men of great vision indeed to see that too many people was a possibility. Even Thomas Jefferson, perhaps our premier visionary, made a profound and uncharacteristic miscalculation by arguing effectively that Kentucky would never become a state because it would never reach the required population of twenty-five thousand voters. In light of such a blind spot in a vision as farsighted as Jefferson's, it is hard to condemn the early emigrants to the Black Hills. It's hard, in fact, to condemn the present inhabitants of the cluttered little housing developments jammed into the once fertile and pristine valleys. Our politicians and civic leaders may be a different story, but probably one should not harbor evil thoughts about the person who turns on that electric light that I see from my porch.

Greed is still a factor in the continuing population growth of our area but more and more now, people are moving to the Black Hills for different reasons. Now many people choose the Hills as a place to live for the quality of life that it has always offered. Of course the twentieth-century irony of the Black Hills is the irony of many places. People come because it is beautiful, sane, and abundant in life. There is relatively clean air, clean water, and still an adequate supply of topsoil. They begin to build an ethic and a heritage around these things and, as the population grows, the very things that brought the people begin to be destroyed, leaving whole communities to discover they are built on eroding and irretrievable foundations.

Rapid City is the second-largest town in the state. Depending on who's counting, the estimates of the city's population run from fifty thousand to seventy-five thousand, perhaps half the total population of the Black Hills. There are few large hardwood trees in western South Dakota and a large portion of them must be in Rapid City. That means there is probably more deep shade in Rapid City than in most northern plains communities. Our neighborhood is the kind of place where Americans live in the movies. Fred MacMurray and his boys could live down the block, Jimmy Stewart could run the local mortgage company. Our end of town is a good place to raise kids. But it is still an American city and so there is another end of town. That's where the Indians live.

North Rapid, as it is called, is not Harlem. It's not L.A.'s Watts or Cleveland's Hough, but it is still a ghetto. And in some ways it is a particularly tragic ghetto. Perhaps the greatest tragedy lies in the fact that the grandparents or great-grandparents of many of these people frequented the Black Hills in pre-European days. Their recent forbears moved in and out of the Hills as freely as the buffalo. Their more distant ancestors, or people like them, existed for thousands of years without altering the environment in any significant way. Whether this was the result of cultural beliefs or the simple fact that they lacked the technology and human numbers to impact the environment is debatable—there were probably less than thirty thousand Lakota scattered over all the western Dakotas, eastern Wyoming, and parts of Nebraska and Montana in the early nineteenth century.

But for whatever reason, it must be difficult for some of those folks living in North Rapid to watch what is happening to the Hills. It must be difficult to watch the gold strip mines of the northern Hills tearing out untold tons of ore each day, must be hard to abide the circus atmosphere of tourist traps and the newly relegalized gambling in Deadwood. It must be hard to take the attempts to turn parts of the Hills into huge garbage dumps for waste from all over the country. It must be difficult watching the deer herds going the way of the buffalo, the water in the trout streams being funnelled off for irrigation, industry, and green golf courses. It must add greatly to their minority sense of powerlessness to see the destruction of the Hills continuing pretty much unabated.

The Lakota Sioux have never given up the dream of regaining the Hills. They fought first in the draws and valleys of the Great Plains with bows and arrows, then in the courts of white cities with legal briefs to accomplish this goal. Finally, the Sioux claim on the Black Hills was upheld by the Supreme Court in 1980. The court ruled that the United States government illegally took the Black Hills from the Sioux nation when they broke the Treaty of 1868. They awarded the tribe the largest cash settlement ever levied against the United States government in an Indian land claim, over $106 million. But the Sioux have refused the money which, with interest, is now closer to $250 million. The official line is that the Black Hills are not for sale. Never mind that in a bigger sense the Hills were sold years ago and continue to be sold every day. Still the Sioux insist that land must be part of any settlement, and that sounds right. Notwithstanding their poor stewardship of the huge reservations to the south and east, it is hard to imagine that they could manage the Black Hills with much less respect and foresight than the United States Forest Service and private owners.

It is true that the Sioux have been deeply wronged but the greater wrong has been to the Hills themselves, and turning over ownership, while it might well act as a salve for our national consciousness, probably would not bring an end to the assault of the Black Hills. It might well turn out to be a failed attempt to step back in time when what is needed are truly bold new steps toward the future. Some people, white and Indian, are more concerned with the welfare of the Hills for posterity than in righting one of many wrongs of the past. When you consider the shaky record of tribal government's ability to look ahead, the age-old jealousies and divisions within the Sioux community, and the fact that many whites who also revere the Black Hills as a special place would be disenfranchised by such a settlement, one begins to wonder if a change in ownership would serve any real purpose other than substituting red exploiters for white ones.

You don't have to be Sioux or live in North Rapid to feel helplessness in the face of the anthropocentricity that is maiming the Black Hills. Many Black Hills residents feel a need to protect the Hills, but almost none have had the courage to focus on the problem. It is not a question of going back in time in search of old solutions, because, in Black Hills time, the problem is very new and more sinister than anything that has happened before. It is a question of going beyond and coming up with fresh, farsighted solutions.

For years, a lot of people have felt helpless over what is happening in the Hills and all over the West. I'm afraid I am one of them. Some nights I lie in our bed thinking about what will become of the land to which I belong. I sometimes get a suffocating feeling that keeps me awake. But at least one night last month I was fast asleep by ten o'clock. My wife and I go to bed early in our little house in the shady end of Rapid City. It's old-fashioned, I realize, but I like to be up before the sun, like to see the morning colors spread across the countryside on my drive to the ranch. Though there has been a Colt .357 in the drawer of the bed stand for twenty years, we have never locked the doors of our Rapid City house. That kind of faith in our security is one of the reasons we live in the Black Hills, and we have always taken a certain amount of pride in the fact that we have never felt a need for dead bolts and safety chains.

That night last month, I was dreaming a pleasant dream of the time when I spent all my nights at the ranch. In the dream there was a cold evening breeze and the smell of stacked prairie hay that I would feed the cattle the next morning. I suppose I was staring at the Black Hills and marveling that there was no light in sight. But there was sound. It was footsteps, and then there was my wife's voice, "Hey. Hey!"

About then I came fully awake. "Get out of here. Get out!" she was yelling. And when I turned, already fumbling in the bedside drawer, I saw a head stuck through the door of our bedroom.

"Hey!" Me this time. Then footfalls ahead of me on the stairs and suddenly I was standing naked and alone in our kitchen. The .357 was in my hand and I was staring at the back door that was now flung open. The cool evening breeze that chilled me was exactly like that of my dream but there was no smell of prairie hay. When I turned, my wife was standing at the dining room door clutching her housecoat at the throat. Our eyes caught and held for several seconds before our shoulders slumped. What on Earth was happening?

The policeman had an accent that I mistook for Chicago. "No," he said. "New Jersey. It's a little mixed up. I've been out here a couple years." He was young and big and exuded confidence. He walked through the house ahead of me, poking his nightstick under all the beds, into the back of the closets. He had done this before, was very professional, and made us feel a little more secure. "It's your business," he said as he readied to leave, "but if it was me, I'd start doing things differently. I'd lock the doors."

Sometimes it seems that the state government's top priority is to make South Dakota as much like Illinois or Ohio as they can. To watch the local news you would think that every farmer, rancher, teacher, merchant, white man, or Indian longs for more factories, more highways, more jobs. But when I move among the people of the Black Hills that is not what I hear. What I hear is that there are only a fraction of the sharp-tailed grouse and pheasants that there used to be, that it's nearly impossible to find a place to cross-country ski or hunt deer where you can be alone. Many conversations end with dazed, shaking heads talking about traffic, lines at restaurants, beer cans thrown into trout streams, the morning smog over the Hills.

When I visit places that I've read were once beautiful and uncorrupted, it strikes me that the human characteristic that is perhaps most unfortunate is our ability to get used to almost any insult to our senses if it comes gradually enough. It's probably the fact that changes have come, and continue to come, so fast out here that makes the sense of loss so profound. I used to feel cheated for never having seen the buffalo. Now I suspect that it's a blessing that they were gone before my time. Maybe if I had waited in traffic as a child I would be adjusting better to Rapid City's rush hour. Maybe I wouldn't notice the cluttered subdivisions along the highway if I had never seen mule deer standing in the meadows that were sacrificed for those housing starts. Maybe I wouldn't notice the topsoil blowing away if I couldn't remember when those wheat fields were prairie, if I didn't remember what switch grass, blue stem, and grama grass look like. And maybe that damned light at the top of the Hills wouldn't bother me if I had never sat on the porch steps and enjoyed the sensation of a few moments of solitude.

I've tried to find that light. I've gotten in my pickup and driven toward it but it always disappears. A ridge of pine trees or a hill blocks it from sight and when I come to where I think it should be visible again there's nothing but the blackness of the Hills. I want to think the light is fastened to a pole above some senseless materialistic venture. I want its existence to be ridiculous. I want it to be simply wrong. But most likely it's not simply anything. Most likely it is someone's home. I may well be seeing a light shining from someone's bedroom window.

So perhaps it is best that I can't find the source of that light. As long as it is just a glow in the distant night I can imagine that it is a huge mercury-vapor light illuminating the night shift's work at a new strip mine, the beacon at the top of another ski hill, the yard light for a sawmill or a factory of some kind. As long as I don't know for sure, I can keep myself out of the equation. I'm not sure what I would do if one night I located that light at the end of someone's driveway. It would sicken me to find a person sitting quietly on their own front porch, staring down-country at a light glimmering from the direction I had just come.

Adele Ne Jame

Poems

from *Nimrod*

Fieldwork, Devil's Lake, Wisconsin

This far north even an early spring
seems insufficient, though starlings
congregate overhead in the branches and
the trees are beginning their work,
though geese, beautiful in their loud
honking, fly in patterns, synchronized,
unpredictable, some wild announcement
you think must have something
to do with mending or perhaps
forgetting that the urgent wind,
like death, dismantles everything,
that even its vibrato which resonates
long in the body is evidence of a diminishing
presence, that love fails. Yet,
I am willing, though arrival seems more
like progressive loss, to attend to this
work of belief, even as a small
creature in the distance breathes evenly,

beautifully in a field of dying fire trees
finding bloodroot, its single pale flower,
willing to say after a long, unforgiving
winter that the sunlight blanching
the lake, after an overnight thaw its current
rushing with the wind's force,
is not just a matter of physics or a metaphor
gone wrong like love's hard turn back,
that in this now perfect light,
the bluffs that circle the lake
are the color of rose quartz,
that this wall of flesh,
in its own time, is equal to
the harsh grace of this landscape,
and that the loud clattering of birds
starting up again is no accident.

from *Ploughshares*

A Ryder Nocturne and *The Temple of the Mind*

Once at night we saw them along the coast's
rough edge, a dozen fishermen torching,
waist-deep in the shallows. The moon
half gone, dragged the tidewater
across the coral and over the reef's
ledge into the open sea.

And as they moved slowly sliding their
glass boxes across the water's dark face,
some held their burning torches high
like bludgeons of fire as if to ignite the glazed-
black water, the light flaring across
their bodies. Lovely,

graceful as the dancers of an ancient hālau,
they pressed their shoulders into the receding
current, and we knew then the fish, stunned
by the light, were giving themselves up
to the net, suffocating in the night wind
as the watery air slid from their delicate open parts.

And when those men were gone—
though they seemed still present by some
trick of the mind that holds
even a violent beauty a little longer

at any cost—I wished them back,
as I wished back our squandered lives,

our love lost somehow to the rushing,
careless night, to the moon's heartless
pull, its argument of pleasure or
despair. But later that night,
as if young again, I wanted
to say to you, see how the three Graces

stand in the world, huddled
outside the lavish temple of this painting
expelled but waiting, the artist said,
for Love to join them; though taunted
by the faun's deadly chant, though the stars
are drowning in the green-golden

night of their expulsion, they wait
as if the lambent wings of night will not
carry them inconsolably towards
what is least possible.

Note: Albert Pinkam Ryder. *The Temple of the Mind.* c. 1883–85

Russell Chatham

The Deepest Currents

from *Esquire*

The first time I ever paid to go fishing was when I took a so-called destination trip to Iceland. It was very expensive, but I had never fished for Atlantic salmon, and I was looking for some romance, for new experiences in new lands. Aside from the actual invitation, which seemed somehow like a privilege, I had just finished a salmon and steelhead season in California, Oregon, and Washington that had me discouraged because of the crowds.

In the real light of high overhead sunshine, a thousand dollars a day for six days to wet a line, no matter how fancy that line might be, was insane for a financially unsuccessful painter. It would take a full year to pay it off. What closed the deal for me was the promise of a river full of fish with no one else on it, a river to which you essentially claimed ownership for a time, a river you could look across without seeing a band of armed loggers in hard hats ready to bean you with an assortment of heavy metal lures bristling with sharp gang hooks.

Our group consisted of ten anglers, mostly older gentlemen ("The old men got all the money," according to Mose Allison), all of them somewhat experienced Atlantic-salmon fishermen. They had been coming to this river for years, and there was a lot of wagering on how many, how big, the first fish caught, and so forth. The year before had been a good one. The high rod for the week had landed about twenty fish. But destination fishermen's lives are ruled by the old axiom, "You should have been here yesterday."

It was the middle of July when we landed in Reykjavík, during a horizontal sleet storm of a velocity sufficient to knock one stout passenger clear off her feet on the long walk across the tarmac to the terminal. First stop was the fishing store to buy flies. Our group went into a frenzy, scooping them up by the handful. My friend Guy de la Valdene asked why I wasn't buying any flies. I said I had plenty already, plus a vise and material if I ran out.

"But you've never even *been* Atlantic-salmon fishing," he said.

I explained to him my theory that the dozen or so varieties of salmon and sea trout worldwide were shirttail cousins and lived more or less similar lives, feeding on similar foods. Their brains were similar in size, which is to say exquisitely tiny and incapable of anything we might recognize as thought. Further, I liked my flies, loved them in fact, having spent decades refining a few simple but exceedingly effective designs, and I planned on using them no matter what.

This kind of talk prompted warnings from the group. The Atlantic salmon was a noble, demanding, and highly selective fish, the subject of centuries of study and hundreds of books; the fly to which it was responding best on the Laxa Whats-its-name this season was the Forktail Rat Face Mary, fished on a dead drift. End of conversation. You didn't mess with tradition when it came to Atlantic salmon.

Our guide was a likable young man who spoke English very well, as do all Icelanders. When we arrived at our beat, the area of the river we had been assigned to fish, we parked and walked to the stream. It seemed awfully small and low.

"Now," our guide began, gesturing toward the river, "what we have here is a pool."

I was mortified. I had never fished with a guide before, and having fished with uncommon frequency—nearly every day for the preceding thirty years—I felt like Michael Jordan might if a new coach, assigned to help him with his game, led him out to the key, pointed at the backboard, and said, "Now, what we have here is a basket."

I walked upstream to the next holding water. I had worked about halfway through it when our guide came up to check on me. He watched a few minutes, then asked to see my fly. He shook his head and asked to see my fly box. He was visibly upset with what he saw and pulled out a box of his own filled with Forktail Rat Face Marys. "You must use this," he said. "And stop moving it. Let it drift dead."

I took it and tied it on. This was not the time for an argument about ichthyological genetics, lunar forces, or behavior of species of fish on the other side of the earth. But privately, I expressed to Guy my opinion that there was not a single fish present in this water.

"How do you know that?"

"I just know, that's all."

In front of the lodge (actually a schoolhouse *used* as a lodge during June, July, and August) there was a steep falls. The river was too low for fish to leap over it, and although a few had passed during the last freshet, most lay waiting below where we were. This made fishing upstream like playing baseball without a ball or bat. "I guess we might as well have taken a nap instead of fishing," Guy said. "A thousand-dollar nap."

At dinner we found out that the four fishermen who'd been lucky enough to fish the two beats below the falls had caught seven or eight nice fish among them. Talk of wagers arose again, along with offers to sell us the correct flies at inflated streamside prices.

At breakfast, however, we learned we would fish the beat directly below the falls in the morning, then in the afternoon the tail-out of the same pool. I immediately wanted to get out of the building and down to the water. Nothing doing. On this river it was strictly banker's hours. You started at nine and stopped for lunch at one. In the afternoon you started at three and stopped at six. At this latitude, at this time of year, it was light all the time. (Given the freedom to do so, I would have fished all night, as I've subsequently done in the Northwest Territories and the Russian Arctic.)

The plan was to drop me off on the near side; then our guide would take Guy across the river to fish. As the car drove off, I was shivering with eagerness. Fish were showing everywhere, and as I ran to the river I was already establishing vectors between boulders and identifying seams in the current. I pulled the monofilament off the reel so hysterically that I backlashed it. The first cast was a bullet, the shooting head turning over quartered downstream, at a hundred feet. The take came in under six seconds, just as I finished the mend. The salmon leaped out of the water upside down. I pressured it hard and had it beached within a few minutes, a beautiful silvery fish about seven or eight pounds.

It took two casts to put the next one on. As I led it to shore, I could see our guide's car crossing the bridge to the other side a mile downstream. Adrenaline was making my ears hot as I carelessly rushed back into the water, tripping and falling. My left arm got wet up to the shoulder. Cold as it was, all that mattered was that this was the bucket of buckets, filled with hundreds of fish. Something happened on every cast: nips, pulls, and takes that came off after a few shakes. The ratio of lost fish to landed fish was three to one.

Instinctively I looked around to see if anyone was watching, and the realization hit me that there was no horde of gear boys spying on the action, ready to sweep down the bank and edge me out, sewing up the hole with an impossible network of lines, sinkers, bait, spoons, and a hundred other doodad curiosities. God damn it, I had paid, and paid big, to keep those bastards at bay. I let out a whoop in celebration and then deliberately made the longest cast I'd ever made with that particular outfit, which converted into another salmon in the air and then on the bank.

When our guide and Guy pulled up across the river, I was playing another fish. The guide got out of the car, pulling a long-handled net with him. I saw him stop and look across at me. Suddenly he was jamming the net back into the car. He was going to drive back to my side to help me land what he naturally assumed to be my first fish.

As his car crossed the bridge, I hooked another one. After landing it, I tried a different position, this time retrieving the fly rapidly at a perverse angle across the current. The take was vicious, the fight short-lived. I was playing another as the guide pulled up, maneuvering his net back out of the car and running down to help. I motioned him back and slid the fish up onto the grass. He ran and picked it up.

"Oh, sir," he said. "Congratulations. It's a wonderful salmon."

"Thank you," I said, getting ready to go back into the water. "Please, you don't need to come all the way over here to help me. I'm managing. Just lay the salmon over behind that big rock with the others."

He walked over and let out a little cry. Scarcely an hour into the day, there was quite a pile of fish back there.

My obsession started maybe forty-five years ago, during an era largely forgotten and in a place that even then existed well outside its own time. In the middle of the nineteenth century, my great-great-grandfather left the Alpine village of Intragna, to search for gold in Australia. He took his find to California, where he purchased five thousand acres from another Swiss family. The elder Piazzoni then sent for his four sons and their families. Today his house stands as it did more than a century ago: no phone or electricity, the lovely old oil lamps working perfectly. When I was a child, the exquisite landscape of Mount Toro in Monterey County formed me. In summer I was encouraged to walk alone in the hills and canyons, to hunt, to paint, and to fish.

My father, uncle, and cousins fished for trout in Chupinas Creek, which flowed past our ranch house and down the canyon to the Carmel River. Steelhead ran upstream to spawn, sometimes past Papa's gate, into our fork, and even up little Irene's creek to the east, though I was never there during winter to see these fish with my own eyes.

They are now extinct, their decline accelerated first by the San Clemente Dam and later by the Los Padres Dam. Thoughtless stocking of hatchery fish from other locations weakened the gene pool, but the final blow was dealt by drought. Back then, though, there was an abundance of steelhead, and when my father decided I was old enough to go fishing with him, we walked down the road past the Favorite Tree, where we had our rope swing, past the big sycamore, where my uncle Phil had carved his son Tom's name in the most beautiful letters deep into the massive tree's trunk, past the bull oak, where there was always a Hereford or two dozing in the deep shade, on to Papa's gate, past the spring from which we drew our drinking water, stopping finally at a small wooded flat near the double creeks.

The equipment was wholly primitive: a three-part steel telescoping pole, well used and dented, and a tiny, ratchety skeleton reel with a short length of waxed line. It didn't matter. It was enough to drop the bait into the holes. The basic skill was to avoid frightening the fish.

My father made me sit away from the creek while he looked for bait. A yellowjacket cruised by, and he stunned it with his hat, then impaled it on the hook. I cowered, remembering the nest we had inadvertently disturbed earlier in the summer while gathering firewood. I was stung more than a hundred times.

My father leaned very slowly forward, cautiously lowering his bait. Within seconds he was lifting a wiggling seven-inch trout into the air. He turned and grabbed it, smacked it on the head with a stick, and put it in his creel. He caught two or three more, then motioned for me to come over to where he knelt behind the shrub he'd used for concealment. "I'll hold you," he said, "and you can look down and see them." He slowly leaned me out over the hole. Six or seven fish darted about, some rushing under the watercress, others nervously facing the current in the deepest part of the pool.

He must have held me there for a long time, because it's one of the clearest images I have from my early childhood. The sun had managed to get through a hole in the trees above, and the little pool, hardly as large as the mattress in a baby's crib, had a laughing quality, as if lit from within.

I watched the deep red tendrils of dead watercress wave in the current below; on the surface, the new growth was bright green and bursting with life. The bottom was half gravel, half sand, heavily flecked with sparkling fool's gold. And the trout were dark and alert, drifting back, waving in the flow, then shooting forward. My father, whom I loved so much, held me there as if time had stopped.

What did the little boy see? Was it a window through which he sensed the shape of his whole life? Or a cosmic mystery, dimly perceived but glimpsed for one split second in a fragile, vanishing element? What was it about this insignificant place that forged such a longing that no matter how wide a circle the boy turned, the man traveled, he would forever seek to return to it?

A year or two after my Icelandic trip, Bob Nauheim, president of Fishing International in Santa Rosa, California, invited me to go with him to Norway to check out a river on which he hoped to book fishermen. The river was the intensely beautiful Gaula, near Trondheim. We fished with several young Swedes, all excellent fishermen and casters. One in particular, Mikael Frodin, exemplified the Scandinavian temperament with respect to fishing: a high level of organization and competence combined with the emotional resonance of an Ingmar Bergman drama. His attention to hook styles and hooking techniques was so intense that I finally had to ask him what percentage of the salmon he hooked were lost to pullouts. (In Iceland I had lost at least 50 percent.) "None!" he said, seriously. An Atlantic salmon expels a fly out its gills, he explained, instead of forward like a steelhead. Therefore, the strike on an Atlantic salmon can never be too slow, only too fast.

Bob and I fished relatively hard for five or six days, and each of us hooked and lost one salmon. We took a few grilse, and every one of them was scarred from passing through the mesh of nets. When Frodin told me that he and Johan Abelsson once caught nearly eighty salmon out of one pool in a single day, the problem suddenly became clear: criminal overharvesting of Atlantic salmon. The Gaula's run had been wiped out.

One afternoon, Frodin and I and some of the other guides and fishermen had a friendly competition. These were the best distance casters I'd ever seen outside California. They gave an impressive demonstration of the effectiveness of the 16-foot, two-handed rod fitted with a 50-foot shooting head. None of them even owned waders.

They fished right off the gravel bars, feet dry, routinely dropping their flies at two hundred feet. But the two best, Frodin and Abelsson, could not beat me with the one-handed rod, and this clearly puzzled them.

My uncle Phil had a pretty good assortment of fishing tackle that he used on the Russian River at Summer Home Park. He started Tom and me fishing for smallmouth bass when we were ten or eleven years old. Of course, we fished with baits of different kinds, baby lamprey eels when we could find them (I still love bait fishing), but Phil spoke rapturously about fly casting. When the shad ran in the spring, he said, they took only silver flies. That was it, then. We had to learn to fly fish or we'd never catch any of these wonderful, mysterious shad.

Phil had several bamboo fly rods, the best of which was a three-piece Granger that he set up for Tom with a size B shooting head and Medalist reel. My dad bought me a similar outfit for my sixteenth birthday. The rod cost twenty-five dollars, a lot of money in those days. The Medalist was $3.95.

Phil decided that the Golden Gate Angling and Casting Club in Golden Gate Park was the best place for us to learn what to do with this equipment. He was still fishing with his Marvin Hedge Seven Taper but quickly saw that a new invention, the shooting head, made this otherwise beautiful silk line obsolete.

"Let's see those outfits, boys," the man on the casting platform said when we arrived for our first lesson.

He stripped off what seemed like a mile of line, made a couple of powerful, amazingly fast false casts, and shot the line forward with such force I thought the rod would break.

"This outfit has a maximum distance of a hundred thirty feet, but you won't get anything like that out of it fishing, especially wading deep. When you shoot it, aim for the top of the eucalyptus trees. Practice out of the pit, not here on the platform. You're not going to catch anything until you can tangle your line around those old men sitting on the bench over there. That's about a hundred feet."

Our instructor, Joe Paul, was one of the best steelhead fishermen and distance casters in California. Later we saw him casting from the pit, a concrete box sunk into the casting pools to simulate wading waist-deep. Forget the old men. His line went over the trees they were sitting under.

When Tom and I got down into the pit, those old men were worlds away. It was eighty feet just to the cement edge of the pool, and we could barely get within ten feet of *that*. We went fishing anyway, of course, but we didn't catch anything—just as Joe predicted.

Our fly lines were made out of tan-colored Dacron from the Sunset Line & Twine Company in Petaluma, California. The colored line was helpful in learning to cast, because you could watch other fishermen and see exactly how their lines were behaving in the air. It was obvious who knew how to cast and who didn't. Joe Paul's been dead for many years, but some of his friends are still around, among them three of the greatest distance casters and salmon and steelhead fishermen who ever lived: Frank Allen, Alan Curtiss, and Bill Schaadt. I've been everywhere in the world where fly fishing is practiced, and I've yet to meet anyone who could carry a suitcase for any of those three.

One day at Watson's Log I watched Schaadt, Charlie Napoli, a friend of Bill's, and Curtiss fish from their boats. They were backlit by the sun, so that every movement was highlighted, their lines illuminated. Bill was still smoking Pall Malls in those days, and the puffs of smoke drifted slowly away from him on the light breeze.

The three casters had unique styles, yet all shared the essential elements of fine casting: tremendous line speed; tight loops; fully extended, perfect turnovers; maximum distance; no bad casts and no tangles, even with the kinky monofilament we had in those days. It was breathtaking and humbling. Another fisherman came walking down the beach, someone I recognized but didn't know. Frank Allen waded in and started casting. A lefty like Curtiss, he was as good as the others were.

That day left a permanent impression on me. Here were four of the best fly casters in the world in the same place at the same time—it was like listening to the best string quartet ever or watching Jordan, Barkley, Bird, and Magic in a pickup game. At the end of an hour I left and went up to the narrows to be alone. I would not have dared fish where those men could see my struggles. I wanted my line to soar out over the river like theirs, but it would not. My monofilament was kinked and fouled up, and even when it wasn't, my fly often hit the water behind me, and on the cast the line tangled around itself, falling in a pile. I cursed my lovely Granger as if it were the problem—a bad workman blaming his tools. I wanted a one-piece glass rod like those guys had. I had yet to learn that the price of a fly rod in no way guarantees its performance. Beautiful rods and reels are nice—I now own a roomful of them—but only one thing counts when you're up your chest in the river and the fish are lying a hundred feet out in front of you: the balance between the action of the rod and the weight of the line.

During the late '50s Frank Allen opened my eyes to a great many things. It was through Frank that I got to know Bill Schaadt, Jon Tarantino, and Myron Gregory. Tarantino held all the world records for distance casting at that time. And Gregory, who had once held the record, was developing the system by which all fly lines are known today, assigning them numbers designating weight instead of letters indicating diameter.

If the rivers were out, we'd go to the pools and refine our equipment, trying out new and different things. Sometimes we watched the tournaments, especially if Tarantino was casting. At the pools, any illusions you might have had about your abilities as a caster were straightened out right away. After all, you were in the company of experts, and the numbers were there on the cement in white paint. Someone was always happy to give you an accurate report on how far your cast went and whether it turned over properly.

I was proud of my friends' accomplishments, and I wanted them to be proud of me. When not fishing, I usually spent an hour or so practice casting, sometimes at home on the grass. In the off-season, when there was little or no chance of finding any fish, I visited the tidewater of Paper Mill Creek (where I was surprised to catch baby stripers, proving that bass spawned there), Walker Creek, Salmon Creek, and

Bodega Bay (where I caught nothing), or the lower pools of the Russian, where I learned how to get big carp to take a fly. Once, I was fishing for sharks and rays with bait at Tomales Bay when a surprise school of stripers surfaced nearby. I had a fly rod rigged, so I dropped a cast into them and caught a twenty-two-pounder, which won the *Field & Stream* contest that year. The catch was especially satisfying because it came in July, when fisheries biologists working in the bay had guaranteed me there were no bass present.

At these beautiful coastal haunts—lonely places where there were never any tourists, swimmers, campers, or boaters—the wind always blew, shaping the trees into mournful sentinels that gave form to the solitude. Early in the fall I always went to Watson's Log, waded the riffle, and walked up to the spot where I had first recognized Frank Allen on that memorable day. I waded out and cast, even though there was nothing to cast for. I peopled the pool with my heroes and imagined myself fishing with them. I could still clearly picture those crisp, bright lines slicing through the air with impossible perfection.

Once in a while I'd go over to the pools on weekday afternoons. The old men weren't there on such days, but their bench was, and I'd start working toward it. Usually I'd get one cast out of five up onto the sidewalk. Finally, after a cast no different from those before it, I saw my line draped over the bench. I set the rod down, climbed out of the pit, walked over, and just stared at it. Had this been a Saturday or Sunday, I thought to myself, with those geezers sitting here lying to each other, I could have jerked their hats off. It had taken ten years, but I had finally arrived at Joe Paul's recommended starting point.

After that first morning in Iceland below the falls, my lunch mates expressed astonishment at the degree to which beginner's luck had penetrated the inscrutable traditions of Atlantic-salmon fishing. When my catch was recorded in the log, the custom for more than a century, my three-hour bag equaled an average week's catch. When "type of fly" was requested and I answered "Comet," there was some hesitation, but it was written down.

Guy, too, began catching fish that afternoon. I had built two special sets of shooting heads, one for myself, one for him. Based upon what I'd been told about the size of the river, I made them short number eights, each twenty-five feet long instead of the normal thirty (on really big water like the lower Eel River in northern California, some of the boys went to AA 35-footers). I made these lines in five densities: floating, slow-sinking, fast-sinking, very-fast-sinking, and lead-core. We could change heads in under two minutes, thereby matching whatever conditions we confronted.

In Iceland, salmon fishing is one part sport, four parts business. There is virtually no public fishing, and the fish themselves are commercial products. One of the rules on this river was that all salmon caught had to be killed. If you wished to take home gravlax or smoked salmon, you gave the lodge three fresh fish in exchange for one that was processed and packed frozen to be taken home. This created a rather gruesome picture. I didn't keep notes on that trip, and lately my memory has turned on me, but by the end of our week we must have had eight or nine dozen fish in the freezer. The lodge keeps precise records in its log, so anyone interested in going to the trouble can look it up. I know that word reached Reykjavík, and that a reporter from the paper drove out to the river to see what was going on, and that after his story appeared, carloads of Icelanders drove out to sit on the bank and watch us fish.

Since we drew the good beats only now and then, we did catch a few of those thousand-dollar naps. We also went into Reykjavík once for dinner and nightclubbing, and the locals gave us a terrific demonstration of what it means to get really drunk.

We had become somewhat unpopular at the lodge dinner table because not only were we trashing the parameters of the possible on the river, but we insisted on bringing to the table armloads of hot sauces from around the world in an attempt to salvage the ever-white food.

One night an old Scottish lawyer asked if he could see one of my Comets. He studied it and said it shouldn't work, but the evidence to the contrary was overwhelming.

"They say you retrieve the fly when you fish it. Why?"

"You cover more water. Show it to more fish. I think it also activates the long tail."

I pushed a few across the table to him, and he wrapped them in a napkin and put them in his pocket. The next day he caught more salmon than ever before—and he'd been coming to the river for years.

The first time I ever saw a Comet, on the Russian River at Austin Riffle one March day about thirty-five years ago, I was fishing just above the mouth of the creek. Al Curtiss was fishing across from me, laying out long casts in my direction, his fly landing within fifty feet of me. His turnovers were so deliberate and perfect that I could easily watch his enormous fly as it settled to the water. It was orange and looked as long as a pencil. He played a lot of fish that day.

Al was secretive about his flies, so I asked Frank what he was using, and he told me it was a fly Joe Paul had come up with. It was big, meant for high, murky water, its most remarkable feature a three-inch tail. Both Joe and Al frequently fished with this fly, which Joe had dubbed his "O-Cedar mop" (a story about this appears in Trey Combs's *Steelhead Fly Fishing,* from Lyons & Burford).

A couple of years later, when I made my first trip to the Smith River to fish for king salmon, Bill Schaadt was using a Comet-style fly that I admired. He called it the Golden Goose, because to enter the annual *Field & Stream* contest, which he frequently won, you had to give the name of the fly on which you'd made your catch. My interest renewed, I tied up a bunch of Comets in different colors and, in deference to the crystal-clear water, made them extremely sparse and thin. They have been my favorites for the last thirty years. Clearly they work as well on Atlantic salmon as they do on Pacific salmon and steelhead. Their versatility was soundly proved in Iceland, then again on two trips to the Kola Peninsula in Russia, where the Icelandic scenario was repeated on the Umba and Pnoi rivers.

When I moved to Livingston, Montana, in 1972, I was running away from what I saw happening in California. The Russian River was dammed to death, then used as a convenient dump for the raw sewage of booming Santa Rosa, which today very much resembles Los Angeles. When Paper Mill Creek and then Walker Creek met similar fates, an era ended. Marin County, once the hunting and fishing backyard of San Francisco, had become one of the two or three wealthiest counties in America, shopping mall on top of shopping mall, freeways jammed to a standstill with BMWs and Jaguars. The wild pigeons we used to hunt on the ridges above Lagunitas now frequently saw gold jewelry flashing up at them as they roosted.

They say a person raised near the ocean can never be really happy away from it, and I'm no exception, but I needed new home water, and freedom and space. Montana had all of those things.

My new home at the head of Deep Creek was only ten minutes from the Yellowstone River, five from Nelson's Spring Creek, and fifteen from Armstrong and DePuy's Spring creeks, waters that were mostly deserted and very lightly fished. In those days there was only one tackle store, Dan Bailey's. Dan had a few guides working for him during summers, but they were not always busy.

I often wondered to myself why anyone needed a guide in Livingston. How hard was it to drive a couple of miles out of town, park, and walk to the river? And what happened to the thrill of discovery when somebody took you by the hand and pointed everything out? When I declined to buy the local flies that day in Reykjavík, I had no secret knowledge, no knowledge at all; I simply wanted to use my own wits and intuition instead of having everything preordained by so-called experts.

This season, tens of thousands of the faithful are expected on the banks of Montana's Madison River. I will not be among them. Nor will I be found on the Yellowstone in Paradise Valley, or Nelson's, DePuy's, or Armstrong's creeks (unless it's the dead of winter). On these last three, you must now pay a fee to fish, and reservations are made years in advance. There are seven fly shops in Park County. The Yellowstone River has hundreds of boats manned by hundreds of guides. The once-peaceful spring creeks, the lonely, quiet alternatives to the big water, resemble county fairs.

The rejuvenation of the human spirit requires periods of solitude in a natural environment. Yet that environment is fast becoming the rarest commodity on earth. Scientists agree that we've done more harm to the planet in the last fifty years than in the preceding million.

In their deepest, simplest manifestations, all forms of fishing—and hunting, too—are the same, which is to say you effectively become married to an experience uncontrolled by, and outside, the self. This year I will fish in Washington, Oregon, British Columbia, Alaska, New Brunswick, Panama, Florida, New Zealand, and a few other places as yet undetermined. All of this will be great fun. My soul, however, does not reside in any of these places. Part of it must remain forever attached to the ruins of California. The rest resides in a secret Montana that tourists will never see.

I know of a little creek with an unfamiliar name, located far from the interstate. You will not find its name on a map or in the governor's letter to potential visitors. I plan on taking my four-year-old son, Paul, there this summer, to a particular little pool I like. If he manages to stay still long enough, certainly something in question, I might hold him so he can watch the trout. Who knows what he'll see? If the television he's so fond of hasn't spoiled his imagination, maybe the spirit of the earth will liven for him, and he'll glimpse his future.

Jennifer Brice

My Mother's Body

First publication

Winter solstice. Festive and frail like the orange globe of a Chinese lantern, the sun hangs on the horizon where it seems to absorb rather than radiate heat. Outside the window of the bedroom where I dress for my sister's wedding, ice fog wisps around the papery shoulders of birch trees, and glittering snow carapaces the frozen ground. With a lamp at my back the window is a mirror into which I lean, struggling with the old-fashioned clasp on my pearl necklace. I see my reflection—a slender, dark-haired young woman in green velvet—and next to it, my sister-in-law, eight months pregnant. She tugs the lace bertha of the bridesmaid's dress up over her shoulders and steps back, cradling her ponderous belly in both hands. "I was crazy to say yes when Hannah asked me to be in this wedding," she says. "I look absolutely obscene." I tell her she's beautiful and mean it, but she shrugs disbelievingly. Then I turn sideways to the window and slide flattened hands over my collarbones, breasts, stomach, hips. My fingers meet at the center of my body where they probe gently for something smaller than the mole above my right breast, something more mysterious than the black spots on the sun. I was never good at keeping secrets. "Can you see my baby yet?" I ask.

Blood ties me to this body and to this winter landscape, separated now by a thin glass membrane. Flawed and familiar, they have pleasured, pained, frightened and sustained me over nearly three decades. I inhabit them; they are me. I bled here, in my mother's house, when I shed the invisible cocoon of childhood. I bleed every time an airplane pierces the sky and carries me away from Alaska for any length of time. And it was a blood test earlier today that explained the feeling of overripeness fraying at my nerves. Below the insulating layers of skin, fat and sinew, my blood now forms a nest for a blastocyst of dividing cells. The desire to be here, in this place, near my family, overwhelms me. The fertilized egg in my womb is a mystery as ineffable as the ties that bind me to this place, these people.

My sister and her groom marry by candlelight in the same log-cabin Episcopal church where my husband and I wed eighteen months earlier. It was June then, the summer solstice, and the church doors were flung open. Purcell's trumpet voluntary shattered the dust motes that hung in the shafts of sunlight. It is midwinter now and the guests shrug into fur or down coats and rush to warm their cars against the 35-below night. In the nearly empty church the photographer shapes my family into a V headed by Helenka, my grandmother, in her sequined evening gown and fluffy bedroom slippers. The slippers catch me unawares. They remind me how everything living is dying: this will be Grandma's last wedding.

When my grandfather died in 1987, he left her eighty acres, a farm, and a construction business. Grandma hired a landscaper to fill in the swimming pool with dirt and she planted a rose garden there with as many bushes as grandchildren. Greenhouse owners laughed at her. "You might as well try growing cacti in Antarctica," they said. But Grandma fertilizes her rose bushes with backbone. They bloom only for her. Whenever one of her grandchildren is ill, she sends a crystal bowl of fragrant roses instead of chicken soup. In the winter when her bushes sleep under a down comforter of snow, their colors tumble off her tongue like the incantation of Abraham's descendants in the book of Genesis: Sterling Silver, Sunflare, Summer Fashion, Summer Sunshine, Allspice, American Pride, Touch of Class, Tropicana, Mr. Lincoln, Legend, Prince Charles, Fountain Square, White Lightning, Double Delight, Sheer Bliss, and Peace. "Jennifer's color is American Beauty," she declared once. Deeper than pink and shallower than red, it is a rare shade. I see it in the northern lights that stain the sky like spilled sacramental wine on my sister's wedding night.

Surrounded by her children and grandchildren, Helenka perches like a plump, bright-eyed chickadee on a barstool in the Gold Rush–era saloon the bride and groom rented for their reception. I tell her I'm pregnant. Because she has a knack for planting familiar words in unfamiliar gardens, I am not surprised when she says, serenely, "I loved making my babies." The way she uses "make" emphasizes the "-creation" end of "procreation," as though a baby were a bowl spun from clay on a pottery wheel and glazed for strength and beauty, or a seed pressed into the womb of the earth and nourished with food and water until it was strong enough to bend in the wind. I've never been good with my hands, never thrown a pot, never painted a still life with fruit, never even grown a Mother's Day geranium from a seed planted in a Styrofoam cup. But my body is making a baby.

Torn between lover and mother, Persephone tarries too long in the underworld. Spring is late this year. Jealous Demeter stirs up blizzards in May. No one is able to coax Helenka's rose bushes, dull green sticks brandishing thorns, into bloom. Melting snow and mud puddles paint a landscape in charcoal grays and dingy browns on the day of her funeral. I wear pearls again, and my first maternity dress. American Beauty. Last week in the ultrasound lab at the hospital I watched my healthy baby girl somersault in her amniotic sac of fluid and blood. Grief for my grandmother is a cherry pit that chokes me when the family joins hands to sing "Amazing Grace." In *The Lives of a Cell,* Lewis Thomas writes: "Everything that comes alive seems to be in trade for something that dies, cell for cell. There might be some comfort in . . . synchrony." Today, my baby's cells multiply by the million; my grandmother's ashes fertilize her rose bushes. There may be some comfort in synchrony, but it is not great.

Spring. I never thought of my mother as beautiful. Evenings when I was growing up, I used to nudge open the bathroom door and roost on the edge of her tub, soaking my feet in the steaming, scented water. "Tell me about your day," Mom would say. As we talked, I studied surreptitously the landscape of her body. Blue-black varicose veins, like tangled rivers and their tributaries, roped their way up to the sparse triangle between her legs. Scarlet moles punctuated a stomach puckered and seamed by surgeries, including the hysterectomy that had proscribed her motherhood. One side of her belly was as firm as a ripe pomegranate; the other hemisphere, molded by scar tissue, collapsed in folds of flab. Illness and childbirth had wounded her body in ways that, with the vanity of youth, I vowed they would never touch me.

Pregnant, I find myself back on the edge of my mother's bathtub where I now study the landscape of possibility while we design flower gardens in our heads. For us, garden talk is a code. "You know the gravel pit off Peger Road?" she asks. "I saw wild iris growing there last week." ("Plant lots of perennials so you won't have to work so hard next summer, with the baby.") The only roses in my mother's garden are portulaca, moss roses, whose silver-dollar-size blooms stitch the sandy soil of her wildflower garden into a pastel quilt. From Memorial Day until Labor Day, Mom lets spiders spin webs in her basement and dust bunnies collect under the beds. Wearing a terry-cloth sunsuit, she kneels outside in the dirt from eight in the morning until seven at night, digging troughs in the topsoil, planting seeds one at a time, sprinkling mounds with fertilized rainwater. In the spring, she is the goddess of the garden, bearing the power of life in a watering can. As the solstice draws near, her role recedes to that of caretaker. She weeds a little every day and coaxes more blooms by snipping off deadheads. By the beginning of July, it can be difficult to find my mother in her garden. Fiddlehead ferns, delphinium, tiger lilies, snapdragons, geraniums, daisies, begonias, pansies, lobelia, Johnny-jump-ups, creeping Jenny, forget-me-nots, lettuce, tomatoes, peas, carrots, radishes, squash and pumpkins: my mother's garden is a healing tonic, a hymn to the regenerative power of the earth, a drunken celebration of life under the midnight sun.

The summer solstice two years ago marked the beginning of the longest winter of my soul. Mom flew to Anchorage for what was expected to be routine gallbladder surgery. Instead, she developed complications and nearly died. Her garden withered while she lay in a hospital bed on life-support machines. Watching my mother weaken and realizing she might die kindled a deep existential fear in me. I was working in Fairbanks from Monday through Friday and flying to Anchorage on the weekends; for the first time in my life, I became afraid of dying in a plane crash. Strangely, I felt safe on takeoff and landing, but once airborne, I dreaded elements beyond human control—turbulence, wind shears, electrical storms—that might tear the jet apart in midair. I left the pressurized cabin of the jet for the silent, gray, temperature-controlled corridors of Humana Hospital. The tinted windows in my mother's room watered down harsh sunlight and drained the landscape of color. With my back to the bed where my mother shrunk daily into a chaos of plastic umbilical cords, I pressed hot tears into cold glass. Intellectually, I knew it was the natural order of things for my mother to die before me. But not in her fifties, not before she taught me how to be a mother. My mother's illness taught me this: my strongest identification is not as someone's friend, sister, granddaughter or wife but as my mother's daughter. She is my road map; without her, I would be completely lost.

Two summers later, Mom is nearly her old self again. Working in her garden, squeezing dirt between her fingers, she grows stronger daily. Unlike her, I lack the patience to let things grow. I overfertilize in a fit of solicitousness or forget to weed in a fit of laziness. This summer, for a change, I crave the physical act of gardening. Mornings, Mom and I visit local greenhouses. She discourages me from temperamental species; I yearn toward hothouse roses. Every afternoon I lug baskets onto the back porch, fill them with dirt, dig shallow holes with a trowel or my fingers, pop the seedlings out of their six-packs, and set them in their new nests. Mosquitos buzz around my head. Hugely pregnant in a denim jumper, I make trip after trip to the kitchen sink for jugs of water mixed with pink fish fertilizer. The front yard is a typical Alaska lawn, which is to say no lawn at all, just a few spruce trees, willow bushes, a delphinium here and there, and a ground covering of ferns, wild roses and cranberry bushes. If I cannot have long-stemmed roses then I want wildness. I strew wildflower seeds everywhere. By midsummer, daisies overflow a rusting wheelbarrow, impatiens spring from the hollows of rotting stumps, and nasturtiums cascade off the roof of the doghouse. My fear for my mother, my grief for my grandmother fade as my garden grows.

Fourth of July. Friends invite Craig and me to float the Chena River with them. The river is a shallow, slow-moving artery that winds through town, binding three-story houses with gazebos to houses with chain-link fences and yapping dogs to houses that are really lean-tos. A radio announcer says it's 75 degrees but a cooling breeze riffles the leaves of birch trees on shore. We paddle the stretch of water below the city power plant because the water there never freezes in winter, not even at 50 below. Now we rest our paddles on our knees and float, trading insults and banter between canoes. I gasp when the first bucket of river water slaps me in the back of the head. I see the second bucket coming and lean to the right. Quicker than regret, the canoe spills all 165 pounds of me into the river. Panicked, I grab for the overturned boat, but my life jacket rides up over my belly, hampers my arms. Lisa mimics me—"The baby, oh God, the baby"—and, laughing, my friends tug me ashore like a harpooned whale.

Later, back on the river, I think about how this baby fills up space inside me that used to be wilderness unexplored by anyone, least of all me. Skiing unroped on glacial moraines, kayaking rivers where grizzly bears fish, landing a small plane in 25-knot crosswinds—these were commonplace risks for me, before. Perhaps the urge to end one's life is next-of-kin to the urge to create it. Hugh Brody, the anthropologist and author, has spoken of finding the center at the edge, in the most remote hut in the most remote village in the most remote region of the country farthest from home. I have found certain truths at the edge but, for me, the center is at the center: in my family's rituals, in my flower boxes, in my womb. For the rest of the afternoon I ride in the middle of the canoe with my hands cupped over the mound of my tummy. An undercurrent of sex enters the conversation; one friend sprawls bare-breasted on the stern of the canoe. I am silent. I want to go home, sink into a warm tub, and wrap peace like a soothing blanket around myself and my baby.

My due date is still six weeks away but I feel like one of those ancient stone fertility figures that I studied in college. When I turn sideways to the mirror, my engorged breasts rest on the jutting shelf of my belly. I used to walk every day but now the baby curls around the steering wheel of the car when I drive the half-mile to my mother's house. She lays down her trowel and fixes us sandwiches of turkey breast, garden lettuce and tomatoes. Afterward we work for a few minutes on Sunday's *New York Times* crossword puzzle. Deeply afraid of giving birth, I yearn for the only solace my mother cannot—or will not—give. Casually, while she looks up a four-letter word for an African gazelle, I ask about labor. She tells me a story about water that breaks in the middle of the night, timed contractions, the urge to push, the moment when the baby wakes in her arms. She never uses the word "pain." During our Lamaze class, my husband and I watched a woman in labor. What I want to ask my mother is this: how does it feel when a woman's lips turn white? My mother knows. My garden grows. There is mystery as well as synchrony. Some comfort.

August 31. The first contraction tears through me at midnight. I feel a giant hand reach inside and try to claw my baby out. Desperate, I cry out for my mother. I want to lay my head on her lap and listen to lullabies. I want her to be my talisman against pain. I want to return to her womb. She walks into the hospital room at 7:30, pale but crisp in a pressed madras jumpsuit, carrying a pile of books and newspapers. To insulate her against my wildness, her helplessness. For a while we tell jokes between contractions. My mother and my husband take turns walking the corridors with me, pushing the IV tree with its bag of sap-like fluid. We stop in front of the nursery windows. I look at the newborns and think, "Soon. Soon. Tomorrow my baby will lie on the other side of the glass." First, though, my body carries me to a place inhabited by insatiable pain, a place where language can never go, a place where I am no longer someone's daughter and not yet someone's mother. The nurse grabs the backs of my hands, spreads my fingers in front of my clenched eyelids. "Jennifer, listen to me. *Listen* to me. Open your eyes. Don't go inside the pain. You'll only make it worse." What is she talking about? This pain is not inside or outside of me; it *is* me. The plate tectonics of childbirth remold the peaks and valleys of my body. The bones of my mother's hand feel as frail as a fledgling's skeleton; it takes all of my strength not to crush them. For a baby, the violent, bruising passage through the birth canal must be like expulsion from paradise. Before, amniotic bliss; after, cold and hunger and hands. As the mother's pain ends, the daughter's begins.

Named for her great-great-great-great-grandfather, Kinzea Grace Jones sleeps on the way home from the hospital. It is September 2, our first outing as a family, my second full day as a mother. Last night, the temperature dipped below freezing. In Alaska, the cusp seasons of spring and fall are often figments of the calendar's imagination. Reluctant to part from the womb of the earth last spring, Persephone must be eager to return this fall. The birch trees have barely begun to shed their chattering leaves when the first snow falls in big, wet clumps. In a defiant blaze of color, the blossoms in my garden face death, their stems and leaves collapsing around them like tattered seaweed. Turbulent postpartum depression runs in my family but still it blindsides me. Grief for my grandmother, who will never name a rose for Kinzea, is a subterranean place into which I burrow every night. Mingled with the grief is an inexplicable sense of loss, as if, in becoming a mother, I became less of a daughter.

I left the hospital after the baby was born without seeing her naked. I was so tired, the nurses so smoothly efficient. Now, as she wriggles and coos in the bathtub, I study her body for the first time: the parallel lines beneath her lips, the pearls of dirt that collect under her chin, her nearly invisible nipples, bracelets of fat at wrists and ankles, a tulip-shaped birthmark on her left buttock, the arch of a tiny foot. Her fifth toes are shriveled like mine, with nails the size of carrot seeds. Our feet foretell a time when our descendants will balance on eight toes instead of ten.

I sit behind Kinzea in the tub, cradling her body between thighs gone flaccid from lack of exercise. My belly slides back and forth in the moving water like a Jell-O mold at a church picnic. Violet stretch marks form a complex root system spreading upward from the fork of my legs where the baby's head rests. My breasts are heavy with milk. Looking down, I recognize my mother's body, my grandmother's body, my great-grandmother's body. Flawed but familiar. There is some comfort—even grace—in synchrony, in being the daughter of a mother and the mother of a daughter. Somewhere, I read that a child needs the care of someone for whom she is a miracle. Mother love, I think, is born of wonder at that miracle.

Contributors

Edward Abbey, author of two dozen works of nonfiction and fiction, maintained considerable influence on the environmental and literary scene for more than twenty years. His second novel, *The Brave Cowboy* (1956), was made into the highly regarded film *Lonely Are the Brave.* His later works included *Fire on the Mountain, Desert Solitaire, Abbey's Road, The Monkey Wrench Gang, The Journey Home, Beyond the Wall, One Life at a Time, Please, The Fool's Progress,* and *Hayduke Lives!* He died in Arizona in 1989.

Rick Bass is fast becoming one of his generation's most accomplished authors. Among his literary works are *The Deer Pasture, Wild to the Heart, Oil Notes, The Watch, Winter Notes,* and *Ninemile Wolves.* His first novel, *Where the Sea Used to Be,* is forthcoming from Norton in 1994. Bass makes his home in the wilds of northwestern Montana with his wife, Elizabeth, an artist who has illustrated several of his books, and his daughter, Mary Katherine.

Jennifer Brice lives with her husband and infant daughter in Fairbanks, Alaska. She is currently writing a book on the last homesteaders under federal law in Alaska. In 1992 she was awarded a Jacob K. Javits Fellowship in the Humanities. Her work will appear soon in a volume featuring the faculty and participants in the Sitka Symposium on Human Values and the Natural World.

Kenneth Brower, son of conservationist David Brower, lives in Berkeley, California, with his wife and young son. He has traveled widely and written prodigiously about the world's great wilderness areas over the past twenty-five years. Some of his books, such as *Earth and the Great Weather, The Brooks Range,* and *Micronesia: Island Wilderness*, are considered classics in the genre.

Russell Chatham is one of America's premier artists. He lives with his family at the headwaters of Deep Creek in western Montana. Chatham's craft as a painter is evident in the intensely visual quality of his prose.

Jan DeBlieu is the author of two books: *Hatteras Journal,* which chronicles life on the Outer Banks of North Carolina, and *Meant to be Wild: The Struggle to Save Endangered Species Through Captive Breeding,* which examines the status of such animals as the black-footed ferret, the red wolf, and the Florida panther. She lives on Roanoke Island, North Carolina, with her husband, Jeffrey Smith.

Annie Dillard, who was born in Pittsburgh and educated in the creative writing program at Hollins College in Virginia, has been one of America's most distinguished authors for nearly two decades. Her first book of prose, *Pilgrim at Tinker Creek,* was awarded the Pulitzer Prize for general nonfiction in 1974. Later works have included poetry, literary criticism, essays, a personal memoir, and a novel, *The Living.* She is married and lives in Middletown, Connecticut. She teaches at Wesleyan University.

Linda M. Hasselstrom lives on a ranch outside Rapid City, South Dakota. Her many books include *Windbreak, Going Over East,* and *Land Circle: Writings Collected from the Land,* which was hailed by reviewers in 1991. She was named Author of the Year by the South Dakota Hall of Fame in 1989 and in 1990 became the first woman ever to receive the Western American Writer award from the Center for Western Studies in Sioux Falls.

Linda Hogan lives in Kittredge, a small town in the mountains west of Denver, and teaches in the creative writing program at the University of Colorado, Boulder. She was born and raised in Oklahoma and is of Chickasaw ancestry. Her acclaimed novel *Mean Spirit* spoke to those roots.

William Kittredge directs the creative writing program at the University of Montana, Missoula. His many distinguished works include *We Are Not in This Together, Hole in the Sky*, and *Owning It All.* Kittredge worked on the screenplay for the film *A River Runs Through It.*

Barry Lopez was born in Port Chester, New York, grew up in southern California, and graduated from the University of Notre Dame. His many acclaimed books include *Of Wolves and Men, River Notes, Desert Notes, Arctic Dreams, Crossing Open Ground,* and *Crow and Weasel.* He writes regularly for *Harper's* and other magazines. When not traveling around the world, Lopez lives with his wife, Sandra, an artist, in the Cascade Mountains of Oregon.

Pat Matsueda, of Japanese-American ancestry, lives in Honolulu, Hawaii, and teaches at the University of Hawaii, Manoa. She also serves as an editor for *Manoa: A Pacific Journal of International Writing.* She has won a number of literary awards and her poetry has been widely published in literary quarterlies and periodicals.

Michael McPherson is a native Polynesian and environmental attorney in Honolulu. He has been published widely in periodicals and is working on his first book, a collection of his poems.

Harry Middleton's widely regarded books include *The Earth Is Enough, On the Spine of Time,* and *The Starlight Creek Angling Society.* Jim Harrison has written of Middleton's work that "he brings to fishing the lyric reverence of Roderick Haig-Brown, a McGuane or Chatham." He lived with his family in northern Alabama until his death in July 1993.

Adele Ne Jame, of Lebanese-American descent, lives in Honolulu, Hawaii. She has received NEA and other awards for her poetry and publishes regularly in various quarterlies and periodicals.

Dan O'Brien owns a cattle ranch outside Rapid City, South Dakota. His first collection of short stories, *Eminent Domain,* won the Iowa Short Fiction Award and was published by the University of Iowa Press in 1988. O'Brien has published an acclaimed work of nonfiction, *The Rites of Autumn: A Falconer's Journey Across the American West,* and two novels, *Spirit of the Hills* and *In the Center of the Nation.* He and his wife, a physician, live in Rapid City.

David Petersen lives in a cabin with his wife, Carolyn, in the San Juan Mountains of Colorado. His books include *Among the Aspen, Racks, Among the Elk,* and *Big Sky, Fair Land: The Environmental Essays of A. B. Guthrie, Jr.* He is also editor of the forthcoming journals of Edward Abbey, *Confessions of a Barbarian,* to be published by Little, Brown in 1994. Petersen is currently writing a book about the grizzly bears of Colorado's San Juan Mountains.

Brenda Peterson writes regularly about nature in the Pacific Northwest from her home in Seattle, Washington. Her first nature book, *Living by Water,* was warmly received. She has contributed to *Sierra* magazine, among others. Recently she traveled to Alaska to cover the Alaska wolf controversy for a Seattle newspaper.

Bob Shacochis has authored two short-story collections, *Easy in the Islands* and *The Next New World,* the first of which won the American Book Award. His work appears regularly in *Outside* and other periodicals. In 1993 Scribner's published his first novel, *Swimming in the Volcano,* to critical acclaim. Bob Shacochis lives in Florida with his wife, who is also a writer.

Peggy Shumaker lives in a log cabin home in Ester, Alaska. Past president of the Associated Writing Programs, which oversees the more than 200 creative writing programs in the United States, Shumaker has taught creative writing at the University of Arizona, the University of Alaska, and Arizona State University. Her books of poetry include *Esperanza's Hair* and *The Circle of Totems.*

Sherry Simpson lives in Fairbanks, Alaska, with her husband. She is pursuing graduate work in Northern Studies and creative writing at the University of Alaska, Fairbanks. Simpson has worked for daily newspapers in Juneau and Fairbanks and currently writes a weekly column for the *Fairbanks Daily-Miner.* She has also edited a book on the area around Juneau for the Alaska Geographic series.

Annick Smith lives and writes in Missoula, Montana. She has traveled widely in the American West. Her writing is often featured in *Outside* and other periodicals.

David Rains Wallace is the author of nine works of natural history, including *The Dark Range, Idle Weeds, The Klamath Knot, Bulow Hammock,* and *The Quetzal and the Macaw.* His book *The Klamath Knot* was awarded the John Burroughs Medal for Nature Writing in 1983. Wallace has also authored two novels, *The Turquoise Dragon* and *The Vermilion Parrot.* He and his wife, Betsy, an artist, make their home in Berkeley, California.

Terry Tempest Williams, who works as a naturalist for the Utah Museum of Natural History in Salt Lake City, has authored three acclaimed nature books: *Pieces of White Shell: A Journey to Navajoland, Coyote's Canyon,* and *Refuge: An Unnatural History of Family and Place.* Her work appears often in *Outside, Sierra,* and other periodicals.

Periodicals Consulted

Alaska Quarterly Review, Department of English, 3221 Providence Drive, Anchorage, Alaska 99508

Antaeus, Ecco Press, 26 West 17th Street, New York, New York 10011

The Antioch Review, P.O. Box 148, Yellow Springs, Ohio 45387

Arizona Quarterly, Department of English, University of Arizona, Tucson, Arizona 85721

The Atlantic Monthly, 745 Boylston Street, Boston, Massachusetts 02116

Audubon, 700 Broadway, New York, New York 10003

Backpacker, 33 East Minor Street, Emmaus, Pennsylvania 18098

Chicago Review, 5801 South Kenwood, Chicago, Illinois 60637

Cimarron Review, 205 Morril Hall, Oklahoma State University, Stillwater, Oklahoma 74078

Colorado Review, 360 Eddy Building, Colorado State University, Fort Collins, Colorado 80523

Denver Quarterly, Department of English, University of Denver, Denver, Colorado 80210

Esquire, 1790 Broadway, New York, New York 10019

Florida Review, Department of English, University of Central Florida, Orlando, Florida 32816

The Georgia Review, University of Georgia, Athens, Georgia 30602

The Gettysburg Review, Gettysburg College, Gettysburg, Pennsylvania 17325

Harper's Magazine, 2 Park Avenue, New York, New York 10016

Hawaii Review, Department of English, University of Hawaii, 1733 Donaghho Road, Honolulu, Hawaii 96822

Kansas Quarterly, Department of English, Denison Hall, Kansas State University, Manhattan, Kansas 66506

The Kenyon Review, Kenyon College, Gambier, Ohio 43022

Manoa, Department of English, University of Hawaii, 1733 Donaghho Road, Honolulu, Hawaii 96822

The Massachusetts Review, Memorial Hall, University of Massachusetts, Amherst, Massachusetts 01002

Michigan Quarterly Review, 3032 Rackham Building, University of Michigan, Ann Arbor, Michigan 48109

Minnesota Monthly, 15 South 9th Street, Suite 320, Minneapolis, Minnesota 55402

The Missouri Review, 1507 Hillcrest Hall, University of Missouri, Columbia, Missouri 65211

Nebraska Review, Department of English, University of Nebraska, Omaha, Nebraska 68182

New England Review, Middlebury College, Middlebury, Vermont 05753

New Mexico Humanities Review, Department of English, New Mexico Tech., Socorro, New Mexico 57801

The New Yorker, 20 West 43rd Street, New York, New York 10036

Nimrod, Arts and Humanities Council of Tulsa, 2210 South Main, Tulsa, OK 74114

The North American Review, University of Northern Iowa, 1227 West 27th Street, Cedar Falls, Iowa 50613

North Atlantic Review, 15 Arbutus Lane, Stony Brook, New York 11790

North Dakota Quarterly, University of North Dakota, Box 8237, Grand Forks, North Dakota 58202

The Ohio Review, Department of English, Ellis Hall, Ohio University, Athens, Ohio 45701

Outside, 1165 North Clark Street, Chicago, Illinois 60610

The Paris Review, 541 East 72nd Street, New York, New York 10021

Prairie Schooner, Andrews Hall, University of Nebraska, Lincoln, Nebraska 68588

Puerto Del Sol, Department of English, New Mexico State University, Las Cruces, New Mexico 88003

Santa Monica Review, Center for the Humanities at Santa Monica College, 1900 Pico Boulevard, Santa Monica, California 90405

The Sewanee Review, University of the South, Sewanee, Tennessee 37375

Sierra, 730 Polk Street, San Francisco, California 94109

Sonora Review, Department of English, University of Arizona, Tucson, Arizona 85721

South Carolina Review, Department of English, Clemson University, Clemson, South Carolina 29634

South Dakota Review, Box 111, University Exchange, Vermillion, South Dakota 57069

Southern Humanities Review, Department of English, Auburn University, Auburn, Alabama 36830

The Southern Review, Drawer D, University Station, Baton Rouge, Louisiana 70803

Southwest Review, Southern Methodist University, Dallas, Texas 75275

Tampa Review, Box 19F, University of Tampa, 401 West Kennedy Boulevard, Tampa, Florida 33606

The Threepenny Review, PO Box 9131, Berkeley, California 94709

The Village Voice Literary Supplement, 842 Broadway, New York, New York 10003

The Virginia Quarterly Review, Department of English, University of Virginia, Charlottesville, Virginia 22903

Wilderness, 900 17th Street NW, Washington, DC 20006

ZYZZYVA, 41 Sutter Street, Suite 1400, San Francisco, California 94104

Permissions

Edward Abbey: "Sheep Count" is from the forthcoming CONFESSIONS OF A BARBARIAN: PAGES FROM THE JOURNALS OF EDWARD ABBEY, edited by David Petersen (New York: Little, Brown, 1994). The text of Abbey's journal is reprinted with the permission of Don Congdon Associates. Copyright © 1994 by Clarke Abbey. Editorial note is by David Petersen. Copyright © 1994 by David Petersen. The note is reprinted with permission of the author.

Rick Bass: "The Fringe," first publication. Copyright © 1993 by Rick Bass. Reprinted with permission of the author.

Kenneth Brower: "Island Beaches" first appeared in *Islands* magazine (July/August 1992). Copyright © 1992 by *Islands* magazine. Reprinted with permission of *Islands* magazine.

Jennifer Brice: "My Mother's Body," first publication. Copyright © 1993 by Jennifer Brice. Reprinted with permission of the author.

Russell Chatham: "The Deepest Currents" first appeared in *Esquire Sportsman* (Spring/Summer 1993). Copyright © 1993 by Russell Chatham. Reprinted with permission of the author.

Jan DeBlieu: "Into the Dragon's Mouth" first appeared in *North Carolina Monthly* (January 1993). Copyright © 1993 by Jan DeBlieu. Reprinted with permission of the author.

Annie Dillard: "On Bellingham Bay" excerpted from THE LIVING, published by HarperCollins: New York, 1992. Copyright © 1992 by Annie Dillard. Reprinted with permission of the author.

Linda Hasselstrom: "The Covenant of the Holy Monkey Wrench" first appeared in *Hembra* (December 1992/January 1993). Copyright © 1993 by Linda Hasselstrom. Reprinted with permission of the author.

Linda Hogan: "The Voyagers" first appeared in *Prairie Schooner* (Winter 1992). Copyright © 1992 by Linda Hogan. Reprinted with permission of the author.

Adele Ne Jame: "Fieldwork, Devil's Lake, Wisconsin" first appeared in *Nimrod* (Fall/Winter 1990). Copyright © 1990 by Adele Ne Jame. "A Ryder Nocturne and *The Temple of the Mind*" first appeared in *Ploughshares* (Spring 1993). Copyright © 1993 by Adele Ne Jame. Both poems are reprinted with permission of the author.

William Kittredge: "Lost Cowboys (But Not Forgotten)" first appeared in *Antaeus* (Autumn 1992). Copyright © 1992 by William Kittredge. Reprinted with permission of the author.

Barry Lopez: "Replacing Memory" is reprinted by permission of Sterling Lord Literistic, Inc. Copyright © 1993 by Barry Holstun Lopez.

Pat Matsueda: "Samurai" and "Wave of Cereus" both appeared in *Manoa* (Spring 1993). Both poems copyright © 1993 by Pat Matsueda. Reprinted with permission of the author.

Michael McPherson: "Maalaea Bay" first appeared in *Manoa* (Summer 1993). Copyright © 1993 by Michael McPherson. "Water" first appeared in *Manoa* (Spring 1992). Copyright © 1992 by Michael McPherson. Both poems are reprinted with permission of the author.

Harry Middleton: "Baja" excerpted from RIVERS OF MEMORY, published by Pruett Publishing Co.: Boulder, Co., 1993. Copyright © 1993 by Harry Middleton. Reprinted with permission of Pruett Publishing Co.

Dan O'Brien: "Life on the Myopian Frontier" appeared in SACRED TRUSTS: ESSAYS ON STEWARDSHIP AND RESPONSIBILITY, edited by Michael Katakis, published by Mercury House: San Francisco, 1993. Copyright © 1993 by Dan O'Brien. Reprinted with permission of the author.

David Petersen: "Where Phantoms Come to Brood and Mourn: A Remembrance of Edward Abbey" first appeared in altered form in *Backpacker* magazine (September 1993). Copyright © 1993 by David Petersen. Reprinted with permission of the author.

Brenda Peterson: "Bread Upon the Waters" originally appeared in *Sierra* (January/February 1992). Copyright © 1992 by Brenda Peterson. Reprinted with permission of the author.

Bob Shacochis: "Greetings from the Big Pineapple" originally appeared in *Outside* magazine (November 1991). Copyright © 1991 by Bob Shacochis. Reprinted by permission of Brandt & Brandt Literary Agents, Inc.

Peggy Shumaker: "The Day the Leaves Came" first appeared in *Ploughshares* (Spring 1993). Copyright © 1993 by Peggy Shumaker. "Exit Glacier" first appeared in *Alaska Quarterly Review* (Winter 1990). Copyright © 1990 by Peggy Shumaker. "Birch Syrup" first appeared in *Northern Lights* (Spring 1991). Copyright © 1991 by Peggy Shumaker. All poems reprinted with permission of the author.

Sherry Simpson: "Where Bears Walk" first appeared in *Permafrost* (Autumn 1993). Copyright © 1993 by Sherry Simpson. Reprinted with permission of the author.

Annick Smith: "The Rites of Snow" first appeared in *Outside* magazine (January 1993). Copyright © 1993 by Annick Smith. Reprinted with permission of the author.

David Rains Wallace: "The Bones from Gracias" first appeared in *ZYZZYVA* (Winter 1992). Copyright © 1992 by David Rains Wallace. Reprinted with permission of the author.

Terry Tempest Williams: "Peregrine Falcon" excerpted from REFUGE: UNNATURAL HISTORY, published by Random House, Inc.: New York, 1992. Copyright © 1992 by Terry Tempest Williams. Reprinted with permission of the author.